Property and Social Re

Property and Social Relations

Edited by
Peter G. Hollowell

HEINEMANN · LONDON

Heinemann Educational Books Ltd
22 Bedford Square, London WC1B 3HH
LONDON · EDINBURGH · MELBOURNE · AUCKLAND
HONG KONG · SINGAPORE · KUALA LUMPUR
NEW DELHI · IBADAN · NAIROBI · JOHANNESBURG
EXETER (NH) · KINGSTON · PORT OF SPAIN

First published 1982
Chapter 8 *The Bureaucratic Collection of Small Consumer Debts* first published 1973 in *Making People Pay*, Routledge & Kegan Paul

British Library Cataloguing in Publication Data
Property and social relations.
1. Property – Social aspects
I. Hollowell, Peter G.
306′.3 HD255

ISBN 0 435 82435 X

Typeset by Sackville Studio Limited, Billericay and printed by Biddles Ltd., Guildford, Surrey.

Contents

The Contributors

Graham Allan has been Lecturer in Sociology at the University of Southampton since 1975, having previously taught at the University of Exeter. He is author of *A Sociology of Friendship and Kinship* as well as various academic papers.

Colin Bell is Professor of Sociology at the University of Aston. He has written *Middle Class Families, Community Studies* and is joint author of *Property, Paternalism and Power* and *Persistence and Change*, and joint editor of *Inside the Whale*, and *Doing Sociological Research*.

Gordon Causer is Lecturer in Sociology at the University of Southampton with special interests in social stratification and industrial studies. He has carried out research on business ideologies, and is currently involved in research into the introduction of electronics-based technologies as a member of the Southampton University New Technology Research Group.

Brian Elliott joined the Sociology Department at the University of Edinburgh in 1965, and became Senior Lecturer in 1979. He is co-editor with Frank Bechhofer of *The Petite Bourgeoisie: Studies of the Uneasy Stratum*, and the author of several articles on urban sociology and social stratification.

Charles Geisler obtained his PhD at the University of Wisconsin in 1979. Since this time he has been Assistant Professor in the Department of Rural Sociology at Cornell University, New York.

Peter Hollowell is Lecturer in Sociology at the University of Southampton specialising in the sociology of work and occupations. He has written empirical studies of lorry drivers and railway locomotivemen.

David McCrone joined the Sociology Department in the University of Edinburgh as a Research Fellow in 1973 to set up a research project with Brian Elliott on Landlordism, and was appointed lecturer in 1975. He is the author of articles on urban sociology, social stratification, and aspects of Scottish culture and social structure.

Howard Newby is Reader in Sociology, University of Essex and Professor of Rural Sociology, University of Wisconsin. He is the author of *The Deferential Worker* and *Green and Pleasant Land*, editor of *International Perspectives in Rural Sociology*, and joint author of *Property, Paternalism and Power* and *Doing Sociological Research*.

Paul Rock, Senior Lecturer in Sociology at the London School of Economics and Political Science, is the author of *Making People Pay, Deviant Behaviour*, and *The Making of Symbolic Interactionism*. He jointly edited *Deviance and Social Control*.

David Rose, Lecturer in Sociology, University of Essex, is joint author of *Property, Paternalism and Power*. He is Convenor of the SSRC Social Stratification Seminar.

Alan Ryan is Reader in Politics and Fellow of New College, Oxford. He has written extensively on issues in the philosophy of social science and the history of political thought. His books include *The Philosophy of Social Science* and *J. S. Mill*. He is at present working on the political thought of Bertrand Russell.

Peter Saunders is Lecturer in Sociology, University of Sussex. He is the author of *Urban Politics: A Sociological Approach; Urban Sociology;* and joint author of *Property, Paternalism and Power.*

Gordon Trasler is foundation Professor of Psychology at the University of Southampton, and currently Head of the Department of Psychology. He teaches courses in personality and individual differences, and in criminal behaviour, and is editor-in-chief of the *British Journal of Criminology*.

Introduction: The Nature of Property

Peter G. Hollowell

Everyday use of the term 'property' indicates no apparent difficulty about its meaning. Familiar experience leads to an easy and unconscious acceptance. People feel they know what they mean when they discuss their own property or that which they would like to own. On a closer inspection, it appears to be a term which the individual may use to indicate a whole range of things, from specific objects usually in his possession, to groups of rights in things not directly controlled.

A cursory examination of even general definitions of property confirms that it is a very complex phenomenon indeed. Some writers open the discussion immediately with an embracing definition.

> Property is a euphonious collocation of letters which serves as a general term for the miscellany of equities that persons hold in the commonwealth. A coin, a lance, a tapestry, a monastic vow, a yoke of oxen, a female slave, an award of alimony, a homestead, a first mortgage, a railroad system, a preferred list and a right of contract are all to be discovered within the catholic category. Each of these terms, meaningless in itself, is a token or focus of a scheme of relationships; each has its support in sanction and repute; each is an aspect of an enveloping culture.[1]

Here the term 'property' is an abstraction for a great diversity of concrete items. In this usage the property items are integrally related to the total social structure of a community. There is an insistence in this definition that any object or custom viewed as property can only be considered as an upper layer supported by an invisible composite social substructure.

Occasionally this type of initial definition is so brief and comprehensive as to be substantially misleading, or even fundamentally incorrect.

> In its widest sense, property denotes the exclusive relationship of a person or a group of persons to an object or complex of objects of material value.[2]

The objection to such a definition is that a person may not have an exclusive relationship to anything without recognition and concession of this fact by other people. Inasmuch as property is conditional upon the existence of certain types of social relations between people, it is essentially a social phenomenon. It is apparent that a cautious and, perhaps unfortunately, more extended approach is to be preferred to succinct embracing definitions. The fundamentals of property need to be inspected to reveal its widely differing elements.

> The essence of property is in the relations among men arising out of their relations to things. . . . Objects over which the rights of property extend are objects conceived of as taken out of the mass of free goods and brought under the exclusive control of a person, and this control is called property.
>
> Property is an exclusive right . . . not a thing but the rights which extend over a thing.[3]

These statements reveal the social and composite nature of property. Property has to be conceived of as a varying bundle of rights each of which are intricately bound up with the general culture pattern.

One of the most basic issues stemming from the range of characteristics amongst the elements of property is that property is always both a subjective and an objective institution. No objective analysis of property can omit the subjective constituents of the phenomenon. People's feelings about property are an essential aspect of it. The statement 'this is mine' is an expression of the sentiment of exclusiveness. Clearly there are severe methodological problems in escaping normative bias while yet recognising and assessing the full importance of the normative element.

Regardless of the political position of the writer, there is frequently a useful concern to escape the treatment of property solely from a particular normative position.

> It is easy enough to say, 'Property is theft' but difficult to prove the assertion. It is easy enough to say 'Property is sacred' but equally difficult to prove it so. The truth probably lies between the two extreme positions – property is neither theft nor sacred, it is just human, and like all things human, imperfect.[4]

Even to justify a partisan point of view, the writer of the above statement, an American lawyer apologist for business property, who died in 1920, found it necessary to defer to the idea of extracting this extreme normative element. Writing from a very different point of view in Europe some three decades earlier, Lafargue scathingly pointed out that similar, ostensibly objective, intellectual justifications for a particular type of normative structure had been and remained an integral part of the capitalist system.

> So great were the zeal, and the ardour which economists brought to bear on their search for capitalistic property in prehistoric times, that they succeeded, in the course of their investigations, in discovering the existence of property outside the human species,

> to wit among the invertebrates; for the ant in her foresight, is a hoarder of provisions. It is a pity that they should not have gone a step farther, and affirmed that, if the ant lays up stores, she does so with a view to sell the same and realise a profit from the circulation of her capital.[5]

A fine example of concern to remain objective is shown in the American lawyer and lecturer, Felix Cohen's penetrating interrogation of his students on the phenomenon of property.

> *C.* What evidence, Mr Black, can you produce to show that private property really exists?
>
> *B.* Well here is a book that is my property. You can see it, feel it, weigh it. What better proof could there be of the existence of private property?
>
> *C.* I can see the shape and colour of the book very well, but I don't see its propertiness. What sort of evidence can you put forward to show that the book is your property?[6]

Cohen's analysis effectively strips property of its normative and ideological connotation, replacing what he calls 'confusion'[7] by a 'realistic' definition of private property in terms of 'exclusions which individuals can impose or withdraw with state backing against the rest of society'. This emergent definition is drawn up on the basis that other definitions already available could not give answers in certain practical situations[8] because they were either too broad or too narrow. The critical importance of avoiding valuational approaches is further emphasised.

> In the first place, such a definition helps us to avoid emotional entanglements. These emotional entanglements are probably more serious in discussions of property than in any other field of social controversy. Property after all, is the essence of all that is proper. How, then, can any reasonable man oppose property? If we define property as value, who will oppose value? If we define property as equities, who is against equities? If the essence of property is enjoyment, who will oppose enjoyment? But if we can distinguish property from all these related terms and achieve an unemotional conception in terms of exclusions and state power, we may have some choice of reaching our objective analysis in trying to determine whether any given type of private property should be socialised, or whether any given type of social relationship should be turned into private property.[9]

This very laudable quest for objectivity should not be allowed to understate the importance of the subjective element. Property is rarely, if ever, neutrally regarded by actors in an empirical situation. Society needs a view of it in relation to individual and social needs. Without such a value structure both individual and society are likely to be in bondage to property. Bishop Charles Gore puts this case eloquently when he says,

> What he [the individual] cries out for, when his conscience is awakened, is not merely personal guidance, but also ideas which can be applied to society; not merely again schemes for law-making, but ideas such as must be behind law-making and without which law-making is in vain. He wants an ideal of property, a principle of property, such as will tend to form a corporate conscience, at first among those who are consciously dissatisfied with things as they are and consciously in want of a theory, and then more widely in society as a whole.[10]

Works of theology and political philosophy show that property receives evaluation because of its consequences rather than as an autonomous phenomenon. The views expounded are often quite utopian but the value references themselves are none the less treatable as objective data. There is also the objective fact that the consequences of property are so immense that a stable evaluation is necessary. The struggle to make this evaluation should not be omitted from any analytic picture.

At this stage it is evident that prolonged effort to procure an even more efficient definition of property, of the type so far examined, cannot be justified. Short definitions, however penetrating yet comprehensive, will usually fail to exposit some important constituent. It seems better to consider the phenomenon in its diversity but with the assistance of two distinct approaches. The first of these, designated analytic, suggests an overriding concern with the universal aspects, while the second, termed empirical, shows the diverse features of property as observed. Every paper has both analytic and empirical elements but the relative emphasis is clear for each of the two sections of the book. Running through the book as a whole is the theme of the social aspects of property. Some interesting questions the material throws light on are: how and with what intensity does property influence social relationships?; how far is property a purely social institution, external to and independent of the individual will?; do many social relationships inherently contain features characteristic of property?

In beginning the analytic section with a paper on concept formulation, the hope is to indicate both the breadth of the institution of property, and the possibility of identification of at least some of its fundamental features. Even a brief survey reveals a truly massive, if very fragmented, literature on the institution. By sifting and arranging this material into three broad categories it is possible to generate an operational concept of property which is feasible for empirical inspection and compatible with broader paradigms in sociology. Social forces are shown to predominate in the developed concept, even in the mental dimension where this might have been less expected.

Although there is no psychology of property in the sense of a unified approach in this area, the discipline clearly makes a major contribution. Consideration of the historical development of ideas and theories in psychology can, by itself, demonstrate some of the problems of assessing the mental aspects of property. The psychoanalytic tradition has particularly illuminating material. Gordon Trasler then uses objective indicators of social context (type of society, socialisation, and crime) to make a statement on property and the self. Possessions are shown to articulate the individual and society by confirming personal identity and self worth. Rather surprisingly; psychology does offer substantial objective support for a sentimental perspective of property, largely through the variety of evidence used.

From experience we all may 'know' that property has many subjective aspects but scientifically satisfactory indication is difficult. In an expression of this kind of feeling Alan Ryan argues that there is more to property than the utilitarian instrumental approach of people such as Hume, Smith and Bentham. He suggests that the writings of Kant, Hegel and Marx show the possibility of an alternative theory of ownership. Property is not simply assets that can be exchanged for what is wanted. The more expressive approach of the romantic theory does enable some of the problems of a purely instrumental theory to be demonstrated. To the working farmer, land is not only an asset, nor is the artist's own painting purely a commodity. Nevertheless the expressive side of property does seem elusive. It appears difficult to say, whether the will to possess can be conceived as being more than rational (Kant), whether there really is spiritual possession of spiritual creation (Hegel), or whether privacy in property is in fact a negation of appropriation (Marx). Although Ryan admits the difficulty of demonstrating these aspects, he is generally convincing on the misleading effects of neglecting the sentimental side of property. Coming away from any philosophical treatment it is very obvious that the empirical social and political consequences of *un*sentimental property are enormous.

Of all the multitude of property objects, land must surely be the most appropriate topic for beginning empirical discussion. It is a fundamental area by any criterion – tangibility, human need, individual sentiment, historical concern, and contemporary social and political importance.[11] An East Anglian study by Rose *et al.* suggests that owner-occupation is very heavily entrenched in the minds of working farmers. As a consequence they make responses showing considerable hostility to perceived threats from price inflation, capital taxation and city institutions. Clearly definable defensive ideologies for occupier landownership are shown to have crystallised as a basis for social action through well established pressure groups. Although no uniformly negative response to current developments in the case of landed property exists, the survey provides excellent empirical insights into both subjective and objective features of ownership as an institution.

In fact land is an excellent empirical subject to demonstrate the fiction of notions like absolute or complete ownership. Constraint on landowners has long existed in the sense of there being legal limitations on ownership rights through recognition of the rights of others. Charles Geisler's account continues the constraint theme evident in the East Anglian study. Just as farmer owner-occupation in England is not always legitimated in terms of economic efficiency so pressure for local control of land in the USA has its source in traditional political values rather than contemporary environmental and social requirements. In his analysis, similar to that of Renner[12] in its implications, Geisler uses a Marxist based materialism to explain the resistance to the social control of land resources. Size of production unit makes control more important than ownership. Private ownership, the basis of the independent businessman in the 'closed' property system, is eroded, first by corporate ownership, and then by government. This produces an 'open' property system, which completes the decline in the common law notion of absolute ownership. The 'public interest state' is a concept stressing the empirical reality of contemporary landed property as rights, either presently or potentially bounded by formal limitations.

Some of the consequences of the decline of the small property-based entrepreneur are discussed in the next two papers. Elliott and McCrone assess the consequences of small capital or 'petty' property in Britain and elsewhere. Theoretically, small capital offers, on the one hand, relief from the exploitation of capitalism, and on the other, a measure of freedom from the alienative effects of bureaucratic paternalism. In this, its virtues may be proclaimed not only by right wing political elements but also by certain socialist groups. In Eastern Europe, Lenin and Kautsky are being used to argue that small capital is not incompatible with a socialist regime. A survey of the historic and present situation of petty property in Britain confirms that small capital has heavily declined in significance. Structural sources, and the retained 'folk devil' images[13] mean that the newly emergent pressure groups will have to make formidable efforts to gain even small improvements in the social position of the small businessman.

In a study of the distribution of wealth in Britain in relation to social stratification, Causer easily manages to confirm the clear persistence of class-based holdings of wealth in the corporate sector. More interesting however, than this already well established fact, is the influence of property in the more critical marginal situation. Though he distinguishes both the small capitalists and the petty bourgeoisie, Causer seems doubtful about the benefits of property to either group. It appears that managers in large corporations, and even independent professionals may have better material rewards than small capitalists whose position is property-based. Even such advantages as do accrue to property-related occupations are not infrequently relinquished by offspring. When the time comes for transfer of the business through inheritance they often prefer to pursue managerial and professional occupations on the basis of achieved qualifications. In any case there is frequently the problem of only one opening and several offspring. Causer thus shows the weak stratification effect of property in the middle ranges of the class structure while maintaining its fundamental importance at the top end of the social scale.

In spite of a demonstrated ambivalence at the margin property still has deep implications for social relations generally in contemporary industrial societies. Three final papers show the influence of property in particular areas of social structure. Paul Rock's essay on debt shows how social relations take the form of attempts at social control when property is threatened through defaults in payment. Graham Allan's paper indicates the consequences of property for kinship structure and solidarity. The last paper investigates property-like features of social relations in a work setting.

Debt collection is a social action in which the subjective aspects of property are clearly demonstrated. By describing the routine practices of people involved in the process, Rock shows the considerable reliance which debt collectors place on the defaulters' *sense* of obligation. The use of threat and bluster in the majority of cases has objectively definable structural supports; a reluctance to estrange what might be a normal customer temporarily deviating; a desire to avoid losses through pursuit of debts; and a need to avoid creating 'incorrigible' or 'professional' defaulters through inappropriate pursuit. In this view, if default is a negation of property rights then reinstitutionalisation is as much a subjective as an objective process.

Property systems have traditionally been considered important in understanding the family, with anthropologists in particular emphasising inheritance and kin grouping. In choosing normal, rather than crisis or other extreme situations, Graham Allan seems all the more convincing on the remaining significance of property for the family in welfare industrial societies. The family is crucial in the transmission of 'symbolic' property (educational and cultural advantage). Life styles are not fundamentally altered but middle class material deficiencies in early career are reduced by gifts between generations.

Neither of these contemporary property transfers enable as much social control as occurred in the traditional 'productive' property inheritance situation of family enterprise. Graham Allan's essay encounters the difficulties of assessing the effects of material property on social relations when so many other factors are involved. The key question here seems to be whether these contemporary features are to be thought of as property equivalents or as transformed substitutes or alternatives. How is property to be defined in these situations?

Property-like relations occur in many spheres of life. Work is no exception. The social theory of property in work activity is well established, while significant empirical studies have already pronounced the objective validity of this idea. A study of steam locomotive men on British Railways shows the social mechanisms underpinning and sustaining such a conception. The locomotiveman's career is seen as a passage through a sequence of increasingly valuable job activities. Career as a claim to job property was undoubtedly central in the steam technology era. However, changes in technology, work organisation, and especially markets, increasingly mean that the job property concept faces challenges. Other systems of job allocation, notably a welfare system, always featured in the locomotiveman's work life. Market contraction places a strain on the seniority/property system through the emergence of a merit/effort system. Nevertheless, even at this stage the work as property theory remains a highly useful illuminator of social action in the locomotiveman's work situation.

Two major points emerge from this collection of essays on property. Property as an institution through either its core features or their consequences is highly diffused throughout any social system. The traditionally limited concern of the institution has been enlarged in modern times, first through the tensions induced by capitalistic industrialisation, and subsequently through recognition of a diversity of rights in advanced industrial society. Private property rights seem to have been mollified while personal and public interest rights appear to have been strengthened. This trend may now have reached the stage where rights in property and other rights are increasingly difficult to distinguish. At a still more general level, such a convergence may mean that any contemporary social relationship may contain elements more specifically associated historically with traditional private property.

The above argument assumes the possibility of an objective definition of property in terms of socially recognised rights in things. What is clearly revealed in this book is the importance of the subjective dimension of property. In the language of the symbolic interactionists, if people define *something* (rather than rights in it) as property, more frequently or more intensely than other things, then this definition has real consequences. An insistence on the importance of the subjective aspects of property reveals that the objective definition (property as rights) is limiting. The real breadth of the institution is pared down since the notion 'right of enjoyment' conveys no sense of the *true* delights or miseries of property.

Notes

1. W. H. Hamilton and I. Till, 'Property', *Encyclopaedia of the Social Sciences*, New York, Macmillan, 1933.
2. W. Friedmann, *Dictionary of the History of Ideas*, New York, Scribners, 1973.
3. R. T. Ely, *Property and Contract in their Relations to the Distribution of Wealth*, London, Macmillan, 1914, Vol. 1, Chapter 3. An excellent summary of the Ely statement can be found in M. R. Cohen and F. S. Cohen *Readings in Jurisprudence and Legal Philosophy*, Boston, Little Brown & Co, 1951, pp.10–17. See also Ely, op. cit., p.108.
4. A. J. Eddy, *Property*, Chicago, A. C. McClurg and Company, 1921, pp.3–4.
5. P. Lafargue, *The Evolution of Property*, New York, Scribners, 1901 (1st edn. 1891), p.2.
6. F. S. Cohen, 'Dialogue on Private Property', *Rutgers Law Review*, Winter 1954, p.359.
7. Ibid., p.378. Cohen talks critically about the confusion of nominalism and says property is a fact and not just a word; the confusion of materialism arising from fourteenth century metaphysics, which regards property as things in space; and the confusion of the semi-materialistic conception of property as a dyadic relation between a person and a thing. Property situations may in fact involve no 'thing' but they essentially consist of relations between people. Lastly Cohen assesses the confusion between the legal concept of property and the economic or ethical concept of 'value' and finds that 'valueless property and propertyless value are among the facts of life'.
8. Ibid. Cohen makes big demands for analytic objectivity with his widely different practical examples of the case of the Montana mules, the ownership of songs, and the difference between capitalism and communism.
9. Ibid., p.379.
10. Charles Gore's Introduction, p.xii in C. Gore (ed.), *Property: Its Duties and Rights*, 2nd edn., London, Macmillan, 1915.
11. See Harrington's 'Oceana' discussed in G. H. Sabine, *A History of Political Theory*, London, Harrap, 1959, p.423 and in C. B. Macpherson, *The Political Theory of Possessive Individualism*, London, OUP, 1962, pp.162–3. See also P. Zagorin, *A History of Political Thought in the English Revolution*, London, Routledge, 1954, Chapter 11. A contemporary view of the importance of land is contained in D. R. Denman, *The Place of Property*, Geographical Pubications Ltd., 1978.
12. K. Renner, *The Institutions of Private Law and their Social Functions*, London, Routledge, 1949.
13. The Milner-Holland Committee Report on Housing in Greater London,

Cmd 2605, London, HMSO, March 1965, was an illustration of aggressive behaviour on the part of landlords suggesting that the 'folk devil' conception is more reality than imagery.

Part I
Some Analytic Approaches on Property

1 On the Operationalisation of Property
Peter G. Hollowell

Property is an ubiquitous feature, yet one of great variety. The problem here is to provide a framework for investigating the phenomenon in all its diversity. This is a twofold process. First, recurring aspects of property are identified through a literature survey. Then follows a suggested operationalisation of the revealed qualities for empirical use. Operationalisation, through the formulation of empirically manageable dimensions is a well recognised process in sociology, even in elusive subjective areas.[1] Indeed, property has itself been operationalised in a remarkable American study focusing on corporate property rights,[2] to give a detailed indication of particular areas. Here, a more comprehensive coverage is attempted through a general formulation of the phenomenon in terms of several broad dimensions.

Identification of Some Major Constituent Elements of Property

As the literature on property is vast, the literature survey is necessarily restricted to the four fields of psychology, political theory, law and sociology. Nevertheless the differing emphases of these disciplines will indicate the breadth of property as an institution.

Psychology is chosen because it deals with feelings about property, and the resultant behaviour at the individual level. Political theory focuses on the need for a stable view of the property institution, as well as its real and ideal functions for civil government. Law presents the more practical and realistic aspects of adjustments in relations between people in property matters. Sociology, by looking at property both as a distinct institution, and as only one element in broader investigations of social structure, suggests that its consequences may be more significant than the autonomous phenomenon.

Psychology, personality and property

Three broad aspects of the psychology of property are of interest. These are the evaluation and acquisition of property objects, the feelings of ownership, and property in relation to personality structure.

Almost any object, material or immaterial must be considered actual or potential property.[3] Children gather up things which arouse their interest. Socialisation reduces indiscriminate grasping and is the source of the evaluation of objects. Collecting, for example involves a process of successful comparison with others to give rewards of superiority, power, and self esteem. Acquisitive behaviour is turned from raw impulse, by the influence of social forces, to an integrated response.[4] Evaluation of property objects is made very complex by the socialisation process, for although basic organic needs are finite, the cultural adaptations to them are not.

Feelings are best viewed as structured emotional responses to particular objects. Need satisfaction is the pivotal element in the transformation of something from a neutral object to one of property.[5] The interplay of individual need and cultural guideline produces a socialised evaluation of objects in the individual so that the individual learns to meet his needs in ways appropriate to the culture. As well as having utility property will also be scarce.[6] The combination of utility and scarcity will serve to intensify feelings of ownership developed in socialisation. Sentiments of ownership are empirically discernible as intense feelings subsequent to an established evaluation pattern and deriving from threats to acquisition in relation to that pattern. Observable sentiments of ownership include possessiveness, jealousy, aggressiveness, domination, security, intimacy, and creativity.[7] The identification of these intensely held feelings is useful in the wider inspection of the mental aspect of ownership.

The relationship between property and personality has several relevant aspects. These are the questions of whether property is inherent in human personality; the effects of property on the development of personality; property as an element in the relationship between personality and social structure; and the moral effects of property on personality.

Property feelings seem easily nurtured in human personality, but variations in the type and intensity of property feelings and behaviour reflecting the diversities of total culture patterns, rule out an explanation of property as some innate psychological force. At the same time particular experiential theories are not well supported.[8] In spite of this, the socially learned evaluation process centres round an analytically small number of needs,[9] which are inherent in the sense of arising from the physiological and psychological constitution of human beings.

Ownership behaviour indicates that property objects are essential instruments in personality development and integration. Security, self identity, self esteem, and self fulfilment are all clearly bound up with the ownership of property. Beaglehole[10] suggests that property objects assist the development of self consciousness and integration of the personality into an ordered system. As property interests are objectified and projected there is also a recognition of the rights of others. Respect for the selfhood of others is part of a process through which the individual gets a conception of the unity of his own self. Acceptance of the property rights of others is thus a necessary step toward the emergence of the developed self.[11]

Property is clearly also a processual element in the relationship between personality and social structure during adulthood. Clothing property is intimately connected with personality as a crucial aspect of the ongoing self. In being used to create appearances, clothes also produce and convey the sense of self, both to the individual and others at a particular time.[12] This representation of the personality through property may be viewed theoretically as an integration between personality and social structure.[13]

Moral consequences of property, meaning evaluation or judgement of its effects on personality, are apparent. Consequences such as freedom or dependence,[14] reason or irrationality,[15] may be analysed both as objective phenomena and as moral conditions.

Property and political theory

Three substantive areas of political philosophers' views on property are of particular interest in the search for a feasible concept of property. Political theorists classify property; they are concerned with its consequences; and, most importantly, they have an interest in its justification.

(i) Classification of property objects Property objects form a highly heterogeneous category. Political philosophers suggest that some are more important (usually in their social and political effects) than others. Two examples make the point about differentiation. The republican theorist of the English civil war, James Harrington, placed special importance on land. Socialist theorists, like Harold Laski, often base many of their proposals on the characteristics of industrial capital.

Harrington's argument is that land is the major source of political power. Land supplies the provisions of life and is thus essential to supply the military instrument actually used in the taking of power.

> . . . but an army is a beast that hath a great belly and must be fed; wherefore this will come into what pastures you have, and what pastures you have will come into the balance of propriety, without which the public sword is but a name or a mere spit frog.[16]

Private property in industrial capital is also a way to power. It is fluid, impersonal, and although its generation and recognition requires co-operative interdependence, it concedes no obligation to the social condition. Capital tends to flow where the financial rewards for its use are greatest without any necessary correspondence between such accrual and human needs. This socialist assessment is simultaneously an analysis and a moral concern about the consequences of capitalist property.

(ii) The political consequences of property In political theory evaluation of property objects is more in terms of their effect on the broader political structure than on the basis of their inherent characteristics. The dominant type of property object is the one having the most widespread effects on the structure of society.

James Harrington's work *The Commonwealth of Oceana*, published in 1656, has the objective thesis that economic power is the fundamental source of political domination. In an agrarian society relative economic power is a function of the distribution of ownership of land. The ruling class is the one which holds the 'balance of property'.

> If one man be the sole landlord of a territory, or overbalance the people, for example three parts in four . . . his empire is absolute monarchy. . . . And if the whole people be landlords, or hold the lands so divided among them, that no man, or number of men . . . overbalance them, the empire is a commonwealth.[17]

Harrington's analysis suggests that the stability of a nation is dependent on achieving the appropriate match between the distribution of land and the governmental structure. Should a change in distribution occur, then equilibrium is re-established when the old ruling group is overthrown by the new group, which owns the major part of the landed property. The important intervening variable between the features of the property object and the effect is distribution. Harrington's theory of the balance of landownership is essentially a theory of the governmental consequences of patterns of distribution of the dominant property object. The forms of government, absolute monarchy, mixed or feudal monarchy, and commonwealth each corresponded to a particular form of land tenure.[18]

Ownership of capital in industrial societies has a clear effect both on individuals and the societies as a whole. Concentration of industrial capital in the hands of a few private individuals means that the owning group necessarily controls all others who depend on the productive use of that capital for a livelihood. Privately owned industrial capital becomes so important that even the state is dominated by capitalists,[19] with the consequence that it is attuned to their will, and protective of them above all. In this situation the rights of property are said to predominate over the rights of men.

> In the absence of other considerations, a political system in which rights are built on property is one in which the propertyless man will have no rights . . . fundamentally, the regime of private property, in the background of industrialism, perpetuates the division into rich and poor, and separates the poor from the conditions which make possible their effective citizenship.[20]

Sharply shelved distribution of capital means that there is a differential access to the means of life and welfare.

(iii) The justification of property A consistent theme in political theory is that societies require consensus on the evaluation of property. Property needs to be legitimated or justified. Many theorists have assessed property, particularly private property, and have subsequently come to justify or condemn the institution.[21] A useful example is Laski who felt the need for there to be a sound justification of property. His interest is in the achievement of a concept of property, which satisfies the moral sense of men, and which thereby reduces the social dangers inherent in an ill formulated view. Laski is extremely critical of the many searches for property justification in psychological, scientific, historical, and especially ethical terms.[22] His own justification of private property is in terms of meeting certain minimum needs of individuals combined with the criteria of their personal efforts and contributions to society.

Another useful assessment of the justification of property is contained in a set of essays on the obstacles to a viable democratic theory, by the Toronto political scientist, C. B. Macpherson. Macpherson's definition of property focuses directly on the need for justification of the institution.[23] His argument is that 'the concept and theory of what the institution is and could be' is always a necessary aspect of the institution, either for its maintenance or for its change.

A genuine democratic society, one enabling 'individuals equally to use and develop their human capacities' is thwarted by the traditional institution of property. The exclusiveness, characteristic of property in a free market society, is underpinned by the labour justification of English utilitarianism – the right to possess, use, and dispose of the fruits of one's own exertions – of which Locke is the major architect. The exclusive property form hinders the democratic goal of maximising men's developmental powers since it maintains 'extractive power', that is man's ability to use the capacities of other men. In the twentieth century, this traditional concept is increasingly challenged by the view of property as the right to revenue.[24] Under the conditions of developed capitalism, three earlier traditional justifications of individual property – the right to the material means of life, the right to a free life, and the right to the current and accumulated fruits of labour – all require equal access to the means of labour for the individual. A relevant contemporary institution of property, therefore, is one upholding the right of the individual *not* to be excluded either from a share in society's total output, or from access to the accumulated means of labour.

Legal aspects of property

In a sense, property only exists because there is law. Law is thus vital for an understanding of the institution.[25] Jurisprudence deals with various interesting aspects of property. These are the types of property object, the holder – object relationship, the varieties of acquisitive action, property as a system, the justification of property, and finally the subjective side of property.

Property is deemed to be either 'corporeal' (rights in material things) or 'incorporeal' (any other proprietory right).[26] In English law a basic division exists within the corporeal category in the distinction between land and chattels. Incorporeal property is a much less tangible category since it may consist of rights in immaterial things. Three major types of immaterial property are discernible: patents, copyrights and trade marks. Incorporeal property also includes a number of different kinds of rights over the property of others, such as leases, tenancies, servitudes, securities and trusts.

Such legal classifications indicate that various property objects may generate different property rules. The empirical reality is a wide range of proprietory protection in a great variety of 'objects'. This differentiation could be the basis of a ranking, giving support to the idea that there are more and less fundamental property objects.

Legal concepts may indicate the variable strength of the relationship between holders of property, and their property objects. Ownership, possession, detention and custody in broad terms represent a continuum of decreasing strength in holder – object relationship. The first of these concepts, ownership, may be thought of as a bundle of rights.[27] These rights include *enjoyment* – the right to use, to yield appropriation, and even to destroy the object; *possession* – the right to occupy, physically control, and exclude others; *transfer* – the right to donate or sell; and finally the right of bequest.

Inasmuch as 'possession' may be lost intentionally or inadvertently by the possessors' relaxation of either physical control over the property object (*corpus possessionis*) or of the intention to possess the object for exclusive use (*animus possidendi*), it is less protected than ownership.[28] 'Detention' involves full physical control in fact but this is not regarded as possession in law. The weakest of all relationships between holder and property object is 'custody' since the holder either does not have full physical control or else has no 'animus' to exclude others.

People obtain property in three broad ways, originally, derivatively, and by succession.[29] Succession is acquisition through bequest or other probate institutions. Derivation involves acquiring property through sale, gift, or statute. Original ownership can come about either through creation, that is my making something, through occupation by staking a claim to ownerless property, or lastly through accession, as in the case of reproducing animals.

Illegal means of acquisition – conquest, violence, coercion, theft, fraud – with stealth as a marginal type – contrasted with legitimate methods locates the boundary between the socially acceptable and unacceptable ways of acquiring property. The prominent treatment given to acquisition in law suggests the importance of this aspect for property generally.

Legal sources support the contention that property can be usefully analysed as a system in two ways. The first method assumes input, throughput and output to be general system characteristics, and attempts to identify parallel features in the legal treatment of property.[30] Input to the system would be the property object – say land or intellectual property. The processing or throughput would involve investigation of title and copyright operations respectively, while output would be valid transfer and prevention of unauthorised performance respectively.

The second method of demonstrating the importance of system features in property is simply to inspect functionalist jurisprudence. Renner's thesis on the institution of private property, which suggests property to be a system with consequences for other systems, is an example.[31] He shows how the private law of property can become an institution of public law with the power of command or control over other people. The practice of limiting the power of property by common law or statute is further support for the conception of property as a system.

The justification of property rules can be seen in relation to the function of law generally. To sustain human life there has to be a purposeful satisfaction of needs. Law exists to facilitate this by providing rules to protect interests and maintain social order. Thus the rules of property would secure the orderly acquisition, use, and disposal of property objects for both individual and social benefit.

> The object of the law of property is to provide a secure foundation, so far as the law can do it, for the acquisition, enjoyment, and disposal of wealth.[32]

Rules of ownership and possession serve to lessen potential conflict which would inevitably limit the benefits from productive use of property objects.

Finally, the legal view of property does throw some light on the subjective aspects of the phenomenon. Intention can be important, even decisive, in possession cases. Some legal minds have held intention to be the essential ingredient, while others have advocated control.[33] Intention itself is not a fixed notion and the type of intention required for possession is likely to be significant. For example there may be an intention to act as owner, or to have an exclusive use. A further issue is the part that knowledge plays in intention. Here the concern is whether intention in possession is to be based firmly on a knowledge of the existence of a property object, its attributes and quantities, and its location at the relevant times.[34] Another point is the degree of specificity required before the intention to control is recognised as a component of possession.[35] The legal uncertainties surrounding intention suggest an elusiveness generally about the subjective aspects of property.

Sociology and property

The contemporary sociology of property has an extremely fragmented appearance. Sociological treatment of other institutions, the family, or formal organisation, tends to be in terms of a distinctive entity. Property is generally analysed from a particular perspective as part of a wider concern, for example as a factor in social stratification.[36] Here selection is made to indicate the potential scope of a sociology of property rather than a comprehensive coverage. First it might be useful to examine the views of a major sociological theorist, Durkheim, on the subject. Secondly, the focus is on the great attention given to the distribution of wealth in capitalist countries. Finally, there is a more general discussion on the consequences of property for social structure as a whole.

(i) A theorist's view – Durkheim Durkheim seeks a definition of property sufficiently general to cover all its forms in different times and cultures. After consideration of property in terms of object or thing, of holder, and of powers, he finally selects exclusivity as the distinguishing right of property.[37] This definition is then used to discuss the origin of property rights. Durkheim discerns an exclusiveness in religious behaviour parallel to that inherent in ownership. The taboos of the Polynesians and the *sacer* of the Romans create a distance

between specified objects and all people, except those who have the recognised qualifications to use them. Explanations of the origins of property must therefore lie in the nature of religious belief since as the effects are similar they are likely to have a similar cause. The connection can sometimes even be direct as when some sacred or taboo person touches an object necessarily converting it into his property.

Numerous analogies are made between sacred objects and appropriated objects. Both types are insulated yet contagious. The sacred draws the profane, while there are accruals to property. Consecration is a form of appropriation. Sacred objects may not be disposed of, and similarly, inalienability (rather than disposability) is arguably the highest development of property in land. Landed property is given a sacredness and consequently inviolability through ceremonies.

It can thus be argued that respect for property has a source external to the person since it is not an extension of respect for the person. Objects are sacred since they were originally appropriated by the Gods. Men take over the property of the Gods through ceremonies. Only those who win the property object (land) from the Gods have rights in it. Hence the inviolability and continued respect for exclusive rights in property continues to exist even after profane appropriation. Property is property because it retains sufficient of the sacred to keep all except the rightful owner at a distance.

Durkheim has other important views on property; how it became individuated through patrimony; the development of moveable property; and the particular significance of contract as a mode of acquisition. No comment is necessary here on the substantive hypothesis of religion (viewed as social representations) as a source of property. It is the functional approach used in his analysis which illustrates the importance of belief systems in defining property rights on an individual and a social level.

(ii) Wealth and its distribution in society This formidable subject has interested a large number of writers.[38] The following summary on the distribution of wealth in Britain must necessarily involve considerable over-simplification.

In the recent past, wealth in Britain has been found to be very unevenly distributed among the adult population. The degree of concentration varies greatly with the type of asset held, but company shares are overwhelmingly held by rich people. Distribution of wealth is more uneven than the distribution of income. Britain shows more inequality in the distribution of wealth than do many other capitalist countries, including the United States. The structure of wealth appears relatively stable over time since redistribution has largely been away from the very rich to the rich rather than to the poor.

In addition to these comments Atkinson offers a useful analysis of the advantages of wealth and by implication the consequences of inequality.[39] He distinguishes three consequences of ownership – the right to income, the right to control, and the right to convey property. The right to income yielded by wealth can give security and freedom of action. Since the rich get higher yields than the less rich on their holdings these unequal accruals to concentrated wealth contribute significantly to economic inequality. In the right to control, the wealthy are likely to be more influential because of the size of their shareholding. The right to convey property is evident from wealth accumulation and concentration through inheritance.

The inference that may be drawn from this summary of evidence on distribution in Britain is that persistent accumulation and concentration of wealth is the 'natural' occurrence, rather than dispersion, which requires deliberate intervention. Property is autonomous notwithstanding the pressures of laws and other social measures, wars, and general economic and social change.[40] Distribution plays a key role in this autonomy. Concentration is likely to be reinforced by differential returns to larger holdings, whether the rewards are purely financial, or mainly consist of influence in company policy, or even of opportunity for transmission and growth through inheritance.

(iii) Property and social structure At the microscopic level, some sociologists have spoken of social relationships in such a way as to make them appear like property relationships. Kingsley Davis discusses jealousy in terms which suggest that the property element is inherent in many types of social relationship. Although the two are distinct in a number of important ways, Davis finds that the 'affectional relationship' does have many features similar to economic property. Most significantly there is the sexual exclusiveness which, after legitimate competition, the community protects.[41]

Sociological discussion of ownership and control in industry gives an example of possible effects of property on social relations at a more intermediate level of social structure. Managerialists suggest that changes in the traditional ownership control relationship have made managers a self aware group with potential professional status.[42] Property also has consequences for the total society through the social stratification system. Ownership as a factor in social inequality has been greatly reduced in capitalist, as well as communist countries but is still influential in both.[43] In the first type, in addition to the inheritance factor, there are also many legally permitted devices for turning income into capital, while in the second, differential access to capital goods produces *de facto* privilege.[44]

The Development of an Operational Concept of Property

This survey of the four perspectives on property conveys the complexity of the subject. Concept development requires that the revealed features be ordered into dimensions. Constraints on the selection and assembly of constituent elements include the need of linkage with broader constructs, the necessity of empirical viability, and the obligation of not offending historical data. The empirical requirement is given most attention in this section since this is the prime purpose of making a definition operational.

From the surveys of psychological, political, legal, and sociological approaches to property, it would appear possible to draw up many dimensions appropriate to the operationalisation of the concept. For clarity, the number should be restricted to three: the mental aspects of possession or ownership, the way in which property is distributed among a population, and finally the methods by which people acquire property and become owners. These aspects are selected as dimensions, since they appear consistently as important themes in the literature survey.

(i) The evaluative dimension: mental aspects of property All four approaches to property mention an essential 'mental' aspect. That is to say they recognise that property exists in the individual's mind as well as being, at times, a concrete material object, or a matter of socially supported rights. This less tangible aspect of the phenomenon may be conveniently viewed as three distinct elements for analytic purposes, though empirically the separation might be difficult, if not impossible, to make.

The subjective element discerns the most individual (as opposed to social) mental aspect. Psychological approaches talk of property as something which has utility, the capacity to satisfy individual organic need. Individuals were said to be likely to express strong sentiments or feelings of ownership if these needs were not satisfied. More fundamentally, it was also suggested that property objects were an important element integrating the personality. Philosophers have also indicated this subjective element in talking of the individual will to appropriate, while lawyers were shown to have a concern with individual intentions to possess or own things. Though such phrases reflect an acknowledgement of its potential significance, the subjective remains the most obscure of all the three elements discussed. Psychology has also been through a similar confusing metaphysical approach to the issue by attributing proprietorial behaviour to innate drives or instincts. More recent psychological approaches have seen acquisitive and possessive activity as a complex process involving a number of different elements. The individual aspects are classified as various types of motive which emerge from broad groupings of organic, psychological, and social needs of the individual. Activity, by individuals in pursuit of need satisfaction is usually normative, that is, conforming to cultural rules.

It is difficult to separate the subjective element from the normative element. The individual is constrained into fulfilling his needs in a socially sanctioned way through socialisation. An individual's needs are socially as well as biologically created. Ways of meeting needs are culturally defined. Property objects are often used to develop the sense of self which is the hallmark of personality. That the institution of property is not simply a matter of individual will is convincingly argued in Durkheim's analysis of a parallel between religious belief and property as institutions. Beaglehole's cross-cultural comparison of some rules of property is a more empirical demonstration that property values are socially based. Responses in individuals, both mental and overt, like jealousy or aggression, are reinforced and even partly created by the values of the normative system.

The third element in this mental dimension of property is what I would choose to term, the moral element. Just as object utilities must be recognised by individuals, who have to learn to acquire and use them to satisfy needs in a socially legitimate fashion, a further essential aspect is the special social process of giving subjective and normative patterns a stable ordering. In other words, the system of assessing the property value patterns in the light of values other than those generated directly by organic utility and social ruling has always been an important aspect of property. Theologians and political philosophers have long struggled with this problem, sometimes in accordance with, but often against, the prevailing spirit of the society in which they live. In the case of property, the concern is not only to define what it is and to order objects of property by importance, but also more significantly, to investigate the justice of distribution patterns and methods of acquisition in general.

These three separate elements, distinguished for analysis and called for convenience the subjective, the normative and the moral, are all part of the mental aspect of property termed the 'evaluative' dimension. Thus

The Evaluative Dimension = The Subject Element (individual organic needs and feelings)
+ The Normative Element (values expressed and held through learned rules derived from social structure)
+ The Moral Element (assessment of subjective and normative through comparison with 'higher' or additional values)

All these elements may be a source of the individual's attitudes to property at any one time. They have important consequences for other dimensions of property, for inasmuch as they constitute the evaluative or mental dimension they are antecedent to overt property behaviour.

(ii) The distribution dimension: the pattern of property holding
Distribution is the second persistent theme which occurs in the property literature survey. On occasions it is neglected, as a phenomenon in its own right, in favour of its consequences. Normative elements have always obscured distribution and though the social climate is now more favourable than previously, they must still be regarded as an inhibition. Yet such social values should not merely be guardedly set aside, since they can be very revealing about the distribution pattern.

Though it is clearly something external to the individual, the psychological message about distribution patterns is a requirement that they meet individual needs in a certain minimum way in the long term. At the other end of the scale there may be individuals who own, and even control, disproportionate amounts of property. Research on wealth distribution in Britain suggests that a tiny minority of the population holds massive amounts of property. It is much more likely that this is a result of historical events and social values than the appetites of particular individuals.

Distribution is thus a systematic phenomenon rather than a matter of the personality characteristics of individuals. This systemic conception could give a view of distribution, either as a distinctive process persistently following a definable sequence in a particular direction, or as a series of interrelated elements linked by understood rules. Both these conceptions can be found in the discussions of the treatment of property in political theory, law and sociology. Distribution is shown as being facilitated through legal institutions which provide rules for reducing challenges and unnecessary disputes. Property has to be transferred by known and agreed methods for ownership to be valid. Thus legal institutions may be seen as defining property by upholding the property rights of those who have followed the recognised procedures against everyone else. Political theorists and sociologists are shown as having a systemic view of distribution inasmuch as they see it as one system in relation to another, namely government and social stratification. Both types of social scientist search for a characteristic pattern of property distribution corresponding to discernible types of political power, while the sociologist is also concerned with the way wealth holding affects social prestige. Considerable attention is given to the extent to which the institutional spheres are initially supportive. Property may not simply or alone be a source of social prestige and political power, but may additionally accrue to those with them more readily than to those without.

Interrelations between systems of the complex kind suggested above make clear statements on the consequences of distribution patterns less possible. In particular they may make the investigator's task of discovering and testing the principles underlying the pattern much more difficult. Perhaps the complexity of system interrelations may be at the bottom of problems arising when the distribution pattern itself is investigated. Social scientists are often uncertain about which property 'objects' should be included when they are defining the total wealth in the community. It is clear from the persistent efforts of researchers in this field that the investigation of the distribution patterns of even the more conventional property objects almost always produces only a best estimate.

To summarise, the distribution dimension must be seen as a systematic phenomenon, a persistent process, or a group of elements supported by rules. A researcher would need to investigate the pattern of distribution itself, the principles underlying it, and the various institutions maintaining it. Wider consequences of the distribution dimension would be treated separately at a later stage of the investigation.

(iii) The acquisitive dimension: the process of appropriation This dimension concerns the crucial issue of how individuals gain access to property. In the first two dimensions, the focus has been on why people require property, why it is created in the first place, and on the ways in which property is apportioned amongst the population of a society. Acquisition is thought of as a process, defined as being a discernible sequence of events, predictable to the people concerned.

There is a dominant process of acquisition, to which most members of any community conform, but there are also likely to be alternative and less approved methods. The legal approach to property is interesting in this respect since it incidentally describes the possible range of acquisitive modes by defining legal and criminal acquisition. Fraud and coercion are certainly ways of acquiring things. They are in sharp contrast with legal methods, which themselves are shown to be varied and complex. Even the legal ways of acquiring property are variously valued by those in the system. Political theorists have viewed inherited wealth differently from that gained by its owner's own effort. The favoured mode of acquisition is thus likely to have a number of institutional supports, which legitimate it above any alternatives.

Sociological evidence suggests that property may be almost self-generating in the sense that those who already have a great deal are likely to know how to come by still more. Those who own property may keep this essential knowledge entirely to themselves or they may favour a limited group with it. Property can in a sense reproduce itself because of the wealth which accrues to it. The legal concept of accession, a variety of original ownership acquisition, which describes the right to ownership of animals borne to animals already owned, is the most direct analogy here. Also relevant in this connection are the findings on the distribution of wealth suggesting that richer people get better yields on their large amounts of wealth than those with less property. Acquisition is thus not simply a matter of equal efforts by all individuals since existing property may autonomously generate still more. An investigator would therefore need to give detailed attention to any rewards attaching to property already owned.

How is it that acquisition is predictable to the individual? Part of the answer to this question is that society concedes ownership only to those individuals, who have the valued characteristics defined as being necessary. The relevant nature and quantity of these attributes is learned during socialisation, as it occurs in childhood. For example a society might have the norm that attributes of intelligence and persistence produce success. In ideational terms at least, the attributes and the outcome of recognised activity are connected in such a way as to insist that the link is causal. The research would thus be concerned to assess the correspondence between groups of attributes and the ownership of property.

Acquisition as a process has individual and social aspects inasmuch as the individual comes to anticipate future situations, not just as isolated incidents or conditions, but as a series or sequence of predictable events which socialisation has led him to expect. The situations themselves are defined socially and are regulated by institutional mechanisms. This final dimension is more complex than the first two since it involves integrating the individual and the social, and also the mental and the behavioural in a patterned sequence over time. This form of operationalisation of property would face its most severe test in this dimension.

Conclusion

Any operationalised property concept is assessible in both a priori and empirical terms. The first group of criteria would certainly include systematic and analytic qualities. System involves coherence between the composite elements. Evaluation, distribution, and acquisition are certainly compatible components though there is more scope for argument about the logic of their sequence. Analytic capacity is measurable in terms of the major canons of theoretical linkage and empirical potential. The proposed operationalised concept would be compatible with each of the positivistic, functional, and *verstehen* types of explanation in sociology, and particularly the social action theory *verstehen* type.

Empirical potential is judged by the extent to which the concept can be seen to penetrate data. The three dimensions of the property concept give coverage and order to property data generally. Development out of the survey of psychology, politics, law, and sociology (as working sources) ensures a useful ideal type in the sense that it is concretely realistic and not simply an artificially derived framework.

Notes

1. For example the treatment of religious belief, alienation, and professional values. See C. Y. Glock and R. Stark, *Religion and Society in Tension*, Chicago, Rand McNally and Co., 1965, especially Chapter 2, 'On the Study of Religious Commitment'; R. Blauner, *Alienation and Freedom*, Chicago, Unviersity of Chicago Press, 1964; A. Hastings and C. R. Hinings, 'Role Relations and Value Adaption: A Study of the Professional Accountant in Industry', *Sociology*, Vol.4, no.3, 1970.
2. A. W. Jones, *Life, Liberty and Property*, Philadelphia, Lippincott Co., 1941.
3. E. Beaglehole, *Property: A Study in Social Psychology*, London, Allen and Unwin, 1931, discusses in considerable detail the varieties of property objects amongst simple peoples. He makes particularly interesting statements on women as property (pp.158–66), on the special significance of land to people in simple societies (pp.138–42, 143–55, 177–97 and 213), on the classification and significance of native ornaments (pp.174–97), and on immaterial property in simple society (pp.140–2, 177). For societies with more developed economies, the range of property objects is wider. See J. R. Commons, *The Legal Foundations of Capitalism*, London, Wisconsin University Press, 1968, pp.18–19. For a clearer list see A. B. Atkinson, *Unequal Shares*, London, Allen Lane, 1972, p.7.
4. Beaglehole op.cit., p.279. Pp.278–84 is the source on evaluation and acquisition as outlined here.
5. Ibid., p.156.
6. Ibid., p.143.
7. Objective descriptions of the sentiments of ownership are difficult to achieve. The following references are a useful beginning: *Possessiveness*, I. D. Suttie, M. Ginsberg, S. Isaacs, T. H. Marshall, 'Symposium on Property and Possessiveness', *The Journal of Medical Psychology*, Vol.15, 1935. *Jealousy*, A. F. Shand, *The Foundations of Character*, London, Macmillan, 1914, pp.256–62; Beaglehole op.cit., pp.164–5; K. Davis, 'Jealousy and Sexual Property', Chapter 7 in *Human Society*, New York, Macmillan, 1966. *Aggressiveness*, R. Stagner, *The Psychology of Personality*, London, McGraw-Hill, 1961, 3rd edn., pp.113–16; Beaglehole, op.cit., p.139; The Milner–Holland Committee Report on Housing in Greater London, Cmnd. 2605, HMSO, London, March 1965, p.173. *Domination*, Beaglehole, op.cit., pp.281, 308–10; G. Simmel, 'Domination' in D. N. Levine (ed.), *Georg Simmel on Individuality and Social Forms*, Chicago, University of Chicago Press, 1971; M. Ginsberg,

On the Diversity of Morals, London, Heinemann, 1956, p.318; M. Young and P. Willmott, *Family and Class in a London Suburb*, London, Mentor, 1967, p.31; F. Bechhofer and B. Elliott, 'Small Shopkeepers and the Class Structure', *Actives Europeenes de Sociologie*, Vol.9, 1968, no.2, pp.180–202; B. Elliott and D. McCrone, 'Privilege, Property and Planning', paper presented at the Fourth Joint Conference on the Behavioural Sciences and Operational Research – held at the London Business School, 19 December 1972. *Security*, C. J. Morgan, *Introduction to Psychology*, 2nd edn., London, Mcgraw-Hill, 1961, p.96; D. McCrone, 'Perception of Housing: A Sociological Study of Two Middle Class Estates', unpublished M.Sc. thesis, Unviersity of Edinburgh, 1971; Jon Gower Davies, *The Evangelistic Bureaucrat*, London, Tavistock, 1972; pp.34, 37–8; Elliott and McCrone (1972), op.cit., pp.6–7. *Intimacy*, Beaglehole, op.cit., pp.142, 146, 298–9. *Creativitys* Beaglehole, op.cit., pp.146–9, 182–3; Young and Willmott, op.cit., p.32; G. Norton, 'The Pleasures arising from the Possession of Land', in C. F. Dowsett, *Land: Its Attraction and Riches*, Land Roll Office, London, 1892.

8. The experimental theories are ingenious and do suggest that property is deeply rooted in the personality without resort to instinct. Psychoanalytic theory, emphasising the remarkable parallel between the early activities of the infant and acquisitive patterns in later life, is initially very attractive. Property interest in adult life is held to be a consequence of the infant's fascination with excretion, and of the management of these desires until there has been a conversion to socially acceptable interests and behaviour. The theory of anal erotism thus seems comprehensive and plausible on the development of the evaluation process, yet it is not matched by sound empirical evidence. Another theory of early socialisation into acquisitive behaviour is provided by L. D. Suttie (*Symposium*, 1935). The infant's 'gradual loss of mother rapport', 'the forced renunciation of the primal baby mother intimacy' produces a tension between the infant and his environment attributable to anxiety about the loss of maternal affection. Property is a source of relieving this anxiety in that 'it is used to give or withhold, to create gratitude or expectancy, to ensure that the possessor will never be ignored by others' (p.60). Both these particularistic socialisation theories may be appropriate depending on the case. The more general idea of early direct socialisation of the infant into a socially acceptable pattern of acquisitiveness to meet recognisable needs seems more appropriate here. I have relied heavily here on Beaglehole, op.cit., pp.267–78, and on Professor G. Trasler's unpublished essay on 'The Psychology of Property', Department of Psychology, University of Southampton, 1951, as well as the 1935 *Symposium*.
9. A. H. Maslow, 'A Theory of Motivation' (1943) in V. H. Vroom and E. L. Deci, *Management and Motivation*, London, Penguin, 1970, pp.27–41. On property meeting basic physiological needs see Beaglehole, op.cit., pp.156–74: on property and the safety need see Beaglehole (1931), op.cit., pp.193, 307; I. D. Suttie *Symposium* (1935), op.cit., p.60, and T. H. Marshall *Symposium* (1935), op.cit. pp.60, 79–81: on property and the higher needs, love and self esteem, see Beaglehole, op.cit., pp.172–3, 219–21, 307–9, and T. H. Marshall, *Symposium* (1935), op.cit., pp.81–3.

10. Beaglehole, op.cit., p.295: Beaglehole sees conational unity (which I interpret as meaning the integrated inception of purposeful activity) as the hallmark of the developed personality.

11. Mead's concept of the fully socialised personality emphasises two levels of social influence on the individual's development. There is the individual's self in consequence of an organisation of particular attitudes of other individuals to him in interaction in specific social situations. The second level operates in the sense that the personality is a reflection of the 'generalised other', that is the organisation of the attitudes of the social group as a whole to which the individual belongs. Generally too elusive for a discussion of the psychology of property, Mead uses property to illustrate the 'generalised other'. Property involves an organised attitude common to all members of the community. A person who claims an object belongs exclusively to him is taking the attitude of the 'generalised other' in that he is appealing to his rights by taking the attitude of the whole group to property. G. H. Mead, 'On Social Psychology' in Anselm Strauss (ed.), Chicago, Unviersity of Chicago Press, 1969, pp.222–8.

12. Beaglehole, op.cit., pp.306–7. Goffman's *Asylums*, Doubleday Anchor, New York, 1961, suggests that depriving the inmates of private property is a vital part of the deliberate process of the mortification of the self in total institutions (pp.18–21, 78–9). More generally the 'performances' of activities require 'expressive equipment' for the performer's personal front of which clothing is an important example. E. Goffman, *The Presentation of Self in Everyday Life*, New York, Doubleday Anchor, 1959.

13. It is also empirically evident that individual and social stability requires the achievement of some congenial balancing interchange between personality and environment in respect of property. Parsonian analysis using the framework of boundary interchanges between isomorphic systems may be a useful starting point here. To begin with see T. Parsons, *The Social System*, London, Routledge, 1951, pp.71–4 for a model with interesting insights.

14. Property can be equally productive of oppositive effects but the evaluation issue still holds. See 'William Godwin's Political Justice. A reprint of the Essay on Property', in H. S. Salt (ed.), London, Allen and Unwin, 1918, on property induced dependence as harmful to the personality. 'Observe the pauper fawning with abject vileness upon his rich benefactor, and speechless with sensations of gratitude for having received that which he ought to have claimed with an erect mein, and with a consciousness, that his claim was irresistible (p.48).

15. For Hegel, property is within the sphere of 'abstract right' (the rights accruing to individuals simply because they are persons). The reasonableness of property is not that it satisfies needs but, that it enables the subjective element in the personality to be replaced by rationality. 'It is in possession first of all that the person becomes rational'. Hegel, *The Philosophy of Right*, cited in M. R. Cohen and F. S. Cohen, *Readings in Jurisprudence and Legal Philosophy*, Boston, Little, Brown and Co., 1951, p.74. Another view is that of Godwin in Salt, op.cit., pp.40–60. The ability consciously to impose the will on a thing does not necessarily

produce rationality and independence of mind, but ostentation, vanity and ambition.

16. Harrington's *Oceana*, cited in G. H. Sabine, *A History of Political Theory*, London, Harrap, 1959, p.423.
17. Harrington's *Oceana*, cited in C. B. Macpherson, *The Political Theory of Possessive Individualism*, London, OUP, 1962, pp.162–3.
18. G. H. Sabine, op.cit., p.425. Also P. Zagorin, *A History of Political Thought in the English Revolution*, London, Routledge, 1954, Chapter 11.
19. H. J. Laski, *A Grammar of Politics*, London, Allen and Unwin, 1934, p.174.
20. H. J. Laski, op.cit., pp.174–5.
21. See for a very brief summary 'Property', in *Palgrave's Dictionary of Political Economy*, London, Macmillan, 1926, Vol.III, pp.231–3, and for more detail R. Schlatter, *Private Property*, London, Allen and Unwin, 1951.
22. H. J. Laski, op.cit., p.178.
23. 'As an institution, property – and any particular system of property – is a man-made device which establishes certain relations between people. Like all such devices, its maintenance requires at least the acquiescence of the bulk of the people, and the positive support of any leading classes. Such support requires a belief that the institution serves some purpose or fills some need. That belief requires, in turn, that there be a theory which both explains and justifies the institution in terms of the purpose served or the need filled. As needs change new theories are developed, and the institution itself is changed by political action.' C. B. Macpherson, *Democratic Theory: Essays in retrieval*, Oxford, Clarendon Press, 1973, p.121. See also C. B. Macpherson (ed.), *Property Mainstream and Critical Positions*, Oxford, Blackwell, 1978.
24. Macpherson (1973), op.cit., pp.40–8, 120–40.
25. Factors here include different histories of legal evolution, differential diffusion of legal rules, the legal function of codifying uncertainty, the autonomy of particular legal institutions, and more general social change.
26. The diagram and discussion in *Salmond on Jurisprudence*, 12th edn., ed. by P. J. Fitzgerald, p.413, on kinds of property is useful here. See also the illuminating discussion of 'Things' in section 114 pp.506–16, in G. W. Paton and D. P. Derham (eds.) *A Textbook of Jurisprudence*, London, OUP, 1972, showing the considerable difficulties surrounding the identification and classification of property objects.
27. The essence of ownership seems clearest in the sense of 'domination', a near absolute institution of Roman law, in which the owner had absolute title to the property object, absolute right to dispose of it, with very few public law restrictions over its use (F. H. Lawson, *Introduction to the Law of Property*, London, OUP, 1958, p.87). The distinction between core and residual rights has been offered as a way of eliciting the essence of ownership (C. R. Noyes, *The Institution of Property*, London, Longmans, 1936). This idea could be used in the distinction between 'ultimate ownership', where the core is left to the owner while the object itself is enjoyed temporarily by another person, and 'complete or beneficial ownership', where the owner enjoys all the rights and privileges which are legally impossible (Paton and Derham, op.cit., p.519). For

Lawson (p.89) the essence of ownership is the core right of the transfer of interest, '. . . the owner of a thing, whether land or a chattel, is the person who can convey the full interest in it to another person'. Although technically there is no ownership of land in English law, the core rights constituting the essence of property in land are shown, in the notion of 'fee simple' holding, to be duration and the extent of inheritability. A. M. Honore in his essay 'Ownership' (in A. G. Guest (ed.), *Oxford Essays in Jurisprudence*, London, OUP, 1961) makes a comprehensive list of the 'standard incidents' attaching to a person who has 'the greatest interest in a thing'.

28. Saying anything definite about possession seems difficult. See R. W. M. Dias, *Jurisprudence*, 3rd edn., London, Butterworths, 1970, pp.341–59 and Paton and Derham, op.cit. In some circumstances possession may have more strength than ownership. Three arguments which seem to carry weight that ownership is generally stronger than possession are that possession is an attribute of ownership, that an owner's claim overrides that of a possessor, and that though possession can be a strong right of limited interest for duration the core rights remain with the owner of the property.
29. Paton and Derham, op.cit., pp.543–52.
30. Supply of resources ('input'), a conversion process ('throughput') and the production of an object or objects ('output') is the definition used by D. Silverman, *The Theory of Organisations*, London, Heinemann, 1970, p.27. The three works used as an 'empirical' basis here are C. R. Noyes, *The Institution of Property*, London, Longmans, 1936; L. F. Vinding-Kruse, *The Right of Property* (trans. by P. T. Federspiel), London, OUP, 1939; F. H. Lawson, *Introduction to the Law of Property*, London, OUP, 1958.
31. Relevant sources here are K. Renner, *The Institutions of Private Law and their Social Functions*, London, Routledge, 1949. For important summary, interpretation, and comment on the approach to and substance of the thesis, reference should be made to W. Friedmann, *Legal Theory*, London, Stevens, 1967; W. Friedmann *Law and Social Change in Contemporary Britain*, London, Stevens, 1951; and O. Kahn-Freund, 'Introduction' to Renner, op.cit.
32. Lawson, op.cit., p.2.
33. D. R. Harris, 'The Concept of Possession in English Law', in Guest (ed.), op.cit., pp.86–7.
34. Ibid., p.75.
35. The example which is given in Paton and Derham, op.cit., p.561, concerns the slave as agent in relation to his master's intention to possess and shows the decline of specific intent.
36. There are exceptions: see R. H. Lowie, *Social Organization*, London, Routledge, 1950, Chapter 6, 'Property' and H. E. Barnes, *Social Institutions*, New York, Prentice Hall, 1946, Chapter 6, 'The Institution of Property in the Light of Sociology and History'.
37. '. . . the right of property is the right of a given individual to exclude other individuals and collective entities from the usage of a given thing. The sole exception is the State and lesser organs of the State, whose right of usage can, however, not be exercised except in special circumstances,

provided for by law.' E. Durkheim, *Professional Ethics and Civic Morals*, London, Routledge, 1957.

38. For example J. E. Meade, *Efficiency, Equality and the Ownership of Property*, London, Allen and Unwin, 1964; Atkinson, op.cit. There are also official reports – Diamond Report, 1975, Royal Commission on the Distribution of Income and Wealth Reports no.1, 2, Cmnd 6172, 6173.
39. 'Wealth provides security, and freedom of action, it allows a person to retire early (or not to work at all); it allows his children to complete their education without financial worries. A person inheriting £1 million can spend £400 a week for the next fifty years. Alternatively he can control the operations of a large company and the jobs of hundreds of workers. Wealth may not be essential to human happiness but its unequal distribution has profound consequences for our society.' Atkinson, op.cit. p.xv.
40. This does not invalidate the contention that property is an institution which has effects on social order generally through its co-ordinating function, as well as being integral to the economic organisation of any society. See A. I. Hallowell, 'The Nature and Function of Property as a Social Institution', *Journal of Legal and Political Sociology*, Vol.1, no.3–4, April 1943, pp.115–38.
41. K. Davis, *Human Society* ,New York, Macmillan, 1966, p.178.
42. Convenient summaries on this topic are to be found in T. B. Bottomore, *Elites and Society*, London, Penguin, 1966, pp.77–82; T. Nichols, *Ownership, Control and Ideology*, London, Allen and Unwin, 1969; J. Child, *The Business Enterprise in Modern Society*, London, Macmillan, 1969, pp.34–59. See also Atkinson, op.cit., pp.38–43 and J. Scott, *Corporations, Classes, and Capitalism*, London, Hutchinson, 1979, especially Chapters 2 and 3.
43. A. Giddens, *The Class Structure of Advanced Societies*, London, Hutchinson, 1973, is a useful summary of sociological thinking on this subject.
44. See D. Lane, *The End of Inequality*, London, Penguin, 1971, p.130 and W. Wesolowski, 'The Notions of Strata and Class in Industrial Society', in A. Beteille (ed.), *Social Inequality*, London, Penguin, 1969.

individual to attend to certain external events or stimuli, to experience a particular emotion, and to strive towards the attainment of some object[7] and believed, therefore, that the instinct of acquisition[8] was the source of the desire to acquire possessions and the satisfaction of ownership – and also, of course, of the collecting, hoarding, acquisitive and predatory behaviour of men and women, and indeed of jackdaws, squirrels and foxes also.

Whether explanations of the institutions of property, or other forms of social behaviour, as the consequences of instinct are admissible at all clearly depends upon the nature of supporting evidence of the physiological and genetic mechanisms through which the instinct is transmitted from one generation to another, is reflected in the neurological characteristics of the individual, and is expressed in his consciousness and his conduct. The failure of the exponents of instinct theory to furnish these essential data – or, indeed, to acknowledge either the need for them or the possibility of investigating the psycho-physical mechanisms involved – was the main cause of the general abandonment by psychologists of the attempt to explain human social behaviour in terms of instinct. The particular question of the relations between the institution of property and the supposed instinct of acquisition raises additional problems. As Ginsberg remarked,

> It may be of some assistance to be informed that the institution of property has a basis in the collecting or acquisitive instinct, but this tells us nothing of what we really want to know, about the different forms which property assumes in different forms of social organisation.[9]

Instinct theories do not necessarily assert that the sentiment of property is derived from a single, specific instinct of acquisitiveness or possessiveness. McDougall's analysis, for example, indicates that a sentiment such as pride in one's home (or in some other possession) is a complex cognitive-emotional system which may have its 'conative-affective roots' in more than one instinct: in this example, the instincts of food-seeking, construction, acquisition and self-assertion together form the instinctual roots of the sentiment which causes the individual to purchase, furnish and defend his house.[10] It would not be difficult to devise similarly complex accounts of the instinctive bases of sentiments related to one's clothing, motor car, sporting equipment or books, for these possessions are valued in different ways.

We may wish to say, then, that possessiveness and the desire to acquire and display personal property have their roots in several instincts, of which the instinct of acquisition is but one. This is essentially Ginsberg's conclusion: '. . . acquisitiveness as such, if it exists at all in man as a specific instinct, plays a comparatively unimportant role in fashioning the institutions and behaviour connected with property'.[11] But however sensible such characterisations may be, they seem to imply such distant and complex connections between the hypothetical instinct of property (or acquisition) and the ways in which men and women feel about, and behave in relation to, their possessions that they amount to little more than saying that these aspects of behaviour are motivated. The notion of an instinct as an inherited disposition to behave in particular ways in certain circumstances, which convincingly describes the complex, apparently unlearned activities of the squirrel or the mason wasp, must necessarily be so diluted and qualified before it can be made to fit human social behaviour that it loses its explanatory value.

Psychoanalytic Theory

Freud's contributions to the psychology of acquisitiveness and possessiveness were initially prompted by the clinical observation that certain individuals exhibited three traits – 'a triad of characteristics which are always to be found together: orderliness, parsimoniousness and obstinacy'[12]; the childhood histories of such people usually showed that they have strongly resisted the attempts of their nurses or parents to train them in regular bowel habits, and had shown extremely strong interests in their own faeces which had persisted beyond the stage of development at which children usually lose this preoccupation. 'One of the clearest signs of subsequent eccentricity or nervousness is to be seen when a baby obstinately refuses to empty his bowels when he is put on the pot – that is when his nurse wants him to – and holds back that function till he himself chooses to exercise it.'[13] Freud thus portrays the toilet training of these individuals as a battle of wills; the infant endeavouring to retain his faeces as long as possible, and resisting the entreaties (or the wrath) of the adult who wishes him to expel them promptly.

The reasons for the child's obstinacy are complex. He is reluctant to give up the valued product of his own body even though his nurse evidently wishes to have it, and shows pleasure and gratitude when he accedes to her request. Secondly, retaining faeces when sitting on the pot results in distension of the colon which is pleasurable. Thirdly, the infant enjoys exercising the power which he has to defy the instructions of his nurse, for a while, and thus to impose his will upon her. The significance of these events for the development of attitudes to property is, of course, that this is the first time that the child has been confronted with the choice between giving or withholding something which is indubitably his and is desired by someone else: 'Interest in faeces is carried over first to interest in gifts, then to interest in money'[14] and it is therefore not unreasonable to expect the obstinacy or compliance with which he responds to his nurse's requests to be reflected in parsimony or generosity in relation to the possessions of later childhood and adult life.

However, Freud does not regard the infant's response to toilet training simply as an early example of his attitude to possessions; he insists that the relationship is a causal one. His reasoning rests upon the notion, central to psychoanalytic theory, of infantile sexuality, according to which the infant derives sensual pleasure from the stimulation of various sensitive areas of his body ('erotogenic zones') in a sequence of phases which reflect the dominant features of his experience. Thus the first erotogenic zone is the mouth, because the most vivid experiences of the earliest weeks and months of life are those of suckling and biting at the breast; toilet training focuses the child's attention upon his sphincters, so that these sensitive areas of his body become erotogenic zones; and in due course the genital zones yield pleasure through manual stimulation. The mature sexuality of the adult includes components or traces of these infantile forms of erotic sensuality.[15] Although the individual later comes to regard his excreta with disgust, the instinct[16] generated in the anal stages of psychosexual development becomes attached to those things which symbolise faeces (possessions, money) and to the actions of acquiring, giving or withholding them. Thus '. . . each one of the three qualities, avarice, pedantry and stubbornness, springs from anal-erotic sources – or, to express it more cautiously and more completely – draws powerful contributions from these sources'.[17]

It is true that Freud set out to explain the miserliness and obstinacy of a small, distinct group of individuals who exhibited what came to be called 'the anal character', but he believed his observations to be relevant to the conduct of other people in relation to their possessions and the acquisition of wealth. Indeed, they are to be regarded as an explanation of the origins of the social institutions of property, since Freud believed, in true reductionist fashion, that '. . . sociology, which deals with the behaviour of man in society, can be nothing other than applied psychology'.[18]

Perhaps the most valuable aspect of Freud's contributions to the psychology of possessions was that it drew attention to the irrationality, the compulsive quality, of much financial activity – a theme which was later developed by Suttie and others.[19] His emphasis on the erotic element in toilet training, and therefore upon the relations between acquisitiveness, hoarding and parsimoniousness, carries less conviction, although, as Beaglehole points out, 'It has such close connections with the general body of Freudian theory that any searching criticism would find it necessary to come to terms first with psycho-analytic doctrine as a whole before it could proceed to treat in detail the theory of anal-erotic character traits and the theory of copro-symbolism.'[20]

Later writers of the dynamic schools of psychology, while generally subscribing to the notion that money and possessions stand in some symbolic relation to the precious bodily products of the infant,[21] have placed greater emphasis on the assertion of independence which is reflected in refusing to perform when asked by one's nurse or one's parent to do so. It seems sensible to discard the picture of the infant on his pot experiencing erotic sensations which he is destined to recall, in disguised form, at his office desk, when calling his stockbroker, or poring over his stamp collection or his bank statement, and instead to treat this as an early demonstration (or as a lesson) that possessions give one power over others.

In his critique of Freud's central thesis, Suttie argued that property had a dual significance. Initially objects are desired for use, for the pleasure or comfort which they promote; but in due course the child's desire for property *to use* becomes transmuted into 'a desire for the ownership and control of property *needed by others*. . . .' Thus

> a secondary meaning becomes attached to the institution of exclusive possession, so that this becomes a means of increasing the social significance of the owner and of commanding on his behalf the *attention* of his social environment; in other words, personal property is a means of overcoming the separation anxiety[22] (emphasis in original).

This description is in close agreement with the observations of Susan Isaacs, to be considered later in this chapter.

Transitional Objects

The significance of the infant's first possession has been investigated by several psychologists. It has been demonstrated that many (but not all) children establish a special relationship with a soft object (typically a piece of blanket, a rag, or a woolly toy) at some time during the first two years of infancy, or in some cases rather later.[23] This possession, which is commonly referred to as a 'cuddly',[24] has certain characteristic features. It is the object of a great deal of physical manipulation – hugging, sucking, chewing, winding about the child's fingers or rubbing between knees or thighs – as a result of which it usually becomes dilapidated or grubby; but its familiar odour, flavour and tactile properties seem to be extremely important to its owner, who resists having it laundered or replaced. The 'cuddly' is always referred to by a proper noun which is commonly a kind of pet name or a word which has become associated with the object, by chance, early in the relationship.[25] The parents generally acknowledge, and perhaps help to define, the infant's special title to the object, and his dependence upon it for comfort, especially when he is settling down to sleep, or when he is distressed, tired or ill. At least in the early stages of this attachment, clinging to the 'cuddly' is part of a soothing ritual which involves sucking the thumb, rubbing the forehead, stroking the nose, or some other comforting, repetitive activity.[26]

The first treasured possession is not, however, simply a source of sensory pleasure; it seems to function as a 'safety signal', as a tangible indication that all is well. Stevenson's case studies suggest that the 'cuddly' is sometimes even more reassuring than the presence of the mother, although it does not appear to stand in a relation of rivalry; the parents explicitly recognise the importance of the child's 'cuddly' to him, and indeed will help him to find it when he needs the comfort it provides. It is to be noted that although this relationship between child and 'cuddly' is most important during the early years of infancy, it typically retains its special significance and properties long after he has acquired more sophisticated toys and other possessions; he may well turn to it again in times of distress or anxiety, and derive solace from its familiar texture, smell and taste.[27]

There is little agreement as to the nature of the infant's attachment to his 'first treasured possession' and its significance for later patterns of ownership. Bowlby argues that such objects can be regarded

> simply as objects towards which certain components of attachment behaviour come to be directed or redirected because the 'natural' object is unavailable. Instead of to the breast, non-nutritive sucking is directed to a dummy; and instead of to a mother's body, hair, or clothing, clinging is directed to a blanket or cuddly toy. Since there is no reason to suppose that (these) objects play any special role in a child's development, cognitive or other, (an) appropriate term for this would be simply 'substitute objects'.[28]

On the other hand, what evidence we have does not suggest that infants who develop an attachment to a 'cuddly' do so because they have special difficulties of access to their mothers. Schaffer and Emerson (admittedly restricting their analysis to infants no older than eighteen months) found that ten out of nineteen infants whose mothers described them as 'accepting, enjoying and . . . actively seeking physical contact . . .' had 'favourite cuddlies', while only one child in a group of nine who 'protested at, resisted and avoided' being picked up, held on the lap, or being kissed or stroked, made use of a cuddly during the first eighteen months.[29] Stevenson reports that children in residential nurseries seldom have 'favourite cuddlies': 'Among twenty children (aged 1 to 5) with whom I worked, not one could be said to cherish a toy or an object for more than a passing hour or two – and then possession was usually maintained to thwart another child.'[30] A similar observation is offered by Provence and Lipton.[31]

In attempting to reconcile these several observations, it is important to take account of Stevenson's case material, which shows that many mothers respected, and indeed supported and perhaps even encouraged their infants' reliance upon their 'cuddlies', while the residential nurseries of that time were likely, on the whole, to discourage a practice which might be regarded as unhygienic and an unnecessary complication for the nurses in caring for the children in their charge. Thus, while Bowlby's view is that the infant's attachment to the 'cuddly' is simply displaced from the unavailable mother, an alternative account might stress the active role of the mother in encouraging her child to realise the reassurance which one can derive from a familiar, physically comfortable, possession of which one is the sole and undisputed owner.

Winnicott points out that the 'cuddly' has a peculiar status as 'the first not-me possession': that it reflects the dawning of the infant's awareness of 'other-than-me' entities, albeit before he has grasped the fact that things in his environment have an independent existence. He therefore proposes 'the use of the terms "transitional object" and "transitional phenomena" for designation of the intermediate area of experience, between the thumb and the teddy bear, between the oral erotism and true object relationship'.[32]

Winnicott's explanation of the special significance of the 'cuddly' – the 'transitional object' – thus intimately connects two processes, one essentially affective (that is, establishing an attachment to an object which, while symbolising the mother's breast, is not),[33] the other cognitive, the first stage in distinguishing between fantasy and fact, between inner objects and external objects',[34] which form the basis for realistic perception of the external world. This is achieved by the mother's willingness to tolerate, and indeed actively to collude in, an illusion which represents the persistence, for a time, of the infant's belief that all that is of value, that yields pleasurable sensation, is part of himself and his own creation.

> The transitional object comes from the environment, as we know, but it is essential to understand that from the infant's point of view it was created by the infant. . . . In respect of these transitional objects the parents, as it were, conspire not to challenge the origin. They easily see that the thumb is part of the child and that the next toy or teddy bear or doll is a gift, but with regard to the object in question they undertake to refrain from challenging the infant as to its origin.[35]

In more mundane language, the parents recognise, and are willing to accept, the child's illusory belief that he has control of his world, that he can ensure that his urgent needs are met and the fearful prospects of being abandoned are warded off by the magical powers of his cuddly which is undisputedly his, because by doing so they can mitigate the trauma of discovering the extent of his defencelessness in the real world.[36]

This analysis ascribes a key role to the transitional object as a bridge between the illusions of omnipotence which characterise early infancy and the realistic thinking of the childhood years. It offers an explanation of the peculiarly comforting and reassuring quality of the 'cuddly', so that (as Stevenson points out) what begins as a progressive phenomenon in children's development may become, as the years go by, a regressive manifestation, in that at times of stress the child turns to the infantile object which comforts and relieves for a time the 'strain of relating inner and outer experiences'.[37] Winnicott does not suggest that the child's relationship with his 'transitional object' forms the prototype for the whole range of his later responses to possessions (indeed, the theory implies that this is emphatically not the case) but it is not unreasonable to suggest that it throws a little light on the mysterious process in which most people gain comfort and reassurance from old and familiar possessions which are often of very little objective worth[38]; and perhaps also, as Winnicott claims, goes some way to explaining certain abnormal patterns and conduct in relation to property.[39]

Acquisitiveness and Possessiveness in the Childhood Years

Conflicts between the child's attachment to greatly loved, but unhygienic and disreputable, possessions and his parents' determination to persuade him into more practical attitudes to property are a common feature of the early years of childhood, and by no means confined to 'transitional objects'. John and Elizabeth Newson report that '. . . the majority of four-year olds seem to have a strongly developed property sense'[40] which frequently leads to conflict with parents who wish to reduce the sheer bulk of the child's accumulated possessions by discarding those that are broken or worn out.

> The logical assumption of the throw-away philosophy is, of course, that when broken goods are replaced by new, the broken ones are put in the dustbin; but where four-year olds and their toys are concerned one is relieved to observe that sentimental attachment confounds logic. . . . It seems very typical of this developmental stage that children should be deeply attached to anything which they regard as belonging to them personally; and this attachment extends not only to favourite toys in a good state of repair, but to all sorts of broken and apparently useless bits and pieces, often of unrecognizable origin, which have come into their possession by casual gift or adoption.[41]

The Newsons' data indicate that the child's right to his own possessions is generally recognised and respected by his parents, who often express some anxiety about the propriety of discarding any of his toys without his consent. Indeed, they report that '. . . there are a very few children who do not present this problem of possessiveness at all. Far from rejoicing in their escape, however, their mothers tend to be a little perturbed at what they correctly regard as an abnormal (in the statistical sense only) indifference to ownership'.[42]

Although hoarding and the accumulation of familiar objects is characteristic of the early years of childhood, it is clear that, even among quite small children, property and ownership are matters of great concern in several quite distinct ways. Susan Isaacs presents numerous case examples which '. . . bear witness to the strength and urgency of the common wish of little children to have exclusive possession or at least the biggest share or main use of whatever properties are the centre of interest at the moment. The satisfaction of having things all one's own is deep, the chagrin at others' having more than oneself very bitter.'[43] She distinguishes four 'forms of the possessive impulse' reflected in her observations: the wish to own and to have exclusive use of an object; proprietorial sentiments (and claims) concerning things which are not objects, such as songs, ideas and proposals; the power which stems from the control of property ('many of the children took it upon themselves now and then to act as dispensers of the public property . . . they got a sense of great power from deciding who should use it and who not, how much they should have, and so on'); and the rivalry and jealousy generated when several children wanted to use a piece of school apparatus at the same time.[44] Isaacs points out that

> Even in the least complicated situation, where the value of the thing owned is intrinsic, as the means of satisfying some (primary or derived) need, the actual wish to *own* it can only be understood in terms of power, or, rather, of *powerlessness*. I want to own it because if I do not it may not be there when I need it, and my need will go unsatisfied. . . . Only by having the means of satisfaction of my need as *mine*, mine to have and to hold, can I feel safe.[45] (emphasis in original).

The burden of Isaacs's discussion of the significance of property to the young is that it has more to do with social relationships, with power and autonomy and prestige, than with the intrinsic worth of possessions or the non-social satisfactions which they can provide; one might perhaps say that, for her, the institutions of property were not devices for promoting and controlling individual enjoyment of objects, but the means by which objects may be used to constrain and to modify the relationships between an individual and his fellows, and his position in the social groups of which he is a member. For that reason she rejects the approach of the classical instinct theorists:

> To think of the motive of possession as a simple irreducible instinct is thus to miss its most significant aspect, viz. its intimate relation with the motives of power, of rivalry, of guilt and of love. It is essentially a *social* response, not a simple direction to the physical objects which may serve individual purposes.[46]

In this respect her analysis closely parallels that of Suttie in the same symposium.[47] However, she places particular emphasis upon the significance of possessions in transactions between individuals:

> Even in the simpler instances of the direct wish to own, it is plain that the relation to another *person* is a very important element. Neither the pleasure of ownership nor the chagrin of envy bears much relation to the intrinsic value of the things owned or coveted. Few objects, other than food when hungry, have absolute and intrinsic value to little children, independent of what other children are having and wanting. What is so desperately desired may be wanted simply because someone else has it or desires it. A thing that has long been treated with indifference or contempt by the owner may suddenly assume great value in his eyes, if another person begins to take an interest in it; an ordinary object in the common environment, which has had no attention from the children, may suddenly become the centre of an intense struggle for ownership, if one of the children . . . shows that it now has value for him.[48]

Such comments are unlikely to surprise a parent or a teacher, but they serve as a reminder of the complex nature of attitudes and sentiments concerning property, even among the very young, and of the importance of possessions in the transactions which children have with one another and with their parents and other adults. These are not exclusively invested in the acquisition and ownership of property; giving is also important. As the Newsons show, parental encouragement (and sometimes coercion) plays an important part in this, although 'some children . . . enjoy being in the position of benefactor'[49]; Isaacs also noted the importance of gratitude for gifts as evidence of the loveworthiness of the recipient, and the security and self-esteem which one may derive from being able to give desirable things and valued services to others.[50]

Collecting behaviour – in the sense of acquiring objects of a particular kind, such as coins, stamps, match-books, or pictures and newspaper cuttings relating to cinema actors or popular musicians – is a common feature of the middle years of childhood; though how common it is seems to be a matter of dispute. The Newsons found that 80 per cent of boys and 66 per cent of girls in their cohorts had specific collections of this kind, the habit being most noticeable, and probably the subject of more parental encouragement, in families of higher socio-economic status.[51] Beaglehole notes the very marked disparity between the findings of several studies of the incidence of collecting behaviour in young children[52]; it seems clear that this kind of activity is subject to fashion and local custom, and not (as some writers have supposed) the expression of some inherent impulse of acquisition.

It might be thought that respect for property and for the rights of ownership must be a peculiarity of capitalist societies, but this does not appear to be the case. Although the notions of common ownership and sharing feature prominently in the training of quite small children in the Soviet Union ('Mine is ours; ours is mine'[53]), they are also taught to value and to take care of their own personal possessions. Thus the Model Programme of Upbringing of the Academy of Pedagogical Sciences includes under Grade One (children aged seven years) '. . . take care of your own things, for example, sew on buttons, iron, shine shoes, keep desk in order'[54] and 'diligence in work and care of possessions' is included as one of the 'stated objectives of upbringing' in Communist morality for Soviet children in the age range 7 – 11 years.[55] The principle appears to be that personal possessions, such as the child's clothing, his books, and his toys, are property held in trust, the ownership of which is ultimately vested in the collective and in the community as a whole – in contrast to the Western notion that an individual is entitled to do as he wishes with objects that he owns, even (if he thinks fit) to destroy them.[56] There is also an emphasis upon the citizen's duty to respect and to take care of public property which is largely lacking in the education of children in non-communist countries.[57]

Property and Individual Delinquency[58]

If one leaves out of account the very large number of offences which arise from the driving of motor vehicles, the great majority of crimes have to do with stealing or damaging the property of others. In England and Wales, for example, thefts, frauds, burglary, the receiving of stolen property and malicious damage to property make up about 95 per cent of all indictable offences recorded by the police[59] and there are good reasons for believing that offences in these categories (particularly those involving damage to public property) are less often reported to the police than crimes which involve some element of violence or the threat of violence.[60] The Uniform Crime Reports in the United States show that about 90 per cent of 'Index' crimes involve theft,[61] and figures for other Western countries are broadly comparable.

It is extremely difficult to estimate the actual incidence of crimes against property, since many offences are not reported[62] and certain kinds of offences, such as shoplifting and thefts by employees in shops and stockrooms, are unlikely to be detected unless the miscreant is actually caught in the act. There is little doubt, however, that the incidence of petty theft is very high indeed. Carter estimated in 1971 that 'the total cost of theft, direct and indirect, private and "social", amounts to around 2 per cent of national income in Britain'[63] of which perhaps £400 million was attributable to theft from shops.[64] A Home Office committee noted that 'Estimates which have been published in the press of losses, in money terms, sustained by retailers by shoplifting have ranged from £56 million to £300 million a year. Estimates of losses from staff thefts range from £135 million to £200 million',[65] and reported that the median estimates of losses through pilfering were between 0.5 and 1.0 per cent of annual turnover for small shops, and between 1 and 2 per cent for large stores.[66]

It also appears to be the case that very many people indulge in thefts and acts of damage to property on occasion. In this respect police records are misleading, since in looking for suspects the police necessarily concentrate their attention on individuals whose criminal activities and methods are already known to them. Investigators who have asked ostensibly law-abiding citizens about their undetected delinquencies have found that 'a very substantial proportion of those men and women who have never been in trouble with the law admit to having done things which could have led to a conviction for stealing or fraud'.[67] For example, 89 per cent of men and 83 per cent of women who responded to a mailed questionnaire in New York State admitted having committed thefts.[68] Studies of young people yield similar findings: for instance, Belson's investigation of 1425 boys, mainly in the age range 13–16 years, in London found that '88 per cent had at some time stolen something from school; 70 per cent had at some time stolen something from a shop, 33 per cent from a stall or barrow' – although many of these thefts were trivial in terms of the value of the object stolen; when only goods worth £1 or more were counted, the figures were 13, 16 and 4 per cent respectively.[69]

What is known of public attitudes to crime seems to indicate that most people regard deliberately damaging property or stealing by means of fraud or burglary as more serious than simple theft, and that they regard dishonest 'opportunism', such as travelling on a bus or a train without paying the fare, or 'stealing by finding', as comparatively trivial. They also distinguish between thefts from individuals and from large businesses or public bodies, generally considering the latter to be less serious.[70] An important component in judgements of the seriousness of a theft seems to be 'who was hurt and how much'.[71]

The little that is known concerning the reaction of the victims of theft and burglary tends to support the notion that the real insult has less to do with the value of the property stolen or damaged than with the violation of the relationship between person and possession. For example, Durant and her colleagues found that the shock of having one's house ransacked is a great deal more important than the financial loss of suffering a burglary or the inconvenience which that involves. Only one in ten of their respondents regarded financial loss as the worst thing about the incident; 'sentimental loss', the distress of finding one's possessions deliberately damaged by an intruder, and 'disappointment in someone known to the informant' (that is, interpreting the attack on one's property as the violation of a personal relationship) were all mentioned by respondents as particularly upsetting aspects of the experience. The most frequent reactions were of shock and the feeling that the theft was 'a mean and horrible thing to do'.[72] It is also, perhaps, significant that only 3 per cent of respondents thought that the most important consideration after the theft was the restoration of his property to the victim, while a third of them thought it more important that the offender should be caught.[73]

Maguire's study of victims of burglary also showed that most were greatly disturbed by the experience. Nearly a third of the victims were angry at the event; 36 per cent reported that their first reaction was one of shock or emotional turmoil. Maguire says: 'Our subjective assessment was that at least 20 (6 per cent) of the 322 victims interviewed had suffered serious distress shortly after discovering the crime. Their reactions included acute shock, trembling, panic and uncontrolled weeping.' This investigation also found the loss of property to be generally less important to the victim than the intrusion on privacy which was involved and the emotional upset and distress to which the experience gave rise. In a minority of cases this was severe and persistent:

> About 12 per cent of all females interviewed used words such as 'pollution', 'violation', or 'a presence in the house'. Many made an explicit analogy with a sexual assault, expressing extreme revulsion at the idea of a 'dirty' stranger touching their private possessions, and had felt impelled to 'clean the house from top to bottom'. . . . The irony is that the event triggering off such responses was often objectively a fairly trivial incident. Most of the victims quoted had lost very little and their houses had not been ransacked. . . .[74]

These reports show vividly the personal significance of possessions – often quite ordinary, utilitarian objects, easily replaced – to mature adults.

Concluding Comments

This brief and incomplete review has illustrated something of the complexity of the relations between men and women and their possessions, and in doing so it has pointed to the daunting difficulties of constructing an adequate psychology of ownership and possessiveness. We can, however, essay one conclusion with some confidence: it is not possible to explain the vast structure of institutions to which we assign the name *property* as the expression, the means of satisfaction, of man's desire for physical objects. Even the earliest possessions, as we have seen, have meanings for the individual which are social, that have to do with his relationships with others and his standing among his fellows. It would be redundant here to try to enumerate the many kinds of social meanings with which possessions are invested; we have already considered the ways in which children and adults depend upon their possessions for security (in several senses of the term), for reassurance, as a means of expressing love and acknowledging loveworthiness, and as the means of exerting power over others and defending oneself against intrusions upon his autonomy. There is much more to be said about the significance of personal property in contemporary society – and indeed a great deal has been written, with characteristic succinctness and clarity, by T. H. Marshall, in his essay of forty-five years ago.[75] The child clutching his 'cuddly', the young business executive purchasing his 'customised' motor car, the Soviet citizen protecting the property of his collective, the warrior engaged in the strange, destructive ritual of the potlach, and even the adolescent housebreaker, are performing actions which can only be described in terms which reflect the particular meanings which possessions have in the societies of which they are members: the curious thing is that although we have no difficulty in recognising this when we reflect upon the strange activities of the Thlingets and the Kwakiutls, we find it more convenient to regard the acquisitive and destructive activities of members of our own society as the expression of some base, non-social (or at least pre-social) appetite or drive.

Some of the most interesting questions concerning property, for the psychologist, relate to the experiences through which infants and children come to understand and learn to make use of the meanings of possessions. If there is a common theme in the work of the many psychologists to whom we have referred in this chapter, it is the significance of possessions in transactions between parents and their children, from the first weeks of infancy. This is surely a topic which may appropriately engage the combined resources of sociologists and psychologists in that regrettably rare activity, interdisciplinary research; there are urgent reasons for wishing to know more about processes which so greatly influence the nature of our society.

Notes

1. G. Wallas, *The Great Society*, London, Macmillan, 1925, p.32. Wallas's own list included, engagingly, 'the queer little instinct which makes us desire to sleep with our feet towards the light'.
2. W. McDougall, *Social Psychology*, 25th edn., London, Methuen, 1943, p.75.
3. Ibid., pp.118–19. This quotation reflects the confusion of the terms acquisition, ownership and possession which is characteristic of the literature.
4. Ibid., p.277.
5. Wallas, op. cit., pp.291–2.
6. McDougall, op. cit., p.25.
7. McDougall, op. cit., p.23.
8. McDougall uses the terms 'instinct of acquisition', 'instinct of possessiveness', etc. interchangeably.
9. M. Ginsberg, *The Psychology of Society*, London, Methuen (University Paperbacks edition), 1964, p.19.
10. See McDougall, op. cit., especially Supplementary Chapter VI.
11. M. Ginsberg, 'Contribution to Symposium on property and possessiveness', *British Journal of Medical Psychology*, **15**, 1935, p.65.
12. S. Freud, *New introductory lectures on psychoanalysis* (trans. by W. J. H. Sprott), London, Hogarth Press, 1933, p.229.
13. S. Freud: *Three essays on the theory of sexuality* (trans. by J. Strachey), London, Imago, 1949, p.64.
14. S. Freud: 'On the transformation of instincts with special reference to anal erotism', in *Collected Papers, Vol.II* (trans. by J. Rivière), London, Hogarth Press, 1924, p.170.
15. Freud, op. cit., 1949, p.83.
16. Freud, *New introductory lectures on psychoanalysis* (trans. by W. J. H. Sprott), London, Hogarth Press, 1933, p.130. Freud uses the term 'instinct' in a special sense: 'The source of an instinct is a process of excitation occurring in an organ and the immediate aim of the instinct lies in the removal of the organic stimulus' op. cit., 1949, p.46.
17. Freud, op. cit., 1924, p.164. See also E. Jones, 'Anal-erotic character traits', in his *Papers on Psychoanalysis*, 2nd edn., London, Baillière, Tindall & Cox, 1918.
18. Freud, op. cit., 1933, p.229.
19. I. Suttie: 'A symposium on property and possessiveness', *British Journal of Medical Psychology*, **15**, 1935, pp.51–62.
20. E. Beaglehole, *Property: a study in social psychology*, London, Allen and Unwin, 1931, pp.272–3.
21. Although, as Suttie points out (op. cit., p.60) while this may be 'a well-established fact in our culture, where excreta and excretory functions are the subject of acute parental interest and anxiety . . . it does not explain the varieties of the institution of property found in other cultures'.
22. Suttie, op. cit., p.59. Suttie quotes a child patient 'who was actually very generous but had an extreme craving for gifts and wanted "all the money in the world . . . so that I can give it *or not* as I like, but they must come and ask me anyhow'. (p.59: emphasis in original).
23. D. W. Winnicott, 'Transitional objects and transitional phenomena',

International Journal of Psychoanalysis, **34**, 1953, pp.89–97; O. Stevenson, 'The first treasured possession', *Psychoanalytic Study of the Child*, **9**, 1954, pp.199–217; M. Wulff: 'Fetishism and object choice in early childhood', *Psychoanalytic Quarterly*, **15**, 1946, pp. 450–71; H. R. Schaffer and P. E. Emerson, 'Patterns of response to physical contact in early human development', *Journal of Child Psychology and Psychiatry*, **5**, 1964, pp.1–13. J. and E. Newson offer a characteristically vivid and well-documented account of the phenomenon in their *Four years old in an urban community*, London, Allen and Unwin, 1968, pp.298–304. They have recently (with Pauline Nye) made a more detailed follow-up study of 'cuddlies', which shows that about 30% of four-year-old children insist on taking such an object to bed as a sleep comforter – more (43%) in Classes I and II than in Class V (20%). Such children seemed on the whole to be better adjusted, and more ready to display spontaneous affection, at the age of eleven, and (surprisingly) less likely to have begun to smoke regularly by the age of 16. (J, and E. Newson and P. Nye: *Persistent infant comfort habits and their sequelae at 11 and 16 years:* not yet published.). See also J. Bowlby, *Attachment*, London, Pelican, 1971, pp.368–73. Stevenson found in her group of forty-three children with 'cuddlies' that this special attachment had begun before the age of 12 months in nine cases, during the second year of life in twenty-two cases, and after the second birthday in twelve instances (op. cit., p.210).

24. Schaffer and Emerson, op. cit., p.9.
25. For example, Olive Stevenson explains how a duster came to be called Say. 'From the first few months of his life Roy clutched a blanket. As he grew older he used to struggle and kick as his mother put on his nappy. If he knocked it off the table, his mother would remark, "Oh, I *say*", and thus she thinks arose the name of the object which did not, however, apparently refer to the nappy. . . . As the cot blanket wore out it was replaced by dusters which became all important at night time and even during the day' and were also called Say (op. cit., p.205).
26. Winnicott, op. cit., p.90, Stevenson, op. cit., p.204. See also B. Spock: 'The striving for autonomy and regressive object relationship' in *Psychoanalytic Study of the Child*, **18**, 1963, pp.361–64.
27. Stevenson, op. cit., pp.203–4 and *passim*.
28. Bowlby, op. cit., p.372. By 'the natural object' Bowlby means 'the object towards which the behaviour is directed in an animal's environment of evolutionary adaptedness'.
29. Schaffer and Emerson, op. cit., p.9.
30. Stevenson, op. cit., p.208.
31. S. Provence and R. C. Lipton, *Infants in institutions*, London, Bailey & Swinfen, 1962. There is some evidence that infants who have undergone separation from their mothers tend initially to show increased dependence upon 'transitional objects'; after some weeks of deprivation of maternal affection this dependence is replaced by indifference, or even (in some cases) active hostility towards the object. It is possible to account for these observations within Winnicott's theoretical scheme, since the transitional object presumably symbolises both the loving mother from whom the infant has become separated and the rejecting mother to whom he attributes continuing deprivation. See C. M. Heinicke and I. J.

Westheimer, *Brief Separations*, London, Longmans Green, 1965, esp. pp.290–1.

32. Winnicott, op. cit., p.89. Note that Winnicott is here using the term 'object' in the psychoanalytic sense. This attachment to an object occurs, first, when '. . . the habitual interest of the child is lured away from exclusive concentration on the happenings of his own body and directed towards those persons in the outside world (the mother or mother substitute) who are responsible for providing satisfaction' – A. Freud, 'Certain types and stages of social maladjustment', in K. R. Eissler (ed.), *Searchlights on Delinquency*, London, Imago, 1949. Thus, as Winnicott points out, 'the first not-me *object* is usually taken to be the breast' (op. cit., p.89).
33. Winnicott, op. cit., pp.91–2.
34. Ibid., p.92.
35. Stevenson, op. cit., pp.200–1. (This introductory comment on Stevenson's paper was in fact a contribution by Winnicott.)
36. Compare Suttie's remark, '. . . personal property is a means of overcoming the separation anxiety' quoted above (see p.36).
37. Stevenson, op. cit. p.202.
38. Compare T. H. Marshall's contribution to the 'Symposium on property and possessiveness', *British Journal of Medical Psychology*, **15**, 1935, esp. p.80.
39. Winnicott, op. cit., pp.96–97. It is notable that pilfering (especially from the foster parents or their own children) is frequently associated with the breakdown of the relationship between foster parents and their foster children. See, for example, G. B. Trasler, *In Place of Parents*, London, Routledge, 1960.
40. Newson and Newson, op. cit., p.139. There are some interesting observations on the same topic in a very early paper by L. W. Kline and C. J. France, 'The psychology of ownership', *Pedagogical Seminary*, **1**, 1891, pp.421–70.
41. Newson and Newson, op. cit., 1968, pp.137–8.
42. Ibid., p.145. See also L. M. Stolz, *Influences on Parent Behaviour*, London, Tavistock, esp. pp.70–80.
43. S. Isaacs, *Social Development in Young Children*, London, Routledge, 1933, p.221.
44. Ibid., pp.221–2.
45. Ibid., p.225. It is interesting to compare Dr Isaacs's typology, arrived at by study of the behaviour of young children at the Malting House school, with T. H. Marshall's reflective analysis; see Marshall, op. cit., pp.79–82.
46. S. Isaacs, Contribution to 'Symposium on property and possessiveness', *British Journal of Medical Psychology*, **15**, 1935, p.74.
47. Suttie, op. cit.
48. Isaacs, op. cit., 1935, p.72.
49. Newson and Newson, op. cit., pp.147–8. See also J. and E. Newson, *Seven years old in the Home Environment*, London, Allen and Unwin, 1976, esp. pp.130–3.
50. Isaacs, op. cit., 1933, pp.272–4.
51. Newson and Newson, op. cit., 1976, pp.124–8.

52. Beaglehole, op. cit., pp.254–260.
53. U. Bronfenbrenner, *Two Worlds of Childhood: US and USSR*, London, Allen and Unwin, 1971, p.21.
54. Ibid., p.29.
55. Ibid., p.30.
56. cf. R. R. Sears, E. E. Maccoby and H. Levin, *Patterns of Child Rearing*, Evanston, Illinois, Row, Peterson, 1957, esp. pp.278–84; also A. S. Makarenko, *A Book for Parents*, trans. as *The Collective Family*, New York, Doubleday, 1967.
57. Bronfenbrenner, op. cit., p.42.
58. That is to say, illegal acts which are not 'corporate' crimes.
59. *Criminal statistics in England and Wales*, 1978, Cmnd 7670. London, HMSO, 1979.
60. cf. R. F. Sparks, H. G. Genn and D. J. Dodd, *Surveying Victims*, Chichester, Wiley, 1977, esp. 151–60; Central Policy Review Staff, *Vandalism*, London, HMSO, 1978, esp. pp.4–5; and R. V. G. Clarke (ed.), *Tackling Vandalism*, London, HMSO, Home Office Research Study no.47, 1978, esp. Chapter 2.
61. *Crime in the United States: Uniform Crime Reports* (published annually), Washington, DC: Federal Bureau of Investigations. (The 'Index' crimes are murder, forcible rape, robbery, aggravated assault, burglary, larceny-theft and motor vehicle theft. It should be noted that receiving stolen property, embezzlement, fraud and vandalism do not feature in the *Index*; these and some non-property offences, are included in Part II of the *Uniform Crime Reports* for which statistics of arrests, and not for offences recorded by the police, are provided.)
62. Sparks, Genn and Dodd estimate that only between 2 and 4 per cent of 'miscellaneous thefts', and 24 per cent of burglaries and thefts from dwelling houses, were recorded by the police in the three London boroughs which they surveyed in 1972 (op. cit., pp.152–3).
63. R. L. Carter, *Theft in the Market*, London, Institute of Economic Affairs, Hobart paper no.60, 1974, p.28.
64. Ibid., p.57. This figure includes thefts by employees.
65. Home Office, *Shoplifting and Thefts by Shop Staff*, London, HMSO, 1973, p.3.
66. Ibid., p.4.
67. R. G. Hood and R. F. Sparks, *Key Issues in Criminology*, London, Weidenfeld and Nicolson, 1970, pp.46–51.
68. J. S. Wallerstein and C. L. Wyle, 'Our law abiding law-breakers', *National Probation*, 1947, pp.107–12.
69. W. A. Belson, *Juvenile Theft: the causal factors*, London, Harper & Row, 1975, p.74.
70. See, for example, M. Durant, M. Thomas and H. D. Willcock, *Crime, Criminals and the Law*, London, HMSO, 1972; Sparks, Genn and Dodd, op. cit.; E. O. Smigel, 'Public attitudes towards stealing as related to the size of the victim organization', *American Sociological Review*, **21**, 1956, pp.320–7; J. C. Eberhart, 'Attitudes toward property: a genetic study by the paired-comparisons rating of offenses', *Journal of Genetic Psychology*, **60**, 1942, pp.3–35; H. D. Willcock, *Deterrents and incentives to crime among boys and young men aged 15–21 years*, London, OPCS, 1963;

P. H. Rossi, E. Waite, C. E. Bose and R. E. Berk, 'The seriousness of crimes: normative structure and individual differences'. *American Sociological Review*, **39**, 1974, pp.224–37.
71. Eberhart, op. cit., p.29.
72. Durant, Thomas and Willcock, op. cit., p.245.
73. Ibid., pp.252–3.
74. M. Maguire: 'The impact of burglary upon victims', *British Journal of Criminology*, **20**, 1980, pp.261–75.
75. Marshall, op.cit.

3 The Romantic Theory of Ownership

Alan Ryan

This essay has a purpose and a theme, but I am rather conscious that it has no very straightforward conclusion. The purpose is to draw attention to the characteristic concerns and claims of those I pick out as 'romantic' theorists of work and ownership; the theme is that what they have in common is best highlighted by a contrast to instrumental and utilitarian accounts of these matters. The absence of a straightforward conclusion reflects the fact that there is no one thing that romantic writers either saw or failed to see, which writers in another tradition would either have failed to see or could not have helped seeing. There are romantic writers who are ardent socialists – in my view the youthful Marx was one such – and there are utilitarians who think that the utilitarian argument favours common ownership rather than private ownership; conversely, there are romantic writers – Kant, for instance – who are as committed to the institutions of bourgeois society as were Bentham or James Mill. What I argue below is not that there were particular conclusions about the gains and losses of work, or about the legitimacy of private ownership, to which romantics came and instrumentalists did not, but that the route by which they got to their conclusions was very different, and that this fact casts doubt on the idea that they were quite the 'same' conclusions.

Before making out my case, there is a preliminary duty I should perform: this is to disembarrass myself of my title. There is a convention among writers on romanticism that the first observation to be made is that romanticism is a very vague word, and that figures who are now called romantics would have resented the label very much indeed. I am quite happy to follow the convention. My subject matter might well be called 'will-based' theories of work and ownership, since it is on working and owning as expressions of the free will that both Kant and Hegel concentrate. But, even that more reticent title would create its own difficulties; one might wonder to what extent Hegel's account of civil society really does rest on the will of the individual, seeing how many constraints the individual finds in his environment.[1] It is true that Hegel seems to justify civil society in terms of its expressing the abilities and characters of persons who are attuned to life in a market society; but these characters and abilities do not look very *willed* much of the time. Still, this is not a reason to despair of finding some characterisation of the 'romantic' tradition in terms of an emphasis on the will, on the will as the expression of character, and on social institutions and activities as ways of 'fixing' or objectifying that will in the outside world. However constrained Hegel's workers and owners become, Hegel's account of their existence begins with the need of the free will to objectify itself; no utilitarian could begin anywhere other than with the need for food, drink and shelter. Anyone who still finds the word 'romantic' objectionable as applied to Kant, say, or to Marx, will lose little by reading it as 'expressive' or 'will-based'.

Instrumental and Utilitarian Theories

If the romantic theory of work and ownership is to be understood by contrast with an instrumental account, our first need is a brief summary of that instrumental account.[2] The elements are these. Work is in itself a disagreeable necessity, forced upon us by the multiplicity of human wants and the meanness of nature. Human beings are more vulnerable than most animals because their wants are more varied and because their wants are changeable over time. The boa-constrictor sleeps off its lunch; the human being wonders about the possibilities of gastronomic innovation. It is a moot point whether this is a 'natural' feature of human beings: Hobbes ascribed it to our constantly changing physical state,[3] while Hume, recognising that competition made it worse, saw it as a more nearly pure social phenomenon.[4] At all events, scarcity exists because our desires to consume outrun what the environment naturally offers. Work is needed to increase the supply of things for consumption; since work is an evil, nobody will do more of it than is needed in order to satisfy whatever wants are in question. This is not to say that all work is of equal unpleasantness. All that is involved is the claim that work is a cost incurred in order to secure a benefit and that the benefit is to be measured in terms of a flow of consumables.

How do these truisms create a basis for property rights? In terms of incentive and security. If we move from individual calculations of how much effort it is worth expending to questions of social welfare, we can see that property rights are essential to social co-operation. An individual may naturally possess his own labour and what it produces in the sense that nobody else has, as a matter of fact, the ability to make him work other than as he chooses or to take from him what he has created. But this is not a property *right*; no titles to his efforts have been allocated, and there is no procedure for enforcing such an allocation. If he is to co-operate with anyone else, some sort of recognised title to a portion of the results is essential: without security for the end result, neither party has an incentive to make the initial effort. Even where it is a matter of an individual deferring consumption rather than co-operation, property rights are needed; if I leave apples on the tree, or if I propose to employ some of them for planting new trees, I have no incentive unless I have security for my enjoyment of the end product. Rules allocating and securing titles, so that people may be got to work efficiently are what the utilitarian and instrumental view would call property rules.

Marxist critics have sometimes seen in this argument a tendency to beg the question of whether a person has a natural, prior property in his own labour and thus to read back into a pre-social state the peculiar position of the proletarian who owns his own labour and nothing else. The illicitness of this is obvious; Aristotle, for instance, could never have derived property rights from a prior property in one's own labour because it was too obvious to him that a slave was owned by somebody else, and hence that his labour was so owned as well. But the utilitarian is in no difficulty. He does not start with any view of men as having rights over their efforts. A man's labour is 'his' only in the sense that it is he who labours; in this sense of his, it is no more his property than his headache is his property. Because in this sense his labour cannot be anyone else's, it cannot be his in the proprietary sense either.[5] The question of whether there *ought* to be slavery or free labour is a utilitarian question to be settled on utilitarian grounds. Men have no natural rights at all; when Bentham dismissed them as 'nonsense on stilts', he spoke for a tradition. Men are neither self-owning by nature nor slaves by nature; there may be very good arguments for having rules about property which make it impossible for one person to own another;[6] and there may be very good reasons for treating employment as a contract between the provider of wages and the supplier of labour; but, whether such rules do exist is a question of what the actual rules of an actual legal system are. The question of whether they *ought* to exist is a question of whether proposed rules will induce men to employ their abilities and the resources of nature as productively of consumable things as possible.

This raises the question of what sort of rights property rights are.[7] Here the answer must be given dogmatically; above all they are rights to exclude others from the control and use of whatever it is that is at issue. This is not a complete account of property, since we also need to include duties owed to others in respect of what one owns, as that *my* car is the one which *I* must keep in a roadworthy state, and it is my cow's damage which I must pay for if she should stray into your field. the degree of control allowed by the law is indeterminate; we should not deny that something was my property just because I could not leave it to whomever I wished, but we might seriously wonder if I had anything worth calling a right to exclude others from use or control if my own rights to control were excessively restricted. There will be cases where the owner would very much wish to divest himself of ownership and yet cannot without this leading us to say that he is not really the owner. In the utilitarian tradition it is generally assumed that the crucial powers that an owner must have for ownership to serve its purposes are those of alienation and the creation of lesser interests in his property which he can exchange for money or money's worth.

By the same token, the utilitarian allows that these rights may be exercised over anything that can be controlled, used and disposed of. Nothing is intrinsically unownable, and there is no repugnancy to appropriation in anything. It would be *silly* to create ownership of, say, individual, uncaught, indistinguishable fish; and it would be *wicked* to allow one man to own another, but in neither case is there any conceptual awkwardness about the idea of owning these things. Again, land is in no way 'special'; its status as 'real property' is a hang-over from feudal arrangements and is of no theoretical interest. Indeed, the chief concern of a utilitarian with land amounts to anxiety about the existence of freehold ownership; the utilitarian who sees the point of property rights as being their tendency to encourage the best use of resources is ready to encumber property with obligations – land ought to be kept in good heart, for instance, and title should be dependent on its being so kept. Morally speaking, therefore, the landowner is never more than a lessee from society at large. Such considerations conflict, to be sure, with the basis of property rights in other ways; security is essential to incentive on most utilitarian accounts, and security is impaired if society is *too* quick to remove a bad farmer. But, the resolution of such conflicts is just what a fully fledged utilitarian theory of property is intended to provide.

The history of utilitarian arguments about property is quite largely a history of arguments about security and rewards. The crucial argument is one which is recurrent in Bentham's work. The point of property rights is to encourage the direction of effort to resources for the production of (eventually) consumables. Yet, the security of tenure and the availability of contractual arrangements on which the value of the institution depends mean that those who work hardest may end with very little, and those who own much may live well without effort. Questions of justice aside, this raises two questions; the first is whether this distribution of rewards is stable, the second whether it is efficient in maximising well being. The obvious answer is that if those who do the work get too little of the rewards they will eventually bring down the system; it also seems clear that the principle of diminishing marginal utility is true enough for a wide class of goods to suggest that their value is maximised if they are distributed equally. Since the losses of the better off are more than compensated for by the gains of the worse off, transfers from richer to poorer are generally justified. But, to make them erodes the security which is the essence of property. The early utilitarians argued, as their successors have often done, that the short-run gain from distributive upheaval would be wiped out by disincentive effects over the longer run. Arguments from 'secondary' utilities tend in the same direction; if there are property rights, then there are the pleasures of expectation – my pleasurable anticipation of the pleasures of owning my father's estate, say. Conversely, the misery of disappointment must be reckoned among the evils of tampering with property rights; not merely am I worse off than if I had my father's estate, but the sense of deprivation is itself a distress.[8] The one argument which no utilitarian can or will employ is that society has no right to envisage such redistribution, because all the goods whose redistribution is contemplated already belong to someone and are not available for redistribution.[9] Writers like Bentham as much as writers like Godwin see owners as essentially stewards.[10]

The Romantic Alternative

Utilitarianism does not find the possessory relationship intrinsically interesting, either as a matter of morality or as a matter of social psychology. Here lies the heart of the contrast with romanticism. The young Marx and Moses Hess claimed that our attitude of *having* prevents us from truly appropriating the world and making it our true property.[11] Stirner claimed that if I take my goods and chattels seriously I cannot possess them but must be possessed by them; even Hegel claimed that it was central to my proprietorship that I should show that the thing I possess is inessential to me.[12] And the connection between work and possession is not a contingent tie, or a tie resting on the civil law for its existence. Because possession is less a matter of one's having something *de facto* in one's hands than a matter of having established a certain relationship with whatever it is, work is often seen as the only way to establish such a relationship. It is important not to exaggerate; Stirner makes playful dealings with things essential to owning them, and there is always a strain in the argument which assimilates work and artistic creation and thus narrows the gap between work and play. Still it remains true that romantics hold that possession is an achievement and that an activity to which 'work' is a plausible label to apply is the most satisfactory or only means to that achievement.

It may seem perverse to locate the starting point of this tradition in Kant's philosophy of law; his bleakly puritanical moral philosophy, and his search for eternal principles of morality and epistemology seem at odds with the characteristic romantic enthusiasm for self-expression and the equally characteristic sense of historical change which romanticism brought into social thought. Nonetheless, it is where we must begin. Kant's derivation of property rights starts from the thought that what property rights are are rights of control; control rather than use is the essence of ownership. So Kant rejects use as a title to property and he rejects labour as a title, too – on the grounds that labour rearranges existing matter, and does not create *ex nihilo*. All that is left is the will to possess; to own something is to will to possess it, and to display the will to possess it in a way that demands recognition from others.[13]

The thought is actually simple enough. If I own something, then whoever uses it without my leave wrongs me; but he does not wrong me in the way he would if he struck me a blow and injured me. I am, as it were, wronged at a distance. To explain this, Kant distinguishes two sorts of occupancy of things by the will – physical and rational. Rational occupation is readily distinguished from physical occupation: I may sit on a park bench I do not own, and I may own a shirt I send to the laundry and am not at that point occupying. To own something is to bring it under the control of my will in such a way that I can defeat subsequent attempts by others to bring it under the control of their will. This is not a matter of power; it is a matter of rights, in that my initial occupancy claims respect even if I am in no position to enforce it.

Before showing how, in Kant's view, this is possible, two things are worth noting. Although Kant's notion of property as a matter of rights of excluding others is much like the utilitarians' notion, the way the argument runs already implies that owning is a matter of a human will taking possession; it therefore already excludes slavery as a possible form of property: persons cannot be owned, even though Kant is prepared to admit a very curious sort of external possession of children, wives and servants which none of his critics have ever much liked.[14] Kant did follow Locke in admitting that slavery might be a legitimate punishment for evil-doers, but like Locke, he held that it required some positive act of evil-doing before a man could *lose* his civil personality and so become an ownable object. But, the thought is clear enough: what defeats appropriation is that something is already occupied by the will of an agent, and what defeats the appropriation of a person is that he is necessarily occupied by his own will. The other point is that this allows a new view of natural rights. Kant thinks that rights require social recognition, so he cannot accept traditional accounts of natural rights. All the same, natural rights now have a place as the presuppositions of non-natural rights. The natural ownership of ourselves and our abilities which we find in Locke, say, re-emerges in the thought that unless our wills were *ours*, we could not become proprietors of external things by taking them into our possession.

One might say that all Kant seems to be doing is endorsing some of the basic ideas of most legal systems; initial occupancy of something unowned is a good title in most systems, and Kant endorses it. When I fence a piece of ground, it is my control and my intention to exercise that control in future that counts, not my present or future use. The interest of Kant's case lies elsewhere, though. For, he brings back the importance of work and use, almost more impressively than if he had founded title on them. Kant obviously agrees that we must work to eat, and that if there were no ownership the incentive to labour would be impaired, but he gives work a role apart from the production of consumable useful things. Work so to speak *fixes* our ownership of the world. Willing to possess is the bare bones of proprietorship; full ownership demands that the world should conform to and reflect our purposes.

The thought which dominates Kant's philosophy of history, though not his legal theory in its narrowest sense, is that history exists to develop human abilities to the utmost; its goal is perfection rather than anything describable as welfare.[15] Work is essentially educative. The obduracy of nature and the diversity of human wants are not to be complained of, for they spur us to develop our talents. To do this, we must treat our talents as forms of property; we must 'thingify' them, treat them as assets to make the most of. The thought could be paralleled by the utilitarian claim that prosperity is increased by giving people the right to sell their own efforts and abilities at will, but it is not that argument. The utilitarian argument treats doing well as the goal; for Kant, the need to do at any rate better is what spurs us on, but the point is to develop human abilities, and to do so in a community governed by rational laws and a strict sense of justice.[16] And all this, of course, rests on a thoroughly non-aggregative moral view; as opposed to the utilitarians' preoccupation with making the greatest use of what lay to hand by way of talents and materials, Kant's philosophy stressed the value of each person's enterprise and each person's freedom as an owner.

He was acutely aware of what he could not guarantee. The development of humanity was not a process that implied that each and every person would develop. In a world where stokers are in demand and poets are not, my capacity for verse might be stunted. It is the history of the species which we are to admire, not any individual life, and Kant seems to have recognised that this might be scant consolation to many of us. Again, Kant's ideal of a society of independent owners and producers engaged in exchanges which threatened nobody's freedom looks modest enough; but he knew that for many people, the reality would be dependence on an employer and little scope for individual initiative. He seems, rashly, to have hoped that the collapse of feudal restraints on property would reduce this dependence, but he was aware that many people would neither find self-expression in work nor fix their purposes in the world through ownership.

Kant's bleakness on this point interestingly matches his bleakness over questions of our knowledge of the world. His epistemology leaves us ignorant of 'things in themselves', and confines us to knowledge of their appearances; his social theory also leaves out relationships with others oddly external. We do not share lives; exchange and work leave each of us untouched in his inner freedom. Even though the terms of his discussion of the purposes of history are very much those of the romantic tradition, he leaves each of us detached from history – we are not merged with our culture, but stand aside, able to look at it and question it. Rights protect each person's independent sphere of action from interference by others; we are tied to others exactly to the extent to which we choose to tie ourselves.

Hegel

It is in Hegel's work that Kant's bleakness is transcended. The greater expansiveness of Hegel's thought is, again, something that can be seen both in his theory of knowledge and in his social theory. Hegel allows the human mind to grasp things in themselves as well as mere phenomena, and he makes an account of social and legal rights the basis for an account of how we share in the lives of one another – and, of course, in so doing he seems much more thoroughly to be working in the romantic spirit.

One first point ought to be made; Hegel's philosophy is sometimes thought to be entirely about work and ownership.[17] The thought is that *The Phenomenology of Spirit* gives an account of the way in which mind creates an external reality which is then an obstacle – misunderstood, endowed with a will of its own, operating according to material forces which are essentially unintelligible, and thus alien – and which after various vicissitudes, mind then appropriates as its own creation. One might say that knowledge in all this is a sort of ownership, and that only what we have made can be fully possessed or fully known. Now, although there is something in this, it is something which must here be ignored. For, although this possessory image of knowledge is important, it is also true that work and ownership themselves do not play a very important part in Hegel's *philosophy*. That is, Hegel certainly thought of them as important social phenomena, and is interesting on them, but he did not think that work in the usual sense had any direct epistemological or ontological implications. There is one small joke against naive realism in *The Philosophy of*

Right, when Hegel suggests that the sheep's consumption of grass shows that not even sheep believe in the self-subsistence of material objects. It is a terrible argument against naive realism, but it does show how little Hegel wanted to found his epistemology on social theory.[18]

The main lines of Hegel's account of property rights are very like Kant's, in that he begins with the right of the free will to externalise itself. Put less opaquely, this amounts to saying that the idea that we are free agents makes little sense unless we are free to do something; what we do makes a difference to the physical world, so we must have the right to control it, alter it and dispose of it in the exercise of our freedom. The thought that we might not be able to appropriate things is incoherent, for what can prevent us? The appropriating will can only be forestalled by another such will, and things have no such will of their own. Savages may think that trees have souls: we know better. Moreover, the world needs an owner; it has no value or point until it is given one.[19] It is this that Hegel expresses in the claim that human beings bring the principle of negation into the world; even the sheep negates the grass, showing that mind may turn matter to its own purposes.

Armed with this equipment, Hegel proceeds fairly predictably. How we bring things into our possession is partly a matter of convention, but partly something with a natural foundation, so that our ability to grasp things founds our control. Like Kant, Hegel treats the presence of a prior will as defeating ownership; but animals do not have this sort of will, and human beings may not have – though Hegel is evasive on the legitimacy of slavery, saying that it had a place only when wrong was still right.[20] In any developed society, there can be no two ways about it. Again, he argues that I must have the right to alienate my abilities, not all of them and for ever since that would be slavery and the alienation of myself, but at any rate any one of them and for periods of time. It does not take much imagination to see the opening this leaves for Marx and other radicals.

Work is important, not so much because it uniquely entitles one to property, nor because people need to be induced to work, but because work is a more complete negation of the world than mere taking. The more that mere stuff is permeated by human will, the more humanised and the more thoroughly appropriated the world is. We no doubt work because we want the end product, but this instrumental motive is not the point of the activity – the point is the activity itself. This suggests, as most commentators agree, that the paradigm of work here is not routine activity, but artistic creation. But it is important not to go far down this path; Hegel agrees that there are continuities, but he is also eager to defend the routine and the efficient.[21] The man he admires is the craftsman who knows his job.

But the crucial stress is that of the fixing of the will in the world, and it is that which causes the characteristic tensions in Hegel's account of these issues. To put it simply, there is a tension between what one might call a natural, psychological interpretation of this view and the more rationalistic, philosophical interpretation. On the natural interpretation, the attraction of a view like Hegel's is that it picks up the rather common aspiration to have one's work reflect one's own abilities, the desire that what we do should be a record of our achievements. Hannah Arendt, distinguishing work from mere labour, emphasises the way in which a man's works are the sort of thing you can put on a shelf or see in the street; the aim of work is to create *a work*, a record of our doings.[22] The more rationalist interpretation rests on the view that what is rational is the work of a whole society, a whole culture, even of 'Mind' or 'Spirit'. Work and ownership make sense, not as expressions of the aims and desires and abilities of particular individuals, but as articulations of the life of the whole community. That Hegel presses in this direction is beyond doubt; he sees rights, for instance, less as Kant saw them, in terms of barriers behind which each individual can get on uninterfered with, than as powers which enable each person to fulfil his social role; the restrictions on a father's ability to disinherit his children, for instance, is not seen by Hegel as a loss of freedom by the individual, but as a way of making the paternal role effective. We appear in *The Philosophy of Right*, not so much as Tom, Dick and Harry but as rolebearers in a system whose rationality is a property of the whole system.

But, if this is so, there is a serious problem here. For the attractions of Hegel's account seem to spring from the way it picks up what is genuinely a romantic emphasis on self-expression. If we then dilute this appeal, we are in some difficulty with the idea that anything like self-expression is achieved. We may, of course, admire the rationality of the way the whole social system is organised; Hegel admired the operation of the 'invisible hand' detected by Adam Smith, and we might – though most critics do not – admire the way the society described by Hegel had allocated social roles to people. It is not at all clear that what we would then admire is the way those roles reflected the wills of those people, for we would surely think that it was rather that those people had been given wills which reflected the duties imposed by their roles.

There are, certainly, satisfactions of a characteristically Hegelian kind to be had; the non-naturalness of social life, for instance, is a theme of which he never tires. The reflective person, contemplating his world, must be aware of the extent to which the world is permeated with human ends, so little in his surroundings owes its presence to the arbitrary operations of blind nature. The world reads us an object lesson in its availability to us, because what we see is so much evidence of what we can do with it. As Marx was later to insist in the *German Ideology,* even what we call 'nature' is by now a residual category – it simply refers to what we have so far left alone, not to something with autonomous powers or quasi-rights of its own. In a way, Hegel is a critic of twentieth century environmental ethics ahead of his time. It is not that we should plough up every inch of soil, and it is not that we should consume everything that we can; it is simply that any concern for an environment is a concern for what we get out of it. But, it cannot be too fiercely insisted on; this does not entail that the satisfactions of the triumph over the brutely material are ones which each individual can have. If one thinks that the Hegelian account seems to start by offering us something of the sort and then backs off into offering us only the triumphs of the species – which is where we saw Kant obliged to leave us – this will seem a deficiency. If one thinks that this takes an altogether *too* individualist, or too simple-mindedly individualist, view of what is on offer, it will not seem anything of the sort.

Marx and Carlyle

The tension I have outlined can be nicely illustrated from two quite famous sources. The more famous is Marx's assault on Hegel, the less famous Carlyle's statement of the gospel of work in *Past and Present*. Marx essentially turns Hegel's weapons against himself, and attacks Hegel for failing to deliver on his own promises. Thus in his critique of Hegel's *Philosophy of Right* Marx complains that Hegel's account of politics just contradicts his account of the nature of property rights; Hegel first says that it is the essence of property that it is disposable of at will, and that it is the property of an individual, but then ends by praising such antique devices as the entail as an aid to political stability. Is this not an admission that property cannot be squared with the needs of society?[23] More importantly, the *Economic – Philosophical Manuscripts* demolishes the justification of private property in the very terms which were supposed to support it. Ownership does not make the world less alien but more; once something is property it must be treated as the market dictates, not as we choose. Because there is a market, things come to dominate us, not the other way about. Of course, a factory does not literally tell its owner what to produce, but it is certainly true that unless he produces what will make him the maximum profit, he will go out of business.

Similarly the process whereby we come to see our abilities as ownable things, to be made the most of, is one which rebounds upon us; we have to sell our labour to whomever will buy it, and since he has no interest in it save in what it will yield in profit, the pressure will be on to reduce our abilities to those sufficient for the simplest machine minding tasks. Marx's hostility to the division of labour in the *Manuscripts* comes out of the same logical stable. Because our ability to work and to express our individuality in work is the central fact about us as human beings, the way we are reduced to working in the fashion and at the pace dictated by current machinery is simply inhuman. Now, the plainest utilitarian might have agreed with Marx that the effects of existing systems of property ownership and their effect on the sort of work people did were in various ways deplorable – hours of work were excessive, wages were too low, the imminence of starvation for many people was greater than could be be justified by any view of incentive and so on. What he could not have said, and what Marx did say, is that men in these conditions were *alienated*. The standards in terms of which alienation is judged are Hegelian standards; it is the humanisation of the world, the bringing of things under human control, the creation of a world which reflects and embodies human needs and abilities that sets the framework for Marx's denunciation. Neither individuals not society fix their intentions in the world under a regime of private property and the division of labour.[24]

Even in Marx's account, though, the tensions persist. Marx does come out clearly enough for the view that if the world is to be truly ours private property must be abolished. More worryingly, he extends the concept of appropriation and with it the concept of work, so that it seems at times that he wants to say that the enjoyment of the world is a form of working on it, as if the eye of the perceptive spectator contributes to the beauty of a painting by making it more than a mere assemblage of paint and canvas. Then the beauty of the paintings is a property appropriated by the appropriate sense; this, then, is a form of human and not private property. But, even if this is an acceptable way of glossing Hess's claim that *having* stops us owning the world, it still leaves some of the tensions between individual achievements and social organisation untouched.

Marx claims that free production is production in accordance with the laws of beauty; this and his attacks on the division of labour seemed to imply that he thought that craftsmanship, and work that approached artistic creation, were the only possible human forms of work. But, he later denounced craft idiocy, so whatever it was that he favoured it can hardly have been skilled craft labour in the usual sense; yet, if one tries to imagine kinds of work that have some utilitarian point and satisfy those who perform them, it is hard to see what other than skilled work of this sort we can have in mind. The difficulty then is to see how this sort of work can survive the growth of large productive enterprises, and how we can combine an elaborate technical division of labour with satisfying work. Of course, we can appeal to the satisfactions we found Hegel offering, though not so much those of the intellect satisfied by the understanding of social intricacy and interdependence, as those of the flesh and the emotions – for whatever else Marx wants he certainly wants us to enjoy the results of social co-operation. This is a good start, and we can go further; Marx plainly envisages that work will be shared out by some democratic process of decision-making, when it ceases to be dictated by the market, and we may all welcome this – if it can be had – as an advance. But, although Marx can engage the utilitarian along these lines, if what is at issue is competing ways of maximising the utility of output while minimising the effort that output costs us, this is not the same satisfaction as that which the workman feels in the job well done. We may all agree that the work we do is what we *ought* to do, and that it has been parcelled out justly and rationally; what that does not show is that the work will be satisfying as self-expression.

Marx, like Hegel, has to lose the empirical individual in the collective subject if human work and human appropriation are to be made universally available. Moreover, in Marx's first thoughts about this, the whole idea of real or human appropriation reveals its implausible face. When we talk about a man tending a garden, we normally know what we mean when we distinguish the worker from the owner or say that the man working in the garden owns it too. We can readily distinguish owner, and worker, from the spectator, who looks at the garden and enjoys it. If we start saying that the spectator who admires it is the true, human proprietor, we stray into nonsense. What seems to be at issue is a perfectly plausible attack on, say, cupidity, and in this context we may well say that it is a mistake to want to *own* something as opposed to wanting to enjoy it; we might cheerfully agree that the owner who thinks of nothing but his ownership of the garden 'gets less out of it' than the spectator who likes the flowers and the trees. But to treat this as an elucidation of the concept of appropriation seems an error. What makes private property an internally incoherent institution, if anything does, is that an institution whose point is to allow individual and social control over the world ends up by defeating both. The suggestion that what we call property therefore is not property, but that something else, namely enjoyment, would be, is a needless addition. It is not surprising that Marx dropped all such talk almost at once and turned upon Moses Hess with a vigour which suggests Marx may have been embarrassed by ever having learned the idiom in the first place.

If the ambivalence between individual and species success is one standing difficulty, the other great difficulty is the role of the will. I have skirted round the obvious problem that what one theory might call 'self-expression' and the imposition of the will, another might treat as self-abnegation and the humbling of the will; I have hinted at the possibility in arguing that Hegel tinkers with the identity of those who get their satisfaction in work and ownership – it is not that individuals are *restricted* in what they can do when they become fathers, but that they become fathers and then *un*restrictedly do what fathers do. Whether this rewriting of the identifying description of an individual is a legitimate move in taking away some of the tension between a methodologically individualist and a methodoligically holistic or structuralist social and moral theory is a large question and not to be settled here.

An issue which is, again, not to be settled here, but which certainly must be raised here is the question of the extent to which various of the disputed elements of romanticism in its everyday sense are consistent. In particular, much of what has gone before has raised the question of the extent to which a rationalist account of the will and its fixing in the world through work and through the institutions of private property is at odds with the idea of self-expression in artistic creation. It is worth at any rate noticing that many artists, whether painters, novelists, musicians or whatever, resist the thought that their art amounts to any sort of work of art it is that needs to be brought into existence; novelists are surprised by what their characters do, painters are startled by the posture adopted by their figures and so on. To the extent that the romantic conception of work assimilates work to artistic creation, there must be some doubt about the connection between work and the will, and by the same token between work and control over things. In a sense one might almost claim that everything I have said about the way the romantic theory of work and possession stresses the lifelessness of mere things is pregnant with problems for the assimilation of work to art; for much art, things must be allowed a life of their own.

A final glimpse of Carlyle's gospel of work will illustrate these points. In *Past and Present* Carlyle introduces the man who ought to be – but in many ways fails to be – an industrial hero, one Plugson of Undershot, a cotton manufacturer. Plugson is a man who is genuinely going to master nature; the pages are thick with the metaphors of military conflict and military organisation. Cotton defies human will; it will not clothe men's backs unless it is picked, ginned, spun, woven; the industrial army is rallied for a fight with cotton, and cotton is duly worsted, or licked into calico at least.[25] The captain of industry is a captain just because he can lead us into a battle with nature – though Plugson is duly condemned because his relations with his troops are mediated by the callous cash nexus and not by the brotherly relations of the band of heroes they truly are.

Here it is immediately clear why we can speak of will and its imposition; the resistence of nature is even to be welcomed in providing the better battle. The implications for theories of ownership are not much spelled out by Carlyle, though plainly the general message is 'to the probable victor the means of production'. But this exuberant and expansive will to conquest is not all there is here; the foot soldier in industry learns patience and self-discipline, and here work shapes the will that it expresses too. Unlike Hegel and Kant, Carlyle envisages hierarchies of expression almost from the first. But there is yet more to it. For Carlyle also offers a different image of the relationship between man and nature that is implicit in work, though without much suggestion that it might be at odds with that involved in the Plugson epic. For when he speaks of agricultural work, Carlyle hymns the amount of unassuming, humble labour that has turned wasteland into a green and smiling world. Here we are not looking at men beating nature into submission, so much as men coaxing the hidden possibilities of nature out of the tangle in which they are hidden. This is not a story of foe against foe, rather one of siding with nature's better self.

This links up with our anxiety about the assimilation of work and art. It is plausible to suppose that the workers who unlock the smiling fields hidden in the waste are doing something of the same sort as Michelangelo when he liberated the prisoners from their marble. He did not scare them into the open, but helped them free; Plugson's military sortie against recalcitrant cotton fits no such picture, though it does fit our intuitive ideas about what the triumph of the will might be like.

What then ought we to conclude? I hope that nobody will wish to conclude only that the romantic theory of work and ownership is a chaos of unresolved problems. For, it is worth recalling that, as the history of orthodox economics shows, the utilitarian varieties of social theory are full of problems of their own. Rather, what these tensions show is what the range of problems is that a romantic theory must tackle – it must concentrate on the nature of the will, on the nature of self-expression; it needs to concern itself with the extent to which different temperaments may find their expression in different sorts of work; it needs to concern itself with the way in which disposability and restricted disposability of property assist the creation and expression of valued forms of character. We cannot conclude that private property or the abolition of private property will emerge as the obvious implication of adopting this approach; all we can suggest is what the argument will be fought over.[26] But, we can also see ways in which a tradition of argument like this will couch its disputes in terms whose emotional and political overtones are radically different from those of the utilitarian tradition. One *can* envisage cost-benefit calculations suggesting that a revolutionary transformation of the mode of production is essential; and one can envisage romantic arguments in defence of the mixed economy. But it is hardly an accident that there are few utilitarian revolutionaries, nor that Hegel's successor was Marx.

Notes

1. G. W. F. Hegel, *The Philosophy of Right* (trans. by T. M. Knox), Oxford, Clarendon Press, 1942, sec.207.
2. cf. my 'Two Concepts of Politics and Democracy: James and John Stuart Mill', in Martin Fleisher (ed.), *Machiavelli and the Nature of Political Thought*, New York, Croom Helm, 1972, pp.76–113.
3. Thomas Hobbes, *Leviathan*, London, Andrew Crooke, 1651, Chapter VI.
4. David Hume, *A Treatise of Human Nature*, Oxford, Clarendon Press, 1888, Book II.
5. J. P. Day, 'Locke on Property', *Philosophical Quarterly*, **16**, 1966, pp.207–21.
6. J. Bentham, *The Theory of Legislation* (ed. by C. K. Ogden), London, Routledge, 1931, pp.201ff.
7. A. M. Honore, 'Ownership', in A. G. Guest (ed.), *Oxford Essays in Jurisprudence*, Oxford, Clarendon Press, 1961, pp.107–47.
8. Bentham, op. cit., 1951, pp.109–23.
9. cf. R. Nozick, *Anarchy, State and Utopia*, Oxford, Basil Blackwell, 1974, p.219.
10. William Godwin, *Enquiry Concerning Political Justice* (ed. by K. Codell Carter), Oxford, Clarendon Press, 1971, p.236.
11. K. Marx, 'Economic – Philosophical Manuscripts', Collected Works, Vol.3, London, Lawrence and Wishart, 1975, pp.299–301.
12. Hegel, op. cit., 1942, addition 26 to sec.44.
13. W. Hastie, *Kant's Philosophy of Law*, Edinburgh, A. & C. Black, 1887, pp.81–4.
14. Ibid., pp.108–13, 237–8.
15. H. Reiss (ed.), *Kant's Political Writings*, Cambridge, Cambridge University Press, 1970, pp.43–5.
16. Ibid., pp.45–6.
17. Marx, op. cit., 1975, pp.332–3.
18. Hegel, op. cit., 1942, sec.44.
19. Ibid.
20. Ibid., sec.57 and addition.
21. Ibid., sec.197 and addition.
22. H. Arendt, *The Human Condition*, Chicago, Chicago University Press, 1958, sec.19, pp.139ff.
23. K. Marx, 'A Contribution to the Critique of Hegel's Philosophy of Right', Collected Works, Vol.3, London, Lawrence and Wishart, 1975, pp.100–1.
24. Marx, 'Economic – Philosophical Manuscripts', op. cit., 1975, pp.306ff.
25. T. Carlyle, *Past and Present*, New York, New York University Press, 1977, p.193.

26. In essence, this is to say that such notions as that of 'self-expression' are indefinitely contestable; see W. B. Gallie, 'Essentially Contested Concepts', Chapter 8 of his *Philosophy and the Historical Understanding*, London, Chatto and Windus, 1964.

Part II
Empirical Studies of Property as a Social Institution

4 Landed Property: Challenge and Response

David Rose, Colin Bell, Howard Newby, Peter Saunders

In this chapter we take as our theme the defence of the central institution of capitalist societies, namely private property. The particular context in which we shall examine this issue is that of landed property in eastern England. We are concerned to explain both how various definitions of private landownership are articulated by two samples of farmers interviewed by us in East Anglia between 1974 and 1976, and how organisations representing farming and landowning interests have responded to various perceived threats to the institution of private landownership.[1] Specifically, we shall discuss three related issues which have recently caused concern, not to say controversy, among landowners and their organisations. These issues are (1) land prices (2) capital taxation and (3) land purchases by City institutions.

A Taxonomy of Landownership

It is currently estimated that about £20,000 million is invested in British agriculture, roughly in the proportion four-fifths landlord's capital, i.e. land and buildings, and one-fifth tenant's capital, 'the money involved in the running of the farm, providing for livestock, machinery, movable plant and equipment, growing and harvested produce plus working capital' (Clery 1975, p.59). Farmers themselves own the overwhelming proportion of these assets as Table 4.1 demonstrates. Land and buildings constitute the largest single element amongst farmers' assets, the land alone being the most significant of the two in terms of farmers' wealth. Given the comparatively recent trends towards owner-occupation (see Table 4.3) and the small scale of farm businesses this is hardly surprising. But for precisely these reasons

Table 4.1 Estimated balance sheet of UK agriculture, June 1975

Liabilities	*£m*	*Assets*	*£m*
Banks	1 100	Land, buildings	15 480
AMC etc.[a]	295	Machinery, plant	1 050
Insurance companies	40	Livestock	1 700
Private loans	300	Crops and produce	1 200
HP and credit	380	Debtors, bank balances[b]	800
Capital owned	18 115		
Total	20 230	Total	20 230

Notes:

[a] A.M.C. represents organisations which lend to farmers to purchase land, and includes The Agricultural Mortgage Corporation, Scottish Agricultural Security Corporation, and Lands Improvement Corporation.

[b] Bank balances means cash held by farmers in the form of bank balances.

Source: Clery 1975, p.28

farmers are extremely sensitive to any changes in the land market which they deem to be against their interests, and this is the case regardless of whether they are owner-occupiers or tenants. Furthermore, because of the typical structure of farm businesses – individually or family owned (see Harrison 1975, pp.18ff) – any increase in land prices inflates the owner-occupier's wealth and consequently increases his tax liability. Similarly, any fundamental changes in the tax structure affecting capital gains, capital transfers or wealth have potentially far reaching repercussions for all farmers and landowners; even tenants are affected because of the situation of landlords (see below).

From our immediate viewpoint this is of great significance, for in the course of the last five years the land market has entered a volatile period and a Labour government was elected in 1974 pledged to a series of new taxes and other measures, some of which were aimed specifically at agriculture but all of which had potentially fundamental consequences for the existing structure of landownership. Farmers and their organisations perceive this as a threat to their position and mobilised against it. In agriculture such fiscal threats are particularly important, for the economic structure of agriculture is very different to that in, say manufacturing. While generally in industry there has developed a divorce between ownership and control, and a concomitant rise of managerialism, in agriculture the situation has reversed. At the turn of the present century 90 per cent of agricultural land was owned by others than those who farmed it and one could discern a *landownership* interest separate from, and often opposed to, a *farming* interest. But the break up of the great estates and the decline of the agricultural landlord resulted in the creation of a new, and now dominant, class of farmer – the owner-occupier. Although, as we have seen this is a very recent historical development, the idea of farmers owning the land they farm is now so rooted that any distinction between owning and farming land is generally overlooked. A threat to landownership as it is presently structured is interpreted by farmers, the NFU, the CLA and even at times by the Ministry of Agriculture as a threat to farming. It is only when we realise how entrenched in the minds of farmers is the idea of owning the land that is farmed, of how much even tenant farmers aspire to own land, that we can appreciate the vehemence with which farmers attack taxation changes and changes in the land market.

The owner-occupiers are certainly the most numerous group of agricultural landowners. Exactly how many there are is impossible to say since official statistics on landownership are not collected, but over one-half of all farm land is now owner-occupied. Nevertheless, despite their decline this century, the traditional private landowners, the agricultural landlords, are still of some importance. In a sense they are even more threatened than the owner-occupiers, for their income from letting land is regarded as unearned and they receive no relief, as working farmers do, under capital transfer tax. Moreover a wealth tax would be a considerable burden to them and the recent extension of security of tenure to agricultural tenants in England and Wales under the Agricultural (Miscellaneous Provisions) Act 1976, will effectively prevent them from gaining vacant possession of their own land. Between these two groups is divided almost 90 per cent of the agricultural land of England and Wales, but the land market itself is beyond their control and the price of land bears no necessary relationship to its agricultural use-value. This has become a great embarrassment to private landowners in recent years.

Apart from private owners of agricultural land there are the institutional landowners. A recent survey of institutional landownership by Gibbs and Harrison (1974) has pointed out that whilst 'the acreage of rented farmland has declined markedly this century, the area owned by public and semi-public bodies has increased and is still increasing' (p.1). In fact figures from their study show that about 10 per cent of the agricultural land of England and Wales is owned by institutions: the distribution is shown in Table 4.2.

There are, then, broadly three types of institutional landowners, viz.:

1. *Traditional institutional landowners* – institutions with a long history of landowning and who generally observe the normative prescriptions of landlord – tenant relationships, e.g. the Church, the Monarchy, Oxbridge colleges.

Table 4.2 Institutional ownership of farm land, England and Wales, 1971

Institution	*Acreage owned*
Monarchy	325 055
Forestry commission	80 555
Ministry of Agriculture	28 112
Other governmental departments	121 663
Nationalised industries	359 233
Local authorities	929 559
Universities	180 385
Conservation bodies	201 452
Agricultural research council	6 622
Church land	157 814
City institutions	170 000
Total	2 560 450

Note: Clery (1975, p.46) estimates the figure for city institutions to be 400 000 acres. The figure given by Gibbs and Harrison is for the UK rather than England and Wales. Our impression is that Clery's figure is an overestimate but that Gibbs's and Harrison's estimate is certainly now an underestimate. City ownership of land will be discussed in more detail later in this paper. It is, perhaps, worth pointing out that the top ten landowners in Britain include only one private individual, the rest being institutional and ranging from the Scottish Department to the Church Commissioners (see *Sunday Times*, 2 February 1975, p.11).
Source: Gibbs and Harrison (1974) p.5

2. *Public landowners* – bodies responsible directly or indirectly to Parliament or whose membership is open to members of the public, e.g. nationalised industries, departments of state, the National Trust.
3. *Financial institutions* – the City element in farm landownership consisting of public companies, especially insurance companies and property groups, some public farming companies whose boards of directors are not related to one another, and pension funds of public and nationalised industries.

This enables us to produce a simple taxonomy of agricultural landownership as shown in Table 4.3.

We are now in a position where we can analyse the responses of farmers and their organisations to certain threats which they currently perceive to landownership. In particular, as we stated in our introduction, we shall examine the threats posed by land price inflation, capital taxation and the entry of city institutions into land purchases. We shall see the various ways in which the private landed interest has sought to defend the system of landownership to which it is so wedded.

Table 4.3 A taxonomy of landownership

Private	*Institutional*
Traditional landlord	Traditional
Owner-occupied	Public
Private trusts/charities	Financial

Note: A very rough calculation, based largely on Ministry of Agriculture tenure figures, would indicate that about 56 per cent of farm land is owned by the owner-occupiers, approximately 33 per cent by traditional private landlords and trusts, 6 per cent by public institutions, 3 per cent by traditional institutions and 1.5 per cent by financial institutions.

Whilst only 56 per cent of land is classified as owner occupied it is nevertheless the case that some of the traditional private landlords, possibly the majority of them, farm some of the land themselves. Some of the land owned by the financial institutions is also farmed by the institutions themselves and not by tenants. Moreover, some land which appears as rented in the financial statistics is in fact owned (on this point see Rose et al., 1977 and below). Consequently the actual amount of land farmed by landowners would be somewhat higher than the 56 per cent figure quoted would indicate.

Land and Inflation

The vast majority of farm landowners have a direct interest in a stable land market in which prices rise only slowly and which ensures that a continuation of private landownership is not threatened by the possibility of such factors as capital taxation. To put our discussion of land prices in a historical perspective Figure 4.1 shows the trend of prices over the last 200 years.[2] We can see from this that the trend since 1945 has been for land prices to rise quite steadily – from £45 an acre in 1945, to £76 in 1949, £101 in 1959 and £299 in 1969. (These are Oxford Institute figures for land with vacant possession.) However the sudden and very rapid rise in land prices that took place in 1972/73 followed by an almost equally dramatic fall in 1974/75 and yet another boom in 1976/77 has put the land market in turmoil and led to a great deal of acrimonious comment in farming circles.

The precise causes of these market events are difficult to analyse but the reaction of farmers is of great interest. Figure 4.2 gives a graphic picture of recent market trends, although the kind of average prices on which it is based hide some of the starker realities faced by farmers in certain areas. In parts of East Anglia, for example, land prices rose from £300 per acre to as much as £1400 per acre in the space of twelve months in 1972/73 and many farmers were somewhat embarrassed to find they were suddenly millionaires. This was a mixed blessing since,

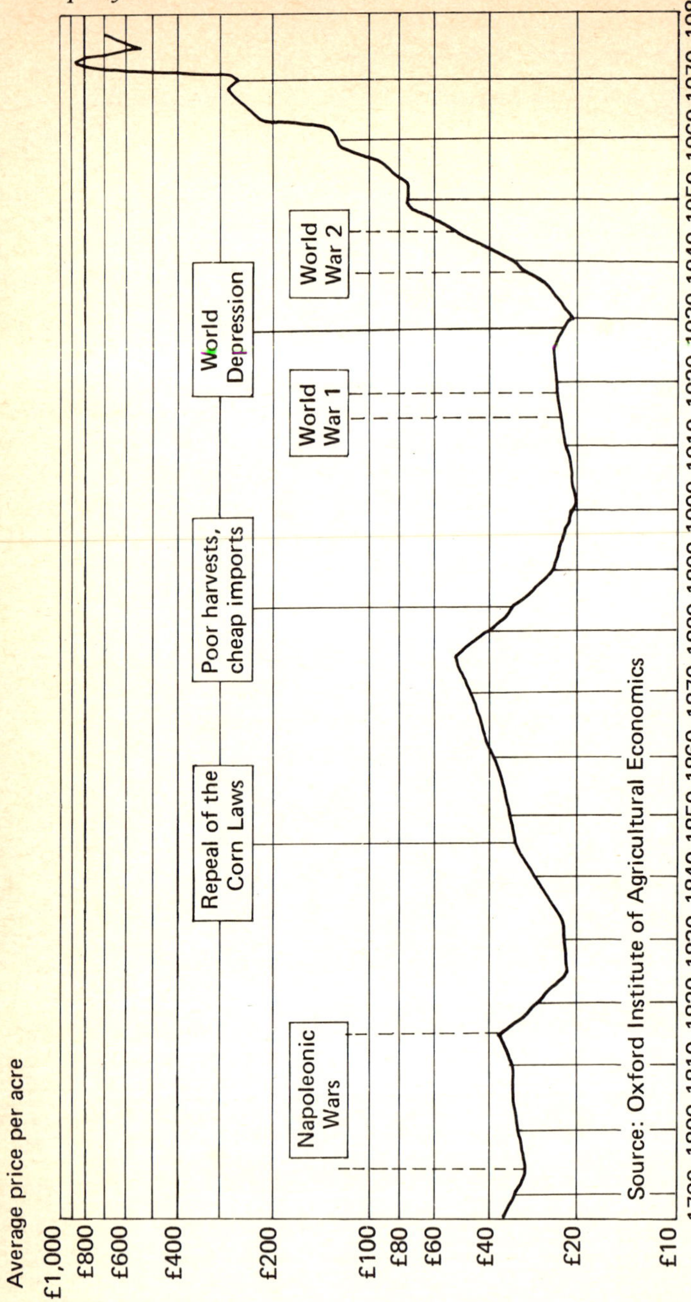

Figure 4.1 The cost of farmland, 1790–1976 (reproduced with permission from the Sunday Telegraph, *19.8.73).*

while it made borrowing easier, it made for a heavy capital tax liability in the future and the possibility of technical bankruptcy if the value of land used for collateral decreased. In a sense the problem for the farmer *vis-à-vis* the land market has been a simple one. The value of land to him is largely dependent upon the prices obtaining in the produce market, but to the non-agricultural investor the anticipated capital growth (together in the past with the knowledge that under the former estate duty system anyone holding agricultural land could claim a 45 per cent relief of estate duty) is the most important factor – and anticipated capital growth is often unrelated to purely *agricultural* prospects. Consequently, because of the differing motives of those buying land, there has been no consistent relationship between the price of land and agricultural prosperity. Sturmey (1955) found that government legislation (e.g. estate duty relief for agriculture) and the level of interest rates were the most important factors affecting land prices but Byrne (1975) suggests that since 1945 there has, in fact, been no relationship between interest rates and land prices. What he does find is a discernible relationship between land prices and share prices:

> . . . while over periods of say five years, no direct relationship can be established, movements in the ordinary share index, subject to occasional lag, are clearly reflected in the price of agricultural land on a year-to-year basis.

However, the more recent and spectacular rises in the price of land after 1970 (Figure 4.2) were in Byrne's opinion brought about by a coincidence of a boom in agriculture, indicated by a 73 per cent rise in the agricultural produce index (1971–3), and a 115 per cent increase in farm incomes (1968–71), and an accompanying boom in the City, with the *Financial Times* ordinary share index rising by 36 per cent (1970–2). In other words the artificially induced growth under the Conservative government of 1970–4 was indirectly responsible for raising land prices: the farmers demanded more land because their returns were increasing and City investors found they had extra capital to invest and chose to extend their portfolios by buying land as a hedge against inflation. Hence a great deal of money was chasing the small amount of land available for sale. Byrne summarises his argument as follows:

> Since the war, the demand for agricultural land has certainly been influenced by the profit motive, social and amenity considerations, and by the prospect of estate duty and capital gains tax roll-over relief. But the enormous rise in land prices, particularly since 1970, seems to have been generated chiefly by investors seeking to protect their capital against erosion.

Unfortunately, even as Byrne was writing land prices were in the process of falling almost as rapidly as they had risen (see Figure 4.2). *Farmland Market* attributed this fall in prices to a variety of factors:

> New taxes, a property market in crisis and high interest rates killed any incentive to speculate; agriculturally (1974) was disastrous; and as prices wavered the institutions withdrew to hold a watching brief.
>
> (no.4, July 1975, p.6)

Articles soon began to appear in the farming press on why land prices were falling, but the interlude turned out to be a short one. By late 1975/early 1976 prices were rising to unprecedentedly high levels once more for much the same variety of reasons as those which accounted for the earlier boom, namely the impetus of high prices themselves, the effects of inflation, and renewed interest by City institutions. Land market experts were forced to dust off their statements of two years earlier, such as the following from *Farmland Market*:

> The overall impression of the market at mid-1976 is one of real buoyancy. The rapid price rises are startling when considered in isolation but, when explained against the background of 1974's heavy losses, they can be seen as a realignment with levels which would have prevailed if the unique cycle of 1972–5 had been discounted.
>
> (no.6, July 1976, p.6)

Whatever the experts might have made of these changes in the land market, the private landowners and owner-occupiers had few doubts: high land prices were not good for farming. The evidence from our interviews was quite clear cut about this, with 84 per cent of those in the 1000+ acres sample and 90 per cent in the 44 parishes believing that the recent inflation in land prices had been harmful to the farming industry. Only four respondents (3.8 per cent) in the 1000+ acres sample and one respondent (1.8 per cent) in the 44 parishes believed this inflation to be positively beneficial (the remainder had mixed reactions). A variety of reasons were given for regarding this inflation as harmful and they are set out in Table 4.4.

Certainly most of our respondents became both animated and voluble when asked about land prices, and few of them would disagree with any of the seven major reasons noted in the table as to why inflation in the price of land was injurious to them. We must also assume that those who did not mention taxation problems explicitly implied them when they cited succession problems and/or a threat to private landownership. A more detailed examination of these replies revealed that taxation problems were mentioned by only 11 per cent of those in the 1000+ acres sample who owned less than 50 per cent of their land, but by 42 per cent who owned more than 50 per cent. In

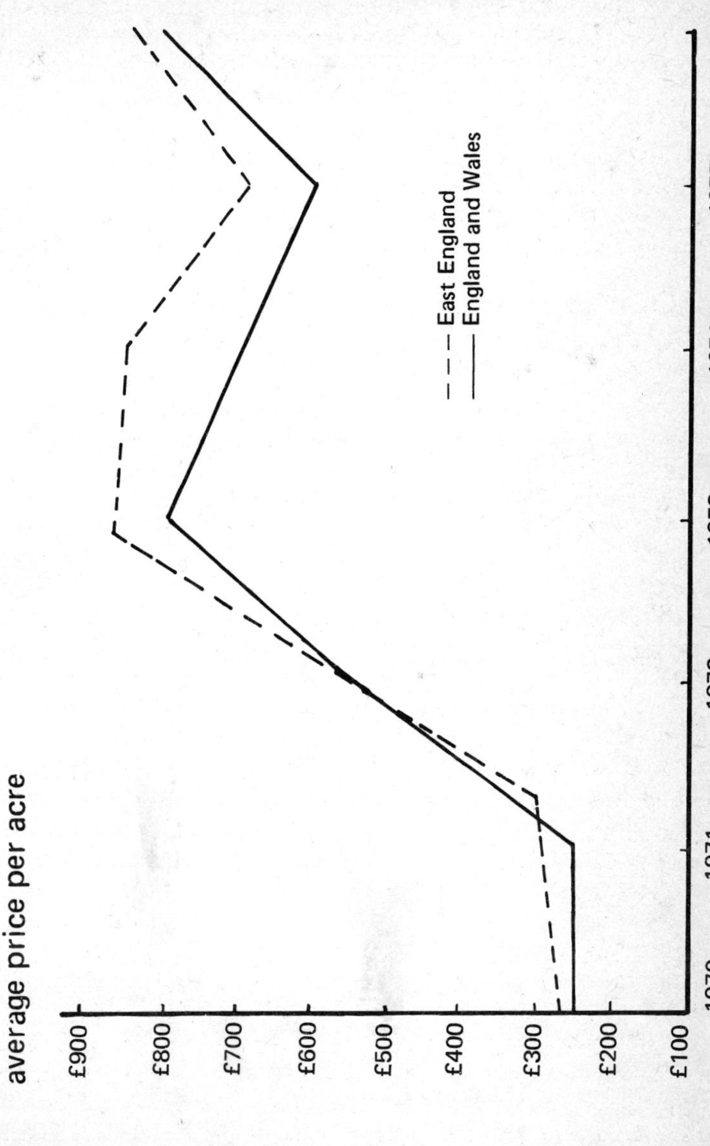

Figure 4.2 Average price of farm land (25 acres and over sold at vacant possession), England and Wales and Eastern England, 1970-76 (Source: Farmland Market*).*

Table 4.4 Reasons inflated land prices are harmful to farmers

Reasons harmful	*1000+ acres (N=95) %*	*44 parishes (N=54) %*
Creates tax problems	36.8	50.0
Restricts recruitment of young farmers	30.5	25.9
Creates succession problems	23.2	7.4
Farming becomes uneconomic	31.6	42.6
Prevents expansion	28.4	27.8
Threatens private landowership	21.1	20.4
Distorts farmers' wealth	8.4	3.7
Other reasons	10.5	5.6

Note: Percentages do not equal 100 as most respondents gave more than one answer.

the 44 parishes sample the equivalent rates were 31 and 50 per cent. Similarly farmers who mentioned succession problems were more likely to be found among those who owned most land. There was thus a relationship between proportion of land owned and reasons given for inflated land prices being harmful. Most tenants recognised that insofar as high land prices caused problems for landlords, then those who rent land are in a vulnerable position. The general point to note, however, is that it is not *farming* which is necessarily put at risk by high land prices, but *landownership and the family business* which owner-occupiers equate with farming. As one tenant put it (a man who made a rigid distinction between *farming* and *owning* land):

> It's harmful to owners but not to tenants. It affected the demand for tenancies but not the rents. It is the family business which really suffers.

Many tenants, however, aspire to ownership and deplore high prices because they make that aspiration less likely to eventuate:

> It makes it difficult to climb the farming ladder. You can't farm land at these prices and that is why the institutions have bought it. If you are sitting on the land you are all right; but for tenants high prices mean high rents.

> You can't make a profit as a farmer . . . and the traditional landowners are being replaced by financial institutions – and that may not be good for farming.

Hence we have the situation where virtually all farmers perceive inflation as a threat to their position as landowners now or at some point in the future. Many of those whom we interviewed laid much of the blame for their problems on those financial institutions who had begun to purchase farm land and who were held responsible for land price inflation. Equally the changes made and proposed by the Labour government after 1974 (and especially capital transfer tax and a proposed wealth tax) were seen in their combined effects with land price inflation to be potentially catastrophic for private land-ownership. We can examine each of these 'threats' in turn.

The City Institutions

Undoubtedly the activities of certain city institutions – insurance companies, unit trusts, pension funds, etc. – in the land market has caused great controversy in farming circles. Most farmers and landowners would maintain that financial institutions have no real concern either for agriculture or the needs of rural communities. Rather they are seen as almost the rural counterpart to the asset strippers.

Since the institutional involvement in the land market was so clearly identified by nearly all farmers as the factor which caused the chaos in land prices, it is hardly surprising that a certain amount of acrimony crept in. Some of this was a result of the persistent tendency among farmers to stigmatise any 'outsiders' connected with the wider urban – industrial world. However, much of this antipathy was directed at institutions who clearly did not intend to take the passive role that had hitherto been associated with traditional institutional landowners. Thus, the debates about the new 'farming institutions' were, in fact, largely concerned with the style of ownership and control of farm land. It was the economic rationality of the City institutions which was so objected to.

If it did nothing else, the rise in land prices in 1972/73 showed that a very great deal of any farm's equity is tied up in land. The CLA, the NFU and the Ministry of Agriculture all made this a central issue in their submissions to the Select Committee on the Wealth Tax,[3] the implication being that if farming did not receive special case status under any wealth tax then private landownership was doomed. What was not asked was whether it is necessary or desirable to own the land that is farmed since it is assumed in farming circles that owning land is practically a *sine qua non* of farming. Yet this is, in a sense, the question which is posed by high land prices. Even the representatives of landowners and farmers, it should be added, do recognise that owner-occupancy can hinder agricultural efficiency, but they fall back on non-economic arguments to justify their position:

> Few proprietors of family businesses of any sort, are motivated by profit *alone* and considerations other than maximisation of profits affect farming and landowning to a varying degree, either consciously or subconsciously.
>
> Maintenance of the countryside and village life, the provision

> of sport, improving amenity, providing continuity of employment, minimisation of taxation and many other considerations provide reasons for doing or not doing something which would improve profitability. These motives are perfectly acceptable on personal social and environmental grounds. . . .
> (CLA 1974, p.3)

Indeed to be a *real* landowner means precisely not to be as efficient as possible. For example, the CLA's recent discussion paper on landownership stated that:

> Other activities of landownership reflect a sense of stewardship which may well be so strong as to dictate courses of action which are totally illogical in terms of maximising the commercial benefits accruing to an owner. The stewardship concept encourages landowners to think and act in the long-term interests of the land and the community it supports. . . . The landowner's vision and his belief in improving his heritage for his heirs encouraged him to subsidise the local community in many practical ways and to improve and maintain the countryside. Despite the economic absurdity of this type of activity many, albeit a steadily reducing number, still carry on.
> (CLA 1976, p.5)

It is not surprising, then, that most farmers react defensively to the activities of the City institutions and generally view their activities as no less threatening to their long-term interests than fiscal measures aimed at a more egalitarian distribution of wealth. For this reason the institutions themselves have been quite keen to publicise their activities in order to demonstrate that their attitude to land is not the rapacious one which many farmers believe it to be. The concern of most farmers has, in any case, been directed less at companies like Norwich Union (which bought its first farm in 1877 and has been quite content to operate as a 'traditional' agricultural landlord) than to those like Property Growth Assurance (PGA)[4] and Fountain Farming Ltd, which represent unknown and innovatory quantities. This is because while farmers are generally less concerned about institutions owning land, provided they let it to farmers, they are suspicious when institutions farm it themselves or take farming profits through some kind of partnership scheme with the tenant. Equally they are concerned when anyone connected with the City predicts the restructuring of agricultural land tenure (a common City preoccupation) and the separation of ownership and control.

The views of our own respondents in East Anglia are summarised in Table 4.5. Clearly we received more responses that were hostile than favourable towards City institutions. There are three basic reasons for this: the impersonal nature of such landownership; the fact that such owners were believed to have other than agricultural interests at heart;

Table 4.5 Farmers' views on City investment in farm land

	1000+ acres (N=93) %	*44 parishes (N=55) %*
Brings in outside capital	30.1	16.4
Institutions are good landlords	12.9	7.3
Other positive views	6.5	3.6
Institutions remote from farming	26.9	34.5
Caused land price inflation	33.3	38.2
Stops real farmers expanding	18.3	40.0
Institutions are bad landlords	4.3	7.3
Other negative views	8.6	3.6

Note: Percentages do not equal 100 as most respondents gave more than one reply.

and economic factors – high prices, unfair competition for land, and succession problems.

Typical of the kinds of comments made by farmers who were most concerned by the financial institutions' land purchases were the following:

> It's all too impersonal. In the past, when land in the village was owned by a local person, the local landlord was the benefactor. He knew everyone in the village by more than nodding acquaintance. Institutions are impersonal and the village suffers and splits up.

> The most efficient and human way to conduct a business is by personal contact. If these insurance companies and so on keep coming in we'll finish up like the rest of British industry, especially in labour relations. You can't make agriculture work on an industrial footing. That does *not* mean we can afford to be yokel about farming – but you do have to *care* about farming. Those who own *must* have a personal interest.

We view it as extremely significant that one-third of the rented land on farms in the 1000+ acres sample now belongs to City institutions. Many of the tenants in this sample, therefore, had first-hand knowledge of the City landlord. Moreover those renting land from such institutions tended to be favourably disposed towards them. Below are a selection of comments of those favouring the City landlord:

> They weren't responsible for the high prices – that was roll-over relief. If we had bought land the amount of money we'd have needed for a farm this size would have been fantastic. As it is we got the leaseback, which I can see nothing wrong with and the insurance company is happy with its 4 per cent return.

> It's good: it creates more tenancies and you can only become really large scale as a tenant. Separation of owning from farming is a good thing and that's what these companies offer. They are investing in agriculture and they are landlords like any other.

Among the farmers with a smaller size of business there was a concern that they would be prevented from expanding their businesses and younger people would be prevented from ever entering farming because of high land prices consequent upon institutional interference in the land market. Equally farmers in the 44 parishes were more shocked at the thought that the institutions should be allowed to purchase land when they had no real love for it. Again, a few quotations from respondents typify this outlook:

> I think it's shockingly bad. Basically these people are not trading in land for agriculture but to safeguard money. They buy large blocks of land farmed by *companies*. Any country that loses its yeoman farmer has lost something.

But interestingly the larger, more go-ahead farmers in the 44 parishes often took a different view. For example:

> The Arabs can buy it for all I care. You can't stand in the way of evolution. . . . The public can take a stake in land through the City and we'll get greater public – not state – ownership. . . . God gave land to the people, not the State.

In summary, when considering how farmers tend to view the entry of the City into land purchase, it would seem that those who have direct experience of their activities are in favour of recent trends. After all they have generally achieved the very security of tenure which is seen as a principal advantage of *owning* land. Those who are more suspicious of the financial institutions either cannot expand or are already guaranteed tenure of their land for at least one more generation. Equally, tenants used to the traditional landlord/tenant system, which guaranteed to them the succession of the next generation, have already experienced an almost *de facto* security of ownership and are wary of innovations in the system. However, as we have argued, innovation in the landlord – tenant system is becoming more likely as government policies threaten to disrupt the traditional system. We seem to be arriving at a point where, as a result of the likely demise of the traditional private landlord, only institutions will be able to offer security of tenure to tenants for succeeding generations. This need not mean fewer tenancies available in the long term (although it may well do so in the immediate future), but it will almost certainly lead to less close relationships between farmers and their landlords. This could have quite profound effects on the rural social structure, especially in a county such as Norfolk where the traditional landlord – tenant relationship has tended to survive longer.

In the meantime, there are those who feel that the financial institutions can be socialised into farming norms:

> It is commonly supposed that the new faceless City Moguls will adopt a ruthless policy of rent revisions or capital starvation to their tenants. . . . Fortunately, there is a buffer of long-standing tradition in the old-established estate agents who act on behalf of the new investors and can surely acquaint them with the more gentlemanly aspects of country living.
>
> (Wormell 1974)

Recently, indeed, the President of the CLA has appealed to the values of a property-owning democracy:

> It is when things look blackest that sensible men remember that the pendulum always swings back, that political wind does not blow for ever in the same direction. . . . We must not lose heart too easily. Private property is not unacceptable to the mass of our fellow countrymen. It is not something of which to be ashamed.
>
> (Barker 1976, p.47)

In other words, the fight is on. Recent legislation, however, to which we now turn, has made the fight harder to win.

The Taxation Threat

It is, of course, precisely to try to ensure a property-owning democracy that successive Liberal and Labour governments have introduced fiscal measures which threaten the continuation of private (capitalist) landownership. Thus the agricultural landlord has been subject for a number of years now to having his rental income assessed as unearned and therefore subject to the top income tax (until the 1979 Budget) rate of 98 per cent. This has encouraged many landowners to take possession of tenanted land as it became available in order to farm it himself ('Taking the land in hand') and thus qualifying for earned income relief. To some extent this has been undertaken reluctantly since estate practice has been to allow son to succeed father into a tenancy, but economic sense dictates having a large earned income with a top rate of tax of 75 per cent. But at least the landowner was in an advantageous position when it came to estate duty. He could claim the 45 per cent abatement relief on farm land, designed to allow his heirs to succeed to his estate, and even, by taking advantage of the seven year rule, could avoid estate duty altogether.[5]

However, he now finds a very different situation under the new capital transfer tax, exacerbated by some of the clauses in the Agriculture (Miscellaneous Provisions) Act 1976. For a private landowner whose income comes entirely or mainly in rents there is no relief under CTT. The only relief goes to 'working farmers'. Moreover, there is no way of escaping CTT since it applies to any major transfers, whether *inter vivos* or at death, except between spouses. Hence the tax can, by skilful juggling, be minimised, but not avoided. Nor can the landowner simply take land in hand and become a 'working farmer', since to qualify for working farmer relief 75 per cent of income in five of the previous seven years must have come from farming. Neither can the landowner claim business property relief as working farmers can. Moreover, the Agriculture (Miscellaneous Provisions) Act extends tenant security to allow close relatives to succeed, almost automatically, as tenants when the existing tenant dies or retires. So taking land in hand will become more difficult. Consequently the position of the private agricultural landlord has been made more tenuous by recent legislation. However, the institutional landlord is, as we have already indicated, entirely unaffected, so the conclusion must be, *ceteris paribus*, that private agricultural landlordism will decline and institutional landlordism increase. The proposed wealth tax can only serve, if implemented, to hasten this process. Of course, an alternative *scenario* is a creeping process of land nationalisation, if land and not cash is used to pay off tax demands; for the fact is that any landowner's assets are illiquid. Many will find it difficult to raise the cash to meet their tax bills and will therefore have to sell land to raise money or offer land in lieu of cash to the Inland Revenue.

The position of the owner-occupier is different but still very much threatened by the tax changes. For less than 1000 acres or £250 000 assets there is a 50 per cent relief across the board and even a 30 per cent business relief above those levels. However, as with the agricultural landlord, the tax cannot be avoided and rising land prices, given that land is the most valuable asset the owner has, cause him to have to pay higher taxes. Once again, of course, a few owner-occupiers will have the cash available to pay the necessary taxes without neglecting future investment and/or mortgaging or selling land – a process which obviously has finite limits. To obtain any of these exemptions from CTT an owner-occupier must again qualify as a 'working farmer', although some of those in our 1000+ acres sample would not have qualified since they received less than 75 per cent of their income from farming. If wealth tax were implemented, owner-occupiers would find the burden hard to carry. The CLA estimates that 30 per cent of *all* those who will be subject to wealth tax in the UK will be owner-occupying farmers. It is thus hardly surprising, considering the above, that farmers would like to see their assets treated in a far different way under CTT and wealth tax. As things stand, however, 'agriculture is bearing a capital burden (land) which it cannot afford' (MacGregor 1973, p.46).[6]

Meanwhile, the institutions continue to buy land, the price rises and owner-occupiers face bigger-than-ever future tax bills. Farmers in our sample were especially bitter about capital taxation which they see as a threat to their continued existence:

> There are no advantages to ownership today because of existing and proposed taxes which threaten to kill agriculture as we have known it. . . . You know, I have had a tough life. I worked myself stupid for ten years to build up this farm and I have succeeded and I'm doing well. But these ten years will have been wasted in vain if taxes take what I have achieved away from my children. I did it for them. If I lose it, I shall regret the loss of my youth. . . . It will be the end if personal gain and initiative for your children are taken away. Why should the hard working half of the country be made to help the scrounging half?

However, as a famous agricultural correspondent has observed, there is an irony in the position of the owner-occupier now faced by the threat of high taxation, for many are the sons and grandsons of those who benefited when the agricultural landlords were driven from their estates due to financial pressures earlier in the century:

> They or their fathers stepped in and bought when others were forced to sell. They did not then worry about the poor rich who were taxed out of their inheritance. . . .
>
> (Cherrington 1975, p.37)

Ownership Ideologies and the Justification of Landownership[7]

In this final section of the paper we wish to make explicit certain points about the ways in which farmers, landowners and their organisations argue in defence of the landownership *status quo*.

To own land as an individual is, of course, to own capital but it is not always easy or satisfactory to justify the ownership of capital in its own terms. That is, it is not easy for landowners to explain their wealth and legitimate their property rights with reference only to the universalistic, impersonal contractual principles of personal gain which are vested in the laws of property. This is especially the case where the landowner is part of a local particularistic social structure in which face-to-face modes of control are necessary. We can briefly describe the way landowners justify their ownership of capital in the form of land by reference to other types of property rights than those associated with capital. It should all the while be remembered that these ideological justifications are important legitimating aspects in contemporary rural society as a whole which can equally be used in defending landownership more generally, for example when landowners feel threatened by capital taxation or financial institutions. The first ideology which we can identify in this context is an individualistic one which sees land as being no different from *any* other form of property. So, for example, what we term (following Lafargue) property of personal appropriation (PPA) – items such as clothes, cars, furnishings, etc. which are widely distributed in advanced capitalist societies – are seen as being no different from capitalist property such as land or factories. Thus, for example, one landowner patiently explained:

> It's human instinct that once you've got something, you hang on to it. It's like your motor car, you'd take a dim view if someone said they were taking it away.

Such an argument has been confirmed and given legitimation by a Cambridge Unviersity farm economist when he writes:

> Ownership of one kind or another is perhaps the most common of human aspirations. A feeling of substance induced by sufficient acres is enjoyed by the traditional landowner, and it is also good to realise how dear to the heart of man is his own small plot, which, like Naboth's vineyard, becomes part of his life and is therefore invaluable.
>
> (University of Cambridge 1947)

Or to take again some of the comments made by farmers we interviewed, each of those quoted here claiming a peculiar personal tie to the land while under-emphasising its profit-generating functions.

> Farming is a way of life, and being an owner-farmer is even more so. It's my inheritance. I feel about it the same way as aristocrats do about their stately homes. It's me, isn't it?
>
> The love of the land and gardens, the wildlife and beauty of our countryside, is in the blood. . . . If more people had a small piece of garden to cultivate, the world would be happier and healthier.

A second group of ideologies, which we term 'collectivistic', revolve around a confusion of private rights of production with communal rights of production, i.e. private landownership is justified in terms of the distribution of real or supposed benefits generated through it. Thus the ownership of landed property inspires not so much personal gain as the production of goods and the generation of wages from which all benefit. Specifically of course, employment is created. Here are some relevant quotes from farmers:

> I know of no one who suffers round here because I earn more. . . . I have to do well if they are to have a decent living. So it's only right that I should be paid for providing others with a living and for my hard work and worry.
>
> I make profit for a purpose – it gives security to my family and my employees. I worked it out that fifty-two people depend on me. . . . I can contribute to the well-being of everyone who drives through here.

> I feel that if it weren't for people like us, others wouldn't get jobs round here. . . . How are you to employ people if someone doesn't have a bit more than others. If farmers could make more profit, there wouldn't be so much unemployment in country areas.

Sometimes *noblesse oblige* or a modern version of it is referred to by landowners. They feel landownership involves duties as well as rights:

> It is incumbent upon me to look after those who are dependent upon me. It is my job to look after them. . . . This is socially desirable. I was brought up to see this as my duty.

> I accept I have to set an example. My wife and I feel we have earned our position but owe it to others to involve ourselves in society. . . . I meet many artisans and am friendly with them. That's my philosophy – responsible Toryism.

The final ideology, which we term 'altruistic' concerns a view of land not as a factor of production but as a matter of consumption, and one enjoyed by the entire community. There is a denial of self-benefit on the part of the owner himself: he becomes a mere agricultural caretaker or, more pertinently, a steward.

Briefly, the concept of stewardship holds that the current title-bearer to a particular piece of land does not 'really' own it. He is, instead, a custodian whose task it is to hand on the land in better heart than he found it to the next generation (who, of course, do likewise). A variation on this popular theme is that land is held 'in trust' for the nation. This ideology of stewardship thus justifies wealth by implying that the landowner is performing a public service by looking after the nation's land, and thus stresses selflessness and altruism rather than any benefit which may be gained by exploiting it. As one farmer said to us:

> A landowner feels it's more in trust for the next generation. You're not out for a quick return.

The concept of stewardship emphasises the non-productive aspects of agricultural land, especially its visual appeal and its aesthetic beauty which it is felt necessary to preserve for the enjoyment of all. This is, of course, a very old notion which, as F. M. L. Thompson points out, was very common in the nineteenth century. It was the stability and continuity of landownership which, in Thompson's words:

> . . . fostered the idea . . . that the owner of an estate for the time being was steward of a trust for unborn generations and temporary recipient of the fruits of his forebears' endeavours.
>
> We can see how Burke, the philosopher of the landed interest arrived at his partnership not only between those who are living,

> but between those who are living, those who are dead and those who are to be born.
>
> (Thompson 1963, p.5)

We have seen already earlier in this paper very similar sentiments to these expressed by farmers, landowners and their organisations, for example the quotations from the CLA documents (see above pp.79–80 and 83).

Once again we see a certain paradox: to be a real landowner is not necessarily the same as being an efficient farmer; yet to threaten the present structure of landownership is to threaten farming. The owner-occupiers have not only taken their land from the old agricultural landlords, but their landownership ideologies, too: '*plus ça change, plus c'est la même chose*'.

Conclusion

For more than one hundred years, the private ownership of land has been under sporadic attack. The major attack has undoubtedly been through the fiscal policies of the state, capital transfer tax being the latest example. Such external threats as taxation and City land purchases have led to a remarkable degree of political mobilisation on the part of landowners. We have seen, for example, how the ideologies of property we outlined relate directly to the arguments used by farmers and their organisations when defending the *status quo*. But what of the future in terms of landownership? There is good reason to believe that if CTT is allowed to operate relatively unhindered in the case of land, and especially if a wealth tax is introduced on top, that there will be a gradual reduction in private landownership. Initially it is the private landlords who will be hardest hit since they cannot claim the reliefs under CTT open to 'working farmers'. But eventually the owner-occupiers, especially the larger ones, will feel the pinch, too. They may well have to sell land, in which case the most likely purchasers will be financial institutions. Or they may offer the state land in lieu of tax. Either way this *could* mean a gradual reversion to a tripartite landed social structure of (i) institutional landlord, (ii) tenant farmer, (iii) landless worker. But this is by no means a certainty. What a Labour government can do, a Conservative one can undo. Equally a favourable movement of affairs in the industrial sector may take the heat out of the land market and financial institutions may decide not to continue with land purchases. What we can say is that the conditions are now present which could lead to a reduction in owner-occupation for the first time in fifty years. What we do not say, knowing what we do about the power of the private landed interest, is that this will happen.

Notes

1. In the course of this paper we shall refer to our recent research (financed by STFC) in East Anglia on farmers. During the course of our work we collected information by interview from 216 farmers in three separate samples. References in this paper are to farmers in two of three samples. We called the samples respectively 'the 1000+ acres sample' and 'the 44 parishes sample'. We should explain something about these samples. The 1000+ acres sample comprised a random sample of all farm-holdings in the counties of Cambridgeshire, Essex, Norfolk and Suffolk (East Anglia) of 1000 acres (250 hectares) or more in area of crops and grass. The 44 parishes sample comprised a random sample of farm holdings regardless of size in an area of 44 parishes in central East Suffolk where one of the authors had originally conducted his research on farm workers (Newby 1977) out of which our research on farmers grew. Further details on our research can be gained from the following: Bell and Newby (1974); Newby *et al.* (1975); Newby *et al.* (1978); Rose *et al.* (1976); Rose *et al.* (1977) and Saunders *et al.* (1978).

   The farming and landowning pressure groups referred to in this paper are the National Farmers' Union (NFU) and the Country Landowners' Association (CLA). This paper does not take account of the Northfield report on landownership nor of proposed tax reforms by the Conservative Government of Mrs Thatcher.
2. Statistics on land prices are not without their problems. Several sets of statistics are produced from various sources, including the Ministry of Agriculture, and all have their advantages and disadvantages. For a short discussion of land price statistics see *The Farmland Market*, no.8, July 1976, p.17. Because the figures produced by *Farmland Market* are based on auction sales, and therefore reflect the open market in land more closely, we shall largely use these figures, wherever possible, in our analysis of recent trends in the market.
3. For example the following exchange is taken from the evidence giving by the CLA to the Select Committee on the Wealth Tax:

   Q. May I ask you . . . have you an idea of the number of farmers plus landowners that would come within the scope of this (wealth) tax?

   A. . . . The calculations are around about 30,000 occupiers would come within the scope.

   Q. You say 30,000 . . . I believe the Inland Revenue puts 100,000 as being the top number of people within the country that will come within the scope, and the farming community, I assume is about 1 per cent, or at the most 2 per cent, of the total population of this country.

   (Chairman) It just confirms the town people's belief that all the wealthy people live out in the country.

   Q. Well, that might be so.

   A. I do not think that any of us would describe it as wealth. I think we should describe it as capital invested on which we have to make a living . . . 80 per cent of capital is invested in illiquid assets which have been recently inflated out of all proportion to their productive value (i.e. land). (House of Commons 1976, p.783).

4. Property Growth Assurance is an interesting combination of city interests, land agents and farmers. The agricultural committee of the group includes a senior partner from a highly respected farming and land agency company which itself manages PGA's land. He is also a director of the largest of all the agricultural trading companies. The other two members of the committee are both farmers and landowners and they, as a committee, direct the farming policy of the group.

   The basic aim of the group is to open up land investment to the small investor by offering agricultural bonds in the form of a life policy. The original minimum investment was £250, now down to £120, with no stipulated maximum. the money thus generated is used to buy farm land largely through sale and leaseback, i.e. an owner-occupier sells his land to PGA who then make him tenant. In fact the original owner generally retains a between 40 and 60 per cent holding in his land with the option to buy back if the fund is willing to sell. Hence there is a co-ownership element. Between 1970 and 1974 PGA bought 18 000 acres of land covering fifty-two separate holdings, half of this land being bought in the heady atmosphere of the 1973 land market. Initially there were spectacular yields – 48 per cent between 1970 and 1974. But as prices fell the company stopped buying land and was eventually forced to sell over 5000 acres, something which the fund's manager had regarded as highly unlikely only two years before. Consequently the value of a single unit in PGA rose from £5 in 1970 to £7.51 in 1974, slumped to £4.64 in 1975 and rose to £5.36 in 1976. But despite selling land in 1975, PGA came back into the land market as prices began to rise in 1976. Moreover they have begun to farm land themselves in common with insurance companies like Abbey Life and the Prudential and pension funds like that of British Airways. PGA's fund manager believes that the lessons learned from farming 680 acres of their own land makes him appreciate his tenants' problems better. But most owner-occupiers remain unconvinced despite PGA's disclaimers that they are not a group of faceless city tycoons out for a quick killing from farming. Further details on PGA can be found in the following: David Campbell, 'The New Landlords', *Farmers' Weekly*, 9 November 1973, pp.68–75; 'We're Not a Bunch of City Tycoons', *Farmers' Weekly*, 25 May 1973, p.63; 'Institutions Return as Land Prices Rise', *Farmers Weekly*, 22 August 1975, p.51; 'A Stake in Land at £10 a Month', *Farmers' Weekly*, 5 April 1974, p.55; 'City Land Buyer Back in Market', *Farmers' Weekly*, 13 August 1976, p.51; Lorana Sullivan, 'Why the City is Going Back to the Farm', *Sunday Times*, 2 May 1976, p.54; Peter Wormell, 'The Landlord in the Bowler', *Big Farm Management*, August 1974, pp.50–3; P. Hutley quoted in the *Essex County Standard*, 27 April 1973. For Fountain Farming see Anthony Rosen, 'Increased Land Prices – Their Implications on the Future Structure of Agriculture', unpublished paper presented to the Rank Hovis McDougall Hampshire Harvest Review, 6 November 1973; Anthony Rosen, 'Who Will Own Britain', *Farmland Market*, no.3, January 1975, pp.9–11; Campbell, op. cit., 1973; Wormell, op. cit., 1974.

5. Under the provisions of the old estate duty, anyone who gave his estate away and then survived for seven years could thereby enable his heirs to avoid the tax entirely. If he did die in the interim, the rate of tax depended on how long he had survived after the transfer. Rosen has made the following comments:

> However, it is not, fortunately, my brief to explain to those poor millionaires, the owner-occupiers, how they should so arrange their affairs to enable the traditional nepotism of owner-occupation to continue unabated. . . . Suffice to say that estate duty is still a voluntary tax and there are only four reasons for paying it –
> 1. If you believe the government can spend your money better than you can.
> 2. A bad accountant.
> 3. A sudden early demise.
> 4. If you do not trust your relatives.
>
> (Rosen 1973, p.2)

6. The CLA in particular has published its views with great energy. While accepting that agriculture must bear its share of capital taxation 'to exact a high tax rate on functional capital, or money tied up in a business (can) only do grave harm to the business and the national economy' (Barker 1976, p.47). CLA investment surveys show cut-backs on large estates because of the threat of capital taxation and the need to build up reserves to pay taxes. After the recent purchase by British Airways Pension Fund of a 1500 acre estate for £2 million, a disgruntled owner-occupier wrote to *Farmers' Weekly* with a typical lament about pension funds not being subject to CTT and so being the likely future owners of the land – but owners who will contribute nothing to rural society (*Farmers' Weekly*, 7 May 1976, pp.39–40).

   But the fact remains that with land yielding a steady 5 to 6 per cent gross per annum, institutions regard it as a good long-term investment, especially as rents are keeping pace with inflation. A recent article in the *Sunday Times* concluded:

   > The financial institutions' agricultural holdings seem destined to increase in coming years. For the past year or so, few top quality farms have come on the market because of indecision caused by legislation. . . . But, as Britain's various taxes on accumulated wealth start to bite, the only British investors who will be able to buy the country's large, good and efficient farms will be the institutions. Small wonder that many are aiming to make farmland as much as 15 per cent of their property portfolios and that their managers are learning more about farming by doing it themselves. (Sullivan, *Sunday Times*, 2 May 1976, p.54).

7. This section is a much condensed version of the final chapter of Newby *et al.*, 1978. See also Rose *et al.*, 1976. We hope that consultation of these sources will make up for some of the theoretical shortcomings of the present paper.

References

Barker, Alan (1976), 'Socialist Peer Rejects State Land Takeover' *Farmers' Weekly* ,4 June 1976, p.47.

Bell, Colin and Newby, Howard (1974), 'Capitalist Farmers in the Class Structure', *Sociologia Ruralis*, **14**, no.1/2, pp.86–107.

Byrne, Nicholas (1975), 'Agricultural Investment: A Guide to Performance (1945–1974)', *Farmland Market*, no.4, July, pp.9–12.

Cherrington, John (1975), 'Cherrington's Diary', *British Farmer and Stockbreeder*, 1 February, p.37.

Clery, Peter (1975), *Farming Finance*, Ipswich, Farming Press Ltd.

Country Landowners' Association (1974), 'Constraints on Business Organisation in Agriculture', London, CLA.

Country Landowners' Association (1976), 'The Future of Landownership – A CLA Discussion Paper', London: CLA.

Gibbs, Richard and Harrison, Alan (1974), '*Landownership by Public and Semi-Public Bodies in Great Britain*', Miscellaneous Study 56 (revised edition), University of Reading, Dept. of Agricultural Economics and Management.

Harrison, Alan (1975), *Farmers and Farm Businesses in England*. Miscellaneous Study 62, University of Reading, Dept. of Agricultural Economics and Management.

House of Commons (1976), *Select Committee on the Wealth Tax: Final Report* (3 volumes), London, HMSO.

Lafargue, Paul (n.d.), *Evolution of Property from Savagery to Civilisation*, Calcutta: Sreekali Prakasalaya.

MacGregor, Alasdair (1973), 'This Inflated Isle', *Farmers' Weekly*, 28 December 1973, p.46.

Ministry of Agriculture (1966), *A Century of Agricultural Statistics*, London, HMSO.

Newby, Howard (1977), *The Deferential Worker*, London, Allen Lane, Harmondsworth, Penguin Books.

Newby, Howard (ed.) (1978), *International Perspectives in Rural Sociology*, London, Wiley.

Newby, Howard, Rose, David, Saunders, Peter and Bell, Colin (1975), 'Field Work', in C. Le Vay (ed.), *The Design and Interpretation of Questionnaires*, Aberystwyth, University College, Dept. of Agricultural Economics, pp.45–73.

Newby, Howard, Bell, Colin, Rose, David and Saunders, Peter (1978), *Property, Paternalism and Power*, London, Hutchinson, Madison, University of Wisconsin.

Rose, David, Saunders, Peter, Newby, Howard and Bell, Colin (1976), 'Ideologies of Property: A Case Study', *Sociological Review*, **24**, no.4, pp.699–731.

Rose, David, Newby, Howard, Saunders, Peter and Bell, Colin (1977), 'Land Tenure and Official Statistics', *Journal of Agriculture Economics*, **XXVIII**, no.1, January, pp.67–75.

Rosen, Anthony (1973), 'Increased Land Prices – Their Implications on the Future Structure of Agriculture', *R.H.M. Hampshire Harvest Review*, September.

Saunders, Peter, Newby, Howard, Bell, Colin and Rose, David (1978), 'Rural Community and Rural Community Power', in H, Newby (ed.), (1978).

Sturmey, S. G. (1955), 'Owner Farming in England and Wales', *Manchester School*, **23**, pp.245–68.

Thompson, F. M. L. (1963), *English Landed Society in the Nineteenth Century*, London: Routledge and Kegan Paul.

University of Cambridge (1947), *Landownership in the Eastern Counties*, Cambridge, University of Cambridge. Farm Economics Branch.

Wormell, Peter (1974), 'The Landlord in the Bowler', *Big Farm Management*, August, pp.50–3.

5 Local Control versus Social Control in Land Use Planning: Sociological Perspectives

*Charles C. Geisler**

> Manifestly we need a modernised philosophy of property. . . . The basis for a social philosophy . . . was laid long ago by Marx . . . nearly everyone accepts as commonplace Marx's idea – revolutionary in his day – that every social institution is the product of development (here some would stop but Marx went on) whose causes are to be found (here again most of us put in some qualification, such as 'partly' or 'primarily') in changing material or economic conditions. Many examples of change in property concepts have already been given, and it is not necessary to remark that when a property concept changes it is because of economic circumstances.
>
> Francis Philbrick (1938, pp.728–9)

Any understanding of American political economy that fails to grasp prevailing views of property rights in the United States, past and present, is meagre. The liberalism of the founding fathers, manifest in the country's earliest social contracts,[1] envisaged decentralised control of land resources amongst 'the multitude' and their local units of government in the making. More recently, levels of growth and economic development unimagined by Adams and Jefferson have fundamentally altered the liberal vision. Decentralised local control of land seems antiquated if not counter to changing 'public interests', both social and environmental. Many contemporary liberals in the United States take as given the desirability of state and federal pre-emptive regulation or 'social control' of land use planning.[2] The French *estatist* tradition as Shonfield (1969) suggests, is gaining respect and emulation in America.

Broadly speaking, the rate of land conversion and utilisation in the United States is sobering. According to Resources for the Future, if present land utilisation rates continue, demand for land resources in all its forms will exceed land available in the United States in the year

---

* Department of Rural Sociology, Cornell University, New York. This Chapter is a revised version of a paper presented in April, 1979, at the European Congress for Rural Sociology held in Cordoba, Spain.

2000 by up to 50 million acres or roughly the combined size of the states of Vermont, New Hampshire, Maine, Massachusetts, Rhode Island, Connecticut and Maryland (General Accounting Office 1977)*. In 1970, according to the US Department of Agriculture (1974), urban areas claimed twice the land they did in 1950. Some expect American cities, and their basic resource requirements, to double again between 1970 and 2000 (Fischer 1970). In sum, historically abundant land reserves in the United States have given way to relative scarcity, and land use conflicts are commonplace.

While the need for uniform social control of land resources at higher levels of government may appear self-evident, local determination to control land remains a potent counterforce. As Rosenbaum has observed:

> The extreme sensitivity of land use governance has resulted in numerous instances of conflict and confrontation between citizens and governments. . . . Citizen groups have demonstrated again and again that, if not satisfied with decisions, they can impede, obstruct, and delay the execution of land use policy for extended lengths of time.
>
> (1976, p.3)

Local control, or the unfettered discretion over land use by property owners and more formally the delegation of land use control to municipalities by state government, evokes a mixture of emotions among most Americans.[3] On the one hand, there is unequivocal evidence that most laws governing the use of private property comprise an inconsistent and irresolute system of planning, are ill-considered from an environmental standpoint, and perpetuate both segregation and social exclusion. On the other hand, impulses to reform such parochialism are muted by several durable realities. We are all 'locals' in some capacity, with an ideological fondness for self-determination and individualism. Local control has a lineage in the United States, moveover, traceable to struggles of considerable historical importance, including the state's rights and home rule movements. The private ownership of property remains deeply embedded in the American dream, even today (Curran 1977).

In sum, decentralised property ownership and control have blended with the identity, the integrity and the status of Americans for generations, often in emotionally charged and confusing ways. It is this confusion about local control which prompts the present chapter.

---

* Resources for the Future is an American non-profit making organisation concerned with the generation and dissemination of knowledge about national resources and the quality of the environment. Established in 1952, it is based in Washington D.C. Source is Healy, R. G. 'Land Use and the States', John Hopkins University Press, Baltimore, 1976.

My chief concern is why, in the face of compelling reasons to the contrary, there exists widely discernible resistance to land use planning reform. To date, inquiries by the scientific community and government have investigated many facets of land use planning – legal, environmental, economic and social. These research agendas are relatively barren, however, when it comes to deciphering resistance to reform and its centrepiece, local control. The area awaits sociological interpretation.

In my view, sociological theory presently extends at least three interpretations of resistance to land use planning reform. The first of these is a demographic explanation for anti-reform phenomenon and can be traced to the work of Emile Durkheim. Another explanation views the resistance as individual irrationalism or social pathology and gives primacy to subjective circumstances. This I term the 'resistance ethos' explanation and associate with the thinking of Max Weber. Finally, Marxist sociology, with certain key revisions, offers materialist insights into opposition to greater social control of land resources. Whereas there is utility in all three traditions, I feel the last perspective has been most seriously overlooked by Marxists and non-Marxists alike in addressing the present course of land use planning. Following a brief exegesis of each theory as it relates to the problem at hand, I shall employ the materialist perspective in arriving at a centre-periphery conceptualisation of property rights and land use control.

The Sociology of Land Use Planning

The prevailing justification for greater social control of land resources bears a marked affinity with the logic of societal development offered nearly a century ago by Emile Durkheim. In his *Division of Labour in Society*, Durkheim poses two modal forms of social organisation. As society progresses from its original, relatively undifferentiated or 'mechanical' form to its more heterogeneous, highly specialised ('organic') counterpart, labour processes become increasingly individuated. This evolution in social organisation is accompanied by intensified social intercourse. Durkheim reasons as follows:

> The division of labour develops . . . as there are more individuals sufficiently in contact to be able to act and react upon one another. If we agree to call this relation and the active commerce resulting from it dynamic or moral density, we can say that the progress of the division of labour is in direct ratio to the moral or dynamic density of society.
>
> (1947, p.257)

Population growth, Durkheim believes, adds to social contact and 'density' under conditions of urban concentration (Schnore 1958). In other words, Durkheim appreciates the importance of human proximity and physical space as essential ingredients in the configuration of social space ('moral density').[4] His view of social organisation in advanced society further presupposes growth in formal regulation by the state, given his assumption that humans possess unlimited appetites for socially desired goods (Giddens 1971). Such social control is, in essence, a codification of prevailing moral rules and, as such, embodies the public interest. Law, 'moral density', and the division of labour are all examples of what Durkheim refers to as *social facts*, that is, realities which transcend individual volition and are more than a mere summation of individual parts.

There could hardly be a closer symmetry between the Durkheimian understanding of complex modern society, with its intricate interdependencies between density and social control, and contemporary rationales for more centralised land use planning. Garret Hardin (1968) argues, for instance, that common lands will be unwittingly overutilised by economically 'rational' humans, a state of affairs presumed to worsen as more humans compete for land. Noting discrepancies between the fixity of land and the flexibility of incomes in 'post-industrial' society, Hirsch (1978) concludes that additional land use regulation and pre-emption of related individual prerogatives is inevitable.[5] As regulation increases, land assumes new meanings. So, too, does the bedrock institution of property itself. Wunderlich depicts the differentiation in modern property definitions in forthright Durkheimian terms:

> As property, objects and people multiply, possibilities arise for creating 'new' property. The property system becomes more complex. Complexity promotes specialisation, so traders, trustees, finders, examiners, appraisers, financiers, assessors and others ply their range of skills in packaging and merchandising property rights. So between the layers of rights holders such as owners, lessees, bailees, grantees, and permittees are the specialists who service the rights.
>
> (1972, p.7)

If the above review fairly establishes the connection between Durkheim's theory and more recent justifications for social control over land resources, what interpretation can be ascribed to Durkheim for popular resistance to such controls? Despite the general evolutionary trend perceived by Durkheim from mechanical to organic social organisation, he nonetheless maintained that 'mechanical solidarity persists even in the most elevated societies' (1947, p.186). The implication seems clear. Even in contemporary society where land use planning is a pressing issue, modes of social control specific to mechanical solidarity coexist with the social control granted the force of law. According to Durkheim's density logic, the former is most likely where population is most dispersed and division of labour lowest (Redfield 1947). Thus, those resisting greater property regulation are apt to reside in open country and smaller communities, places in which social control is akin to moral consensus and cohesion rather than law.[6]

Like Durkheim, Max Weber gave lengthy consideration to the advent of western capitalism, an authority system and social order distinguishable from its more primitive, feudal antecedents. But where Durkheim concentrates on individuation tied to the division of labour, Weber places attention on individualism and the subjectivism it implies. He argues in *The Protestant Ethic and the Spirit of Capitalism* that capitalism owes much to aesthetic protestantism as well as to personality types (Gerth and Mills 1958). In his posthumously published *Economy and Society*, Weber (1978) characterises modern bureaucracy as a pre-eminently rational system of controlling society (Marcuse 1971). Capitalism, for Weber, is as much a cultural form of legal – rational governance as it is a distinctive form of economic organisation.[7]

The subjectivism in Weber's sociological theory is pervasive. Humans are accorded volition and free will,[8] regardless of the division of labour, physical or social density, or other 'social facts'. Whereas for Durkheim autonomous human behaviour is of little account, Weber defends the relative autonomy of individuals amid a mixture of compelling economic as well as cultural – ideological forces. Indeed, Weber's defence of value-free research in *Methodology for the Social Sciences* only affirms his basic belief that individual values are real and can affect the larger society of which they are a part.

There are both general and specific reasons for summoning Weber in bringing sociology to bear on popular opposition to land use regulation and reform. The general reason is most straightforward. Discourse among planners, resource managers, public officials and social scientists commonly locates responsibility in the opponent's subjective state – psychological, cultural or ideological. Allegedly, opponents are irrational or parochial; they place provincial local interests over the public interest of society and display phobic responses to 'outside interference'; they are enmeshed in rural subcultures or are alienated from society's mainstreams;[9] they lack the education and sophistication needed to grasp the ecological side-effects of private land use; or they are given to ultra-conservative ideologies which sanctify private ownership. These views share in one form or another, Weber's paramount concern with ethos and periodically border on psychological determinism.[10]

There is a more specific relevance in Weber's theory as well. It emerges from flaws in legal – rational bureaucracies, foreseen by

Weber and capable of provoking popular resistance to controls imposed by the bureaucracy or interests it might come to represent. On the one hand, he sees rational – legal bureaucracy as indispensable to capitalism. On the other he anticipates that the very virtues of bureaucracy will become its vices, prompting reversion to less rational, more traditional authority systems.[11] Despite the public interest ends served by rational – legal systems in their pure form, Weber acknowledges that class interests help define system legitimacy through religion and ideology (Birnbaum 1965).

Thus, in shifting from ideal type to the real world, Weber identifies significant flaws in rational – legal systems which vitiate their effectiveness and raises questions as to their legitimacy (Mommsen 1974). Where rational – legal order is perceived as neither rational nor legal, citizen resistance to such 'rationalism', and to centralised control into which it translates (Ostrum 1974), is not unthinkable. In other words, Weber's theory is applicable to anti-reform sentiments if it is assumed that opponents view government regulation in some sense as illegal. The premier example of such sentiment is the common allegation, echoing Oliver Wendell Holmes in his historic *Mahon v. Pennsylvania Coal* decision of 1922, that government regulation of land may produce unconstitutional 'taking' of property.[12]

For Karl Marx, the ownership and control of property is basic to understanding the disharmonies of society. The 'laws of motion' of capital which Marx sought to isolate may be restated as laws of property transmission from one class in society to another. Whereas the preponderance of Marxist analysis is devoted to the dispossession of labour from the working class, the materialist perspective likewise illuminates the dispossession of property rights from independent producers in the course of capitalist development. From this standpoint, therefore, resistance to land use planning emanates from material deprivation of property rights, particularly among those with close occupational ties to real property.

Independent commodity producers, or the petty bourgeoisie, are those people who own their means of production and who rely on personal or family labour to make their living rather than on wage labour. As capitalism replaced feudalism, these small-scale producers either expanded their share and scale of property ownership, and emerged as nascent capitalists requiring hired labour, or they gradually relinquished ownership to other capitalists and were themselves absorbed into the working class. Thus, it is commonplace to depict independent producers then and now as a 'transition class' (Goss *et al.* 1978; Wright 1978), the members of which are headed for new and very often inferior (proletarian) class positions.

The dispossession experienced by independent producers assumes two forms, both forms being types of property. One involves artisan skills. As industrialisation spreads in the train of capitalist mechanisation, worker versatility is replaced with worker specialisation – a relative loss of control by individuals over production (Braverman 1974; Holland 1976). The other is a more tangible form of property, namely, land. The Enclosure Movement of England, beginning in the fifteenth century, evicted and displaced free peasant proprietors. This massive expropriation of property rights was referred to by Marx (1973 Vol. 1, p.714) as the 'historic divorce' of the means of production from actual producers and was the basis for the whole process of subsequent capitalist development (p.716).

This historic divorce or dispossession did of course not happen uniformly in all places or at one point in time.[13] On the contrary, it was both gradual and spatially uneven, advancing furthest in more urban areas where the factory system concentrated and least in the countryside where traditional forms of ownership were most entrenched. In their own way, Marx and Engels acknowledged this spatial division of labour between town and countryside:

> Here first became manifest (as civilisation arose from barbarism) the division of the population into two great classes which is directly based on the division of labour and on the instruments of production. The town already is in actual fact the concentration of the population, of the instruments of production, of capital . . . while the country demonstrates just the opposite fact. . . . *The separation of town and country can also be understood as the separation of capital and landed property, as the beginning of the existence and development of capital independent of landed property.* . . .
>
> (1970 p.69, emphasis added)

Needless to say, the monopoly capitalism which has emerged in the century since Marx compiled his views has rendered the town–countryside dichotomy somewhat obsolete. Today more than ever, large-scale capital has outgrown its loyalty to jurisdictions on the basis of size and scale alone. What is not obsolete, however, is Marx's notion of differentiating space on the basis of how production is organised, a necessary dimension of which is the prevailing property system. It thus becomes plausible to substitute the more flexible concept of 'centre' for town and 'periphery' for countryside. The centre (Marx's 'town') has been the focal area of capitalist organisation and administration, first under competitive capitalism and currently under advanced monopoly conditions. The periphery, wherein earlier and even pre-capitalist modes of production endure, coexists with the centre. This coexistence is not without conflict, however, for dispossession is most threatening in the periphery where survival is closely tied to private ownership. Resistance to social control initiatives, from the materialist perspective, is therefore a reflection of historical tensions underlying centre and periphery production systems.

The three preceding sociological perspectives suggest a variety of ways in which classical theories can illuminate opposition to land use planning. The first emphasises demographic imperatives, land use planning opponents being poorly integrated into the conventions of complex ('organic') society. The second stresses subjective states which may produce opposition to various forms of social control when government legitimacy is in question. Material dispossession, spread unevenly across class and place, distinguishes the third theory. The remainder of this essay will argue that resistence to social control of land resources remains obscure without an analysis of material dispossession of property rights. This involves assessing the class positions of land use planning opponents, of opponent reliance on private ownership for survival, and of the expendability of independent producers in the larger scheme of advanced capitalist development.

An American 'Enclosure Movement'

At risk of straining the analogy, it may be stated that the enclosure movement of which Marx wrote persists today in the United States in the form of expanded social control over property rights. It is frequently assumed by students of the 'historical divorce' and 'primitive accumulation' that dispossesson ran its course in the infancy of capitalism. In fact, dispossession continues today though not always in the form of overt expropriation. Whereas in the English enclosure movement actual ownership changed hands, the American enclosure movement (France and England may also provide examples[14]) rests principally on the redistribution of control. The one is the functional equivalent of the other. The result for independent producers having direct or indirect occupational ties to the land is the same – alienation of property rights.

The redistribution of control over property in the United States is essentially the product of land use planning which makes private property rights public. Moreover, the trend has been to invest discretion over how these rights will be used in higher, more centralised units of government (Finnell 1978; Popper 1979). The name commonly given this trend, 'quiet revolution on land use control' (Bosselman and Callies 1971), is the name by which the American enclosures movement has come to be known.

Perhaps the most salient feature of the quiet revolution in land use control is the degree to which its historical significance is misunderstood. Typically, because the term came to light in the heyday of the environmental movement, the quiet revolution is thought to be recent. This impression is bolstered empirically by the appearance of numerous state and federal land use controls, following the passage of Hawaii's comprehensive land use plan in 1961, and by the popularisation of Aldo Leopold's (1966) environmentally based 'land ethic'. Public regulation of private property is undeniably on the increase (General Accounting Office 1977) which in turn has contributed to basic redefinition in the meanings of 'property' (Wunderlich 1972) and 'land' (Bosselman and Callies 1971).

From the materialist perspective, however, the quiet revolution in land use control is part of a longer term corporate revolution which has transformed the basic nature of economic organisation in the United States (Geisler 1979). This corporate revolution manifested itself outwardly in terms of scale. That is, by late in the last century monopoly units of production were displacing or absorbing smaller units of capital. There was a less manifest but no less important aspect of the corporate revolution as well. As agrarian capitalism of the nineteenth century gave way to the highly concentrated and more centralised economic organisation of the twentieth, the common law notion of absolute ownership declined in relevance.[15] Control of property replaced ownership in importance. Independent producers, dependent on private ownership or a 'closed' property system, were and continue to be class fatalities as the property institution of which they are a part are transformed.[16]

Thus, with the differentiation of capital into competitive and monopoly forms, fee simple ownership ceded ground, both literally and figuratively, to the 'open' property system in which rights of use were severely abridged. The corporate revolution and the dispossession it signalled is implied in Max Lerner's well-known essay on 'The Property Revolution':

> Industrial property became centralised, family ownership waned, the corporate form pushed aside the others, the size of the property unit shifted – and America, which had once been a society mainly of small property owners, became a society not only of the Big Technology and the Big Corporation, but also of Big Property.
>
> (1957, p.298)

Of retreating, small property interests, Lerner says this:

> Small Property still exists in the form of small farms, small businesses, and tiny shops, but the independent farmer is a dwindling fraction of the population, the small manufacturer is being crowded by the great corporations, and the little merchant finds himself precariously caught in an economy of big department stores, chain stores, mail-order firms, and discount houses.

Where Lerner offers little guidance is with respect to the legal mechanisms by which the transfer from Small Property to Big Property occurs, that is, with respect to the legitimating role of the state.

The 'Public Interest State'

Earlier in this chapter the classical liberal underpinnings of competitive capitalism and the private property system which accompanied it were identified. The *laissez-faire* state was, in its circumspect use of regulation, hardly a menace to private interests. In contrast to this 'private interest state' is what legal scholar Charles Reich (1964) calls the 'public interest state'. Here, the government presides over and gives legitimacy to an essentially transformed (i.e., 'open') property system and, implicitly, the production system of which it is part. In other words, the state in advanced capitalism intervenes in traditional property relationships and authorises myriad new property forms, all in the 'public interest'. Though Reich does not focus on land *per se*, his observations clearly pertain to real property developments.

The public interest state is of singular importance in the interclass transfer of property rights. Consider, for example, what transpires when the police powers of government are exercised to regulate the land:

> An uncompensated transfer of land use options is made from the owner to a government. The use options are held in trust by government, and benefits therefrom are granted to persons in the public. Some persons of this public will be more favourably treated, by virtue of their more frequent use, than other persons.
> (Wunderlich 1974, p.20).

To 'frequent use' must be added the additional criteria of economic and political power. Though land use controls are frequently developed with laudable social and environmental goals in mind, the historical record is replete with instances of such government policy favouring the monopoly sector of capital.[17] Thus, there are those, including unimpeachable authorities on the increasing social control over real property rights (e.g., Mason 1958; Dunham 1964; Healy 1977; and Castle 1978), who question the regulatory neutrality of higher levels of government. Reich, himself cynical regarding the impartiality of the so-called public interest state, writes:

> The public interest state . . . represents in one sense the triumph of society over private property. This triumph is the end point of a great and necessary movement for reform. But somehow the result is different from what the reformers wanted. Somehow the idealistic concept of the public interest has summoned up a

doctrine monstrous and oppressive. It is time to take another look at private property, and at the 'public interest' philosophy that dominates its modern substitute, the largesse of government.
(1964, p.771)

In the final analysis what permits the state to intervene in private property affairs is not so much its public sector status as its public interest claims. One must bear in mind that the supreme law of the land, the US Constitution, forbids dispossession without just compensation *and* a public purpose.[18] If these conditions are unmet, courts of law (which, representing the most conservative branch of government, harken to laws generally conceived under competitive capitalism) are apt to find land use controls to be unlawful, confiscatory seizures of property. Conversely, if a public interest basis for land use planning can be shown, regulation is likely to proceed and private property rights shift to the public domain without the substantial (perhaps prohibitive) burden of compensation.

Thus, the battlefield on which the American enclosure movement is waged is in large part ideological. For property rights are inviolate except in case of war or overriding public interest considerations providing elected officials a mandate to condemn or regulate these rights. To no one's surprise, the 'public interest' has proven to be unashamedly *ad hoc* in American history, even according to reports by the American Bar Foundation (Finnell 1978). In essence, this means that the police powers of the state, an authority almost without peer, are subject to the political economy surrounding the public interest. The ideological hegemony of large units of capital thus translate directly into a legal transfer of property rights to the public sector where certain private interests are better represented than others.

From Political Economy to Political Ecology

Only when the foregoing materialist perspective on land use planning is given a spatial dimension does its relevance to local control become apparent. As stated earlier, the closed property system has languished as social control over property rights has advanced. And as this has occurred, the mode of production most irrevocably tied to such rights has been threatened. Independent producers have been marginalised in terms of their overall contribution to the larger economy, and spatially as well. As I have shown elsewhere,[19] the proportion of self-employed producers in the labour force provides one approach to actually mapping the residual closed property system in the United States.

In the vocabulary of the foregoing discussion, this residual property-production zone may be thought of as the 'periphery' and contrasted to the property-production 'centre'. Even in the face of massive hinterland relocation by large capital, there remains a discernable geographic patterning of this centre and periphery. Further, the centre-periphery demarcation provides a conceptual 'map' for the political economy terminology already introduced. These are shown in Table 5.1, and include systems of production, property, ideology and governance. Each varies according to centre-periphery location.

Table 5.1 *The division of key concepts within the materialist perspective according to 'centre' and 'periphery'*

System Referent	*Spatial Divison of Labour* *Centre*	*Periphery*
Production system	High ratio of capital to labour and 'Big Property' referring to revolutionalised (high concentrated and centralised) corporate forms.	High (relative) ratio of labour to capital as well as high incidence of production not based on wage labour.
Property system	Open property prevalent (less-than-fee forms of ownership and myriad 'new property' driving out conventional forms).	Closed property prevalent (absolute fee simple ownership rights) but 'losing' ground to invading monopoly property-production forms.
State system	Public Interest State which wields broad police powers in regulating land use rights, thereby replacing local control with social control and redistributing property rights away from independent commodity producers.	Local decentralised units of government reflecting values of the nineteenth century Private Interest State wherein regulation, if it exists at all, protects private property rights and values.
Ideological system	Leopoldian land ethic based on revised public interest concepts justifying the open property system.	Traditional, *laissez-faire* land use ethic justifying the closed property system.

Local resistance to land use planning may now be viewed from the standpoint of political ecology. That is, on a day-to-day basis, local control is a territorial expression of what some might consider an anachronistic mode of production resisting extinction. This extinction, while not necessarily deliberate, is functionally determined by the revolution in property rights associated with maturing capitalism. Being dysfunctional for independent producers, this revolution evokes a strong protectionist stance on behalf of private property via the mechanism of local government. True, local control encompasses many additional interests. But so long as land use planning is legally delegated to local jurisdictions in the United States, local control is likely to receive its primary existential inspiration from those who survive by independent production.

Discussion

I suggested at the outset that, of the three perspectives presented, the materialist view has been most seriously neglected in addressing developments in land use policy. As shown, both the Durkheimian and Weberian perspectives offer insights into why such policies face local opposition. Yet neither develops a satisfactory theory of property, without which there can be only limited understanding of popular reaction to land use planning reform. The materialist perspective, whatever its shortcomings, can be accused of no such lacuna. As sociology takes greater account of property variables, as argued by Gouldner (1970), Firey (1976), and Newby (1979), the richness of the materialist position will likely emerg ›.

The present study rests on the assumption that property systems are dynamic rather than static, a consequence of changing modes of production interacting with assorted forms of government, some more centralised than others. The closed property system is slowly giving way to its open property counterpart, as if by some property equivalent to Gresham's Law. By having associated the open property system with advancing monopoly capitalism, however, I have understated the considerable potential of open property coupled with local control. To be sure, further research is needed exploring how the open property system might be decentralised in its administration, thus returning social control to the local level of government and freeing local control from its close ties with private property.

Notes

1. Language appearing in the Declaration of Independence, namely 'the pursuit of happiness', is commonly interpreted even today to mean one's right to own land and exercise broad discretion in its disposal and use. In the United States Constitution, Article 5 and the Fourteenth Amendment guarantee just compensation and due process when the Tenth Amendment has emerged as a potential limitation as the federal government's ability to 'coerce' state and local administration of federal programs, with implications for future land use planning at the local level [e.g., EPA *v.* Brown U.S.,97S.Ct.1635(1977)].
2. This use of social control has become somewhat of a convention among land economists in the United States (e.g., Ely and Wehrwein 1938; Clawson 1975) in reference to more land use planning and control by more centralised units of government. I have discussed this phenomenon, also referred to as the 'quiet revolution in land use control' (Bosselman and Callies 1971) in detail elsewhere (Geisler 1979).
3. Readers interested in local control and its institutionalisation as part of

formal home rule policies in the United States are referred to Sandalow (1964). More home rule charters, according to that author, have been granted since World War II; this suggests an amplified potential for inter-governmental conflict over land use control.

4. The asserted primacy of spatial arrangements in Durkheim's model has, according to Benoit-Smullyan (1948), caused him to be accused of sociological materialism. Leo Schnore (1958), to whom we are indebted for synthesising Durkheim's diverse writings, argues that such allegations are based on misreadings of Durkheim's work, a view supported by Giddens (1971).
5. The tendency to reason that social and economic growth occurs only with significant environmental (including land use) trade-offs requiring additional public interest regulation is commonplace. The reader is referred to Bosselman and Callies (1971), Hardin (1968), Healy (1977), and Nelson (1977) for examples.
6. Social control under conditions of mechanical solidarity is exercised primarily through what Durkheim termed the conscience collective, that is, the totality of beliefs and sentiments common to average members of the society. In simpler societies, the conscience collective is, according to Durkheim, embodied in religion (Lukes, 1973, p.518). Here the parallels between Durkheim's thinking and that of Leslie White (1967) seems obvious. The latter understands the Judeo – Christian tradition broadly to reinforce the 'natural' right of humans to exploit nature as they see fit.
7. 'Legal – rational' refers to policy formation based on systematic calculations of cause and consequence and consideration of means and ends as opposed to mere tradition, religious doctrine, or ruler edict.
8. For discussion of the meanings Weber assigned to freedom as well as democracy, see Gerth and Mills 1958, pp.70–4.
9. Here, the theoretical views of Weber and Durkheim intermingle insofar as the psychological portrait offered is believed by many to fit small town or rural people. The difference remains that Durkheim traced dominant causality from the macro-social unit to the individual whereas for Weber, causality works at least partially (if at all) in the opposite direction.
10. In the *Protestant Ethic*, Weber renounces any intention of replacing one-sided materialism with a one-sided spiritualist interpretation of history. More generally, he continually qualifies his theoretical findings to allow for multi-causal explanations of social phenomena.
11. This degenerative process predictably results in new forms of charismatic leadership, the endpoint of which might be benign or despotic. Gerth and Mills review this pessimistic strain in Weber (see pages cited in reference, note 8).
12. In dicta to this famous decision, Holmes alluded to the 'petty larceny' of the police powers, that is, the formal authority by which government regulates private property (see Bosselman *et al.* 1973).
13. This idea is not widely shared among Marxist scholars, most of whom believe that primitive accumulation was a historically specific, pre-capitalist phase of economic activity. Just as Wright (1978, p.64) stresses that the loss of control over the labour process under capitalism is not an all-or-nothing phenomenon, however, having occurred gradually over a long period of time and still unfolding, primitive accumulation recurs at

home and abroad and may prove to be an essential counter-crisis tendency within advanced capitalism (that is, a mode of offsetting the falling rate of profit).

14. Harbingers of expanded social control over property rights appear elsewhere, for example, in France (Lefebvre 1976) and in England (Ehrenfeld 1978).
15. According to Shonfield (1969, pp.385–6); 'Britain and the United States, both holding to the common law tradition, were brilliantly inventive in using their legal systems to create an environment in which a great reserve of previously suppressed business initiative was liberated. They concentrated the main weight of their effort on the protection and enlargement of the rights of private property: the arrangements governing society were turned into a series of contracts between owners of various things, including the owners of their own labour, about the terms on which such property was to be used.'
16. The works of Poulantzas (1975), and most recently Wright (1978) each reckon with property forms as affected by capital concentration. Poulantzas (p.146) addresses the gradual 'dissolution' of competitive capital *vis-à-vis* monopoly capital, that is, dispossession defined as eroding *real ownership* (the ultimate say over what is produced via investment prerogative and eroding *possession* (control over physical production decisions). Wright brings further refinement to Poulantzas's insights on both property and on the make-up of the modern petty bourgeoisie. In so doing, he emphasises that 'the old petty bourgeoisie [the independent producer to whom I have referred] is constantly threatened by the growth of monopoly capitalism.' (p.58).
17. This commenced in the nineteenth century, when broad powers of eminent domain devolved to and served as subsidies for large private enterprise (Scheiber 1973; Horwitz 1977). Additional examples of land use policies couched in the public interest but redistributing property wealth to monopoly capital are found in Harvey (1974), Kehoe *et al.* (1975), and Geisler (1979).
18. See Article V of the Constitution ('no person shall be deprived of life, liberty or property, without due process of law'). Moreover, the due process and equal protection clauses of the Fourteenth Amendment, products of the nineteenth century, require that state land use controls bear a rational relationship to 'legitimate state interests'.
19. See Geisler (1979). Here, I separated the counties of Wisonsin according to high (periphery) and low (centre) proportions of self-employed producers of the overall workforce and, using multivariate statistical manipulations, found this centre-periphery variable to be a strong predictor of opposition to further land use planning.

References

Benoit-Smullyan, Emile (1948), 'The Sociologism of Emile Durkheim and His School', in Harry Elmer Barnes (ed.), *An Introduction to the History of Sociology*, Chicago, University of Chicago Press, pp.499–538.

Birnbaum, Norman (1965), 'The Rise of Capitalism: Marx and Weber', in Neil J. Smelser, Jr. (ed.), *Readings in Sociology*. Englewood Cliffs, NJ, Prentice-Hall, pp.2–16.

Bosselman, Fred and Callies, David (1971), *The Quiet Revolution in Land Use Control*. Washington DC, Council on Environmental Quality.

Bosselman, Fred, Callies, David and Banta, John (1973), *The Taking Issue*. Washington DC, Council on Environmental Quality.

Braverman, Harry (1974), *Labor and Monopoly Capital*, New York, Monthly Review.

Brown, Peter G. (1975), *The American Law Institute Model Land Development Code, the Taking Issue, and Private Property Rights*. Washington DC, The Urban Institute.

Castle, Emery, N. (1978), 'Property rights and the political economy of resource scarcity' *American Journal of Agricultural Economics*, February, pp.2–9.

Clawson, Marion (1975), 'Economic and social conflicts in land use planning', *Natural Resources Journal*, **15**, July, pp.473–89.

Curran, Barbara A. (1977), *The Legal Needs of the Public: The Updated Final Report of a National Survey*, Chicago, American Bar Association.

Dunham, Allison (1964), 'Property, City Planning and Liberty', in Charles M. Haar (ed.), *Anglo-American Planning Practice*, Cambridge, Mass., Harvard University Press, pp.28–43.

Durkheim, Emile (1947), *The Division of Labour in Society*, first published 1893, Glencoe Illionois, Free Press.

Durkheim, Emile (1962), *Socialism and St. Simon*, New York, Collier Books.

Durkheim, Emile (1964), *The Rules of Sociological Method*, first published 1938, New York, Free Press.

Ehrenfeld, David (1978), *The Arrogance of Humanism*, New York, Oxford University Press.

Ely, Richart T. and Wehrwein, George S. (1938), *Land Economics*, Madison, University of Wisconsin Press.

Finnell, Gilbert L., Jr. (1978), 'The federal regulatory role in coastal land management', *American Bar Foundation Research Journal* No.2, Spring, pp.168–288

Firey, Walter (1976), 'The Application of Sociology to Land-Use Tenure', paper presented at annual meetings of the American Sociological Association, New York.

Fischer, John (1970), *Land Use in the United States*, New York, H. W. Wilson Company.

Geisler, Charles C. (1979), A Sociological Interpretation of Land Use Planning in Capitalist Society. Unpublished Ph.D. Dissertation, University of Wisconsin, Madison, Wisconsin.

General Accounting Office (GAO) (1977), *Land Use Planning, Management and Control*, Government Accounting Office Staff Study (28 July).

Gerth, Hans H. and C. Wright Mills (1958), *From Max Weber: Essays in Sociology*, New York, A Galaxy Book.

Giddens, Anthony (1971), *Capitalism and Modern Social Theory*, London, Cambridge University Press.

Goss, Kevin, Buttel, Frederick H. and Rodefeld, Richard D. (1978), 'The Political Economy of Class Structure in US Agriculture: A Theoretical Outline', paper presented at the Annual Meeting of the Rural Sociological Society, San Francisco, California (September).

Gouldner, Alvin, W. (1970), *The Coming Crisis in Western Sociology*, New York, Basic Books.

Hardin, Garrett (1968), 'The tragedy of the commons', *Science*, **162**, December, pp.1243–8.
Harvey, David (1974), 'Class-monopoly Rent, Finance Capital and the Urban Revolution', in *Regional Studies*, London, Pergamon Press, pp.233–55.
Healy, Robert G. (1977), *Land Use and the States*, Baltimore, Johns Hopkins.
Heyman, Ira M. (1968), 'The great 'property rights' fallacy' *Cry California*, Summer, pp.29–34.
Hirsch, Fred (1978), *Social limits to Growth*, first published 1976, New York, Twentieth Century Fund.
Holland, Stuart (1976), *Capital Versus the Regions*, New York, St. Martin's Press.
Horwitz, Morgan J. (1977), *The Transformation of American Law, 1789–1860*, Cambridge, Harvard University Press.
Kehoe, Dalton, Morley, David, Proudfoot, Stuart B., and Roberts, Neal A. (1975), *Public Land Ownership: Frameworks for Evaluation*, Toronto, Lexington Books.
Lefebvre, Henri (1976), 'Reflections on the Politics of Space', *Antipode*, **8**, May pp.30–7.
Leopold, Aldo (1966), *Sand County Almanac*, first published 1949, New York, Ballatine Books, Inc.
Lerner, Max (1957) *America as a Civilization*, New York, Simon and Schuster.
Lukes, S. (1973), *Emile Durkheim*, London, Allen Lane.
Marcuse, Herbert (1971), 'Industrialisation and Capitalism', in Otto Stammer (ed.), *Max Weber and Sociology Today*, New York, Harper Torchbook, pp.133–51.
Marx, Karl and Engels, Frederick (1970), *The German Ideology*, New York, International Publishers.
Marx, Karl (1973), *Capital* Vol. 1, first published 1861, New York, International Publishers.
Mason, Edward S. (1958), 'The Political Economy of Resource Use' in Henry Jarret (ed.), *Perspectives on Conservation*, Baltimore, Johns Hopkins Press, pp.157–72.
Mommsen, Wolfgang I. (1974), *The Age of Bureaucracy; Perspectives on the Political Sociology of Max Weber*, Oxford, Blackwell.
Nelson, Robert H. (1977), *Zoning and Property Rights: An Analysis of the American System of Land-Use Regulation*, Cambridge, MIT Press.
Newby, Howard (1980), 'Rural Sociology–A Trend Report', *Current Sociology*, Vol.28, No.1 (Spring).
Ostrum, Vincent (1974), *The Intellectual Crisis In American Public Administration*, Alabama, University of Alabama Press.
Philbrick Francis S. (1938), 'Changing concepts of property in law', *University of Pennsylvania Law Register*, **86**, May, pp.691–732.
Popper, Frank (1979), *The Politics of Land-Use Reform*, New York, Twentieth Century Fund.
Poulantzas, Nicos (1973), 'On social classes', *New Left Review*, **76**.
Poulantzas, Nicos (1975), *Classes In Contemporary Capitalism*, London, New Left Books.
Redfield, Robert (1947), 'The folk society', *American Journal of Sociology*, **52**, pp. 292–308.
Reich, Charles A. (1964), 'The new property', *Yale Law Journal*, **73**, April, pp.733–87.

Rosenbaum, Nelson (1977), *Land Use and the Legislatures: The Politics of State Innovation*, Washington DC, The Urban Institute.

Sandalow, Terrance (1963–64), 'The limits of municipal power under home rule; a role for the courts', *Minnesota Law Review*, **48**, pp.642–721.

Scheiber, Harry N. (1973), 'Property law, expropriation, and resource allocation by government; the United States, 1789–1910', *Journal of Economic History*, **33**, March, pp.232–51.

Schnore, Leo F. (1958), 'Social morphology and human ecology', *American Journal of Sociology*, May, pp.620–34.

Shonfield, Andrew (1969), *Modern Capitalism*, New York, Oxford University Press.

Tarlock, A. Dan (1972), 'Notes for a revised theory of zoning', in Gene Wunderlich and W. L. Gibson, Jr. (eds.), *Perspectives of Property*, Institute for Research on Land and Water Resources, Pennsylvania State University, pp.17–24.

Torrence, John (1977), *Estrangement, Alienation and Exploitation*, New York, Columbia University Press.

US Department of Agriculture (1974), *Our Land and Water Resources*, Miscellaneous Publication no.1290, Economic Research Bureau Service, May.

Weber, Max (1958), *The Protestant Ethic and the Spirit of Capitalism*, first published 1905, New York, Charles Scribner and Sons.

Weber, Max (1978), *Economy and Society 1-11*, first published 1913, Berkeley, Unviersity of California Press.

White, Lynn, Jr., (1967), 'The historical roots of our ecological crisis', *Science*, **155**, 10 March, pp.1203–7.

Wright, Erik Olin (1978), *Class, Crisis and the State*, London, New Left Books.

Wunderlich, Gene (1972), 'Toward a New Idea of Property', in Gene Wunderlich and W. L. Gibson (eds.) *Perspectives of Property*, University Park, Pennsylvania State University, pp.1–8.

Wunderlich, Gene (1974), 'Who Owns America's Land: Problems in Preserving the Rural Landscape', paper presented to the American Association for the Advancement of Science.

6 The Social World of Petty Property

Brian Elliott and David McCrone

Introduction

It seems appropriate to begin with a reference to C. B. MacPherson's work, for more than any other contemporary social scientist he has kept alive a curiosity about the institution of property in modern capitalist societies. His writings on Property echo the approach of Morris Cohen, a legal theorist of the 1920s:

> we must recognise that a property right is a relation not between an owner and a thing, but between the owner and other individuals in reference to things. A right is always against one or more individuals.
>
> (1978, p.159)

The quote makes one thing plain: to write about property is to write about power. Property establishes relationships of superiority and inferiority and the rights and obligations it enjoins, the customs and sentiments that surround it, provide many of the most fundamental elements in any social order. Property defines basic interests and as such it lays down a framework of alliances and oppositions which structure a society.

Our concern in this essay is with property in some of its most familiar guises. We are interested in *petty* property – not in major blocs of capital which make up the multinational corporations or other big businesses, not with the sprawling empires of the property companies or the banks or the insurance firms but with little enterprises. We shall look at the small fry of our economy: the companies with fewer than 200 employees – the minor manufacturing plants, the small shops, the family-run hotels and services enterprises, the small trading companies and the petty rentiers.

The fact that we are dealing with petty property may be taken by some to indicate that our focus is on petty, that is to say, trivial relationships. Wc shall try to persuade them otherwise. In our view the mundane, taken-for-granted encounters with petty property are extremely important for it is in these everyday dealings with small employers or shopkeepers or landlords that some of our most durable impressions of property relations are formed. It is here that we experience most intimately the power of property and out of our own recollections and those of our families and neighbours we fashion prejudices which we employ in a general way. Relationships formed around petty property are the stuff from which folk-images and folk-memories are made, and these, of course, profoundly affect the social and political life of communities and whole societies. There is also another reason why petty property should be taken seriously: it still matters economically. True, the commanding heights are held by the giant enterprises, but still the vast majority of all businesses in western countries are *small* businesses. Even in Britain where the decline of the *petit bourgeois* stratum has gone furthest, small concerns matter, for there are still around two million self-employed people producing a quarter of the national wealth.

In the past five years or so the owners of small property have been noisy. In many countries they have formed new groups and associations to publicise their grievances and put pressure on politicians. If we are to make sense of the recent agitations in Britain we must work with an historical approach, for the current unrest is really intelligible only when we see it as a response to long-term changes in the patterns of social relationships. Thus our task is to look at shifting structures of relations, not simply at an aggregate level but also in terms which allow us to understand the individual perceptions and responses. We shall try to illustrate the truth of Gramsci's well known observation that:

> each individual is the synthesis not only of existing relations but, of the history of these relations. He is a precis of all the past.
> (Gramsci 1976)

In doing so we shall draw on three interrelated studies in which we have been involved over the last ten years.[1]

The Social Relations of Petty Property

The growth of British towns in the nineteenth century created a stratum of petty rentiers who bought and sold land and housing hoping to benefit from the enormous demand for accommodation. Large estates bordering the towns were sold off, frequently in small parcels, to entrepreneurs who organised the building of tenements and back-to-backs for the workers, and suburban villas for the swelling middle class. Developers, builders and those who bought property for rent were rarely 'big' businessmen. Of course a few astute characters did make fortunes, but mostly local property markets were highly fragmented with numerous *petit bourgeois* or even artisan families and individuals investing in property. Before there were insurance schemes and state pensions and superannuation plans, rented property was commonly used by those who had a little money put by, as a secure, durable but unspectacular investment. They were, says Gauldie

> . . . the very kind of people to have low expectations of returns from investment, to choose safety in the form of a small yearly income rather than greater possible profits over a longer period of time.
>
> (Gauldie 1974)

The quality and character of the housing they invested in could, of course, vary considerably. Some was well-built and provided accommodation for middle class groups or for skilled men whose jobs afforded a good measure of security and reasonably high wages, but much of the housing thrown up in the scramble of breakneck urbanisation was poor, jerry-built stuff. With probably no more than 10 per cent of the population owning their own homes the rental market was large and highly differentiated. Not surprisingly the quality of service provided by landlords varied widely too. Periodic, local gluts of housing for the middle income groups saw landlords actually competing for tenants but in many of the poorer districts the tale was altogether different. In the areas of greatest 'housing stress' property was commonly bought and sold with tenants knowing nothing about it; absentee landlordism was the norm; house 'farming' or rack-renting common and abandonment of property by no means unknown. It was typically in the crowded inner districts of the cities that the power of the property holders manifested itself in the starkest, most visible and most exploitative forms. Given the vagaries of the competitive market economy, given the changing economic demands made on a family at different points in the domestic cycle, poverty and firsthand encounters with exploitative landlordism were common experiences in the working class. When they first came to the towns, when their families were young, in times of unemployment or in old age, workers could find themselves at the bottom of the housing market, forced to pay the 'house farmers' exorbitant rents for rudimentary furnished accommodation. John Butt describes the system of daily rents with its discounts for regular customers – 8*d*. a night for an old customer, 10*d*, for a new – which still operated in Glasgow in the early years of this century. In this way the power of petty property was known and recognised and frequently embedded in social consciousness through the recounted tales told in families or neighbourhoods.

It was also to the inner city slums that crusading clergymen, philanthropic businessmen and government or municipal officials came collecting gaudy details of the misery of urban living. Often their reports depict the landlords as rogues. Take, for instance, Andrew

Mearns's famous pamphlet, *The Bitter Cry of Outcast London*, (1893):

> If by any chance a reluctant landlord can be induced to execute or pay for some long-needed repairs, they become the occasions for new exactions. Going through these rooms we come to one in which a hole, as big as a man's head, has been roughly covered, and how? A piece of board from an old soap box has been fixed over the opening by one nail and to the tenant has been given a yard and a half of paper with which to cover it: and for this expenditure perhaps 4*d*. at the outside – 3*d*. a week has been put upon the rent.
>
> (1971, p.65)

Mearns was not the only man to develop a critique out of powerful moral and religious precepts. In Scotland where poverty and appalling housing conditions had long gone hand-in-hand, we find a journalist Robert Bremner's condemnation:

> I am told that slum landlords are deemed worthy to enter the membership of, and hold office, in, the Christian Church. The day, I believe, is coming nearer when the man who deliberately invests in slum property will be deemed less worthy to enter society than the drunkard or the harlot whom his greed helps to manufacture.
>
> (Quoted in Butt 1977, p.86)

The periodic efforts to stir middle class consciences about the housing conditions of the working class in nineteenth century Britain frequently laid much responsibility at the landlord's door and as the number of reports and pamphlets and articles mounted one could trace the creation of a common image. The landlord was an unprincipled, rapacious oppressor whose actions contributed to crime, disease and moral degeneracy. The landlord became a 'folk-devil'. In the latter part of the Victorian period and into the Edwardian era landlordism was the target of a great many attacks. W. T. Stead in the *Pall Mall Gazette* gave great publicity to the Mearns pamplet. Henry Lazarus in 1892 wrote an indictment simply entitled *Landlordism* and elsewhere Henry George (*Progress and Poverty*, 1881) had taken up the cry.

To a number of commentators it was evident that in the building and renting of property there were several actors involved and that it was not only the landowners who exercised the power of property. Kaufman, in his tract, *The Housing of the Working Class and the Poor* spelled out the interrelationships between landed aristocrats and the 'rack renters'. The former were:

> . . . as a rule, liberal, kindly and considerate in their dealings with their tenantry. But in permitting the employment of middlemen

> as intermediaries who themselves delegate the work to others less scrupulous than themselves, they indirectly encourage rack-renting of the most objectionable kind.
>
> (1907, p.51)

Two decades later we find George Bernard Shaw commenting in his Fabian way on landlords and their agents. Mr Lickcheese is the rent collector and speaking of his employer, Mr Sartorious he observes:

> I don't say he's the worst landlord in London; he couldn't be worse than some; but he's no better than the worst I ever had to do with. And though I say it, I'm better than the best collector he ever done business with. I've screwed more and spent less on his properties than anyone would believe that knows what such properties are.
>
> (*Widower's Houses* 1927, p.80)

There is little doubt that by the 1920s this view of property owners and those who acted for them had become well established in popular consciousness. Of course, it would not be totally accepted by the solid middle class, but it seemed to distil the experience of a great many working class people and the landlord certainly became an element in the demonology of the left in Britain.

Another figure in the urban landscape who also enjoys a place in popular consciousness – though this time a more ambiguous one – is the small shopkeeper. Here too we can observe the power that even the most petty property once gave. By the end of the last century it was not only the middle class which made extensive use of shops for food and other basic necessities of life. Many areas of working class housing were far removed from street markets and increasingly the small retailer became an established part of the workers' community. Often the shopkeepers were themselves from the ranks of the poor, having set up shop in a desperate attempt to cope with unemployment or under-employment. To begin with they would often practise a miniscule form of trading – selling the tiniest quantities of food, selling cigarettes singly – but if the business survived and expanded they would become involved in the networks of debt and credit which did so much to structure working class life.

In the nineteenth century, and well into this one, many working class families found it impossible to pay their way each week. This stemmed partly from the levels of wages and partly from the uncertainties of employment with 'layoffs' and seasonal working all too common. Few were able to avoid falling into debt from time to time so family budgets often had to accommodate repayments of previous credit and attempts to save and 'insure' against the next period of illness or unemployment as well as coping with 'current' demands. The weekly budget usually included payment of arrears, to the landlord, the grocer or the baker as Booth's evidence showed (Booth, 1897). On a 'typical' working class budget of £2. 3*s*. 9*d*. a week, rent accounted for 13*s*. which included 2*s*. arrears, and the baker's bill of 3*s*. 9*d*. with 1*s*. in arrears. Tressell's *The Ragged Trousered Philanthropists* further illustrates the point:

> 'How much rent do we owe now? asked Eaton. 'Four weeks, and I promised the collector the last time he called that we'd pay two weeks next Monday. He was quite nasty about it.'. . .
>
> 'If we pay the two weeks rent that'll leave us 12*s*. to live on.' 'But we won't be able to keep all that', said Ruth, 'because there's other things to pay . . . we owe the baker 8*s*. for the bread he let us have while you were not working, and there's about 12*s*. owing for groceries. We'll have to pay them something on account. . . . Then there's the instalments for the furniture and oil cloth. . . . I've been paying that bit by bit all summer. I paid the last of it the week you finished your last job. Then you were out three weeks and as we had nothing in hand I had to get what we wanted without paying for it'.
>
> (1955 edn., pp.54–6)

In order to be in debt, it was necessary to convince the shopkeeper or the landlord that you would eventually be able to pay and that your character was good. The petty property owners became moral arbiters. Roberts in *The Classic Slum* gives an insider's view of how credit was awarded. His mother ran the corner shop:

> 'In the hardest times', she said, 'it was often for me to decide who ate and who didn't.'
>
> 'If bankruptcy, always close in a slum shop, was to be avoided, one had to assess the careful judgment, the honesty, class standing and financial resources of all tick customers.'
>
> (1973, p.81)

The criteria for 'tick' were rigorous – not only the financial standing but also the abstemiousness and time-keeping of the husband would be assessed as well as the family's debts elsewhere. The tick book and the clear rent book were the badges of integrity. There were many who could never attain them. They were turned away by the storekeepers, evicted by the landlords, after which they had to 'pay their way', buying the morsels of food, finding a night's shelter as best they could. To them the exclusive character of property rights were plain enough.

The system of debt and credit into which most workers were locked served as a means of social control. In *Outcast London* Stedman Jones describes it as follows:

> In order to escape starvation and in order to ensure against the possibility of being thrown onto the streets . . . it was essential to establish good credit relations with the landlords, the local shop

> and the local pub. Landlords in poorer areas would be paid up in the summer. Local stores and pubs came to similar arrangements. 'Being known' in a district was thus of considerable economic importance. From the viewpoint of the labourer, it provided a further incentive against mobility. Credit arrangements which had been built up in one neighbourhood over a period of time, could not immediately be transferred to another.
>
> (1971, p.88)

To the petty property holder wanting a continuous flow of rent or profit the bonds of indebtedness between landlord and tenant or shopkeeper and customer produced a desirable stability in the community. As in all debt relationships there was the risk that too much credit might be given in which case the debtors would begin to acquire influence over the creditors – but usually that could be guarded against. The shopkeeper limited the 'tick' he would grant. The landlord would cut his losses and evict the tenant who had amassed too many arrears.

In Scotland the law underpinned the position of landlords in a quite remarkable way. There existed, until this century, something called 'the right of hypothec' by which, according to the Guthrie report of 1907:

> Tenants' furniture, furnishings and tools were liable to sequestration by a landlord immediately after they enter on possession of a house, as security for rent not then accrued, due or payable.
>
> (Para 76a)

Thus, the landlord had the right to deprive the tenant of *all* his personal belongings. The right was rarely exercised but when political pressure was exerted to rescind it the representatives of landlords and factors defended the arrangement on the grounds that, like eviction, it could be used from time to time *'pour encourager les autres'*.

A tenancy was really more than a commercial transaction, it was the means whereby those with property could exert not just material influence but moral authority too. The landlord in the nineteenth century could set rents at any level he liked or raise them at will. Before letting a property he could demand evidence of probity and worth – the tenant had to bring his 'character' with him – and he could grant or withhold similar documents, if a tenant wished to leave or was evicted. It is these powers which even today are carried as collective images of 'the landlord' and which do most to cast him as a folk devil.

But we should not leave our discussion of the power of petty property without noting that such social and economic influence frequently translated itself into political power. The work of writers such as Hennock (1973) or Fraser (1976) or Garrard (1977) provides ample evidence of the fact that petty property owners, local businessmen, landlords and shopkeepers often appeared on the town councils and from time to time established effective control of municipal affairs. Our own study of property and politics in Edinburgh turned up a startlingly clear illustration of the power of local property holders, (Elliott, McCrone and Skelton 1978).

In 1875 no fewer than 80 per cent of the councillors were Edinburgh landlords, and most of the property held was residential not commercial or industrial. Though they may have had many reasons for entering local political life there can be little doubt that once there they found that many of the issues they debated touched their property interests in various ways. These men of property effectively controlled the growth of the city, its physical expansion, its incorporation of other districts and of course the internal developments including the rudimentary planning of districts and the shaping of what today we would call the infrastructure. They were in charge of what Harvey Molotch (1976) termed, in another context, the 'growth machine', and precisely because local government depended so heavily on local property taxes they kept a sharp eye on the costs of development which would fall on men and women like themselves. We analysed the composition of committees and found that on the most important ones – like the Lord Provost's Committee or the Treasurer's Committee the landlords were even more heavily represented. In addition we looked for what we called the 'Building Interests' and combining the numbers of builders, factors and building craftsmen we could see that in 1875 some 23 per cent of the council were directly involved in the building trade.

Our analysis covered the one hundred years, 1875 to 1975, within which we distinguished three broad periods. The first from 1875 to 1918 was the period when local administrations had the greatest autonomy, and in Edinburgh this was the phase during which landlords – a few of them operating on a large scale, but most of them petty property owners – were most evident in the City Chambers. From 1919 to 1939 we are able to show that there was an obvious decline in the proportion who were landlords – 57 per cent in 1925 and 45 per cent in 1935, and that land, shops, factories and other forms of commercial property had become relatively more important among their holdings. And some of those who had the most successful political careers were no longer men who built or invested directly in the construction business, rather they were estate agents or factors who made money from the *management* of property. The inter-war years saw the town dominated by the so-called Progressive Association, a right wing grouping dedicated to defending local autonomy and opposing the forces of socialism.

Even after World War II, in the last of our periods, this Progressive Association held sway so that for more than forty years Scotland's capital was run by a parochial association consisting mostly of small businessmen. With the decline of private landlordism in Britain as a whole, with the growth of public housing on one side and owner-occupation on the other, the involvement of landlords as such waned markedly. Many of those who have replaced them though still have ties to the building business. A good few in 1975 were surveyors, architects, heating engineers, insurance and mortgage brokers and there was one very wealthy 'professional' property developer. The 'property interests', in the 1970s were less direct. They involved those whose role was to 'service' real estate development. There was still in 1975 a marked tendency for these interests to be disproportionately represented on the committees that were most concerned with the development of the city – with its housing and with physical planning.

Looking over the whole one hundred year period one cannot fail to be impressed by the fact that the small property interests established and maintained a hegemonic control over local politics for most of this century. Bigger businessmen and professionals retreated from municipal politics and only recently have reappeared in any number. The working class, except for a few months right at the end of our period, have acquired control of the council and at every turn obstacles to working class representation and socialist policies were erected by a passionately anti-left alliance of petty property holders.

Local government then has been the arena in which the public power of small property holders has been exercised. In most cities, though, they have not been so successful in their attempts to cling to power. The general decline of petty property, the shrinkage of its material base has usually been reflected in a much weaker grip on the machinery of municipal politics.

But the traditional political influence of landlords and shopkeepers and local employers and their manoeuvrings to sustain their superiority are remembered by those who were also their tenants or customers or employees. Such memories help generalise the recollections of personal hurts.

The Decline of Petty Property: Structural and Ideological Factors

Petty property holders occupy an awkward, interstitial location in capitalist societies and this affects profoundly their attitudes and ideologies and their relations with members of other classes and occupational groupings. The petty rentiers and small businessmen do not enjoy the routine, taken-for-granted superiority of the big bourgeois, but neither do they experience the consistent pattern of subordination which stamps the life of most manual workers. Uncertainty and contingency are the hallmarks of many *petit bourgeois* lives. Running their own businesses, they are frequently forced into some awareness of their vulnerability to change, to the booms and recessions in the economy, to the fiscal and other impositions of the state, to pressure from organised labour. Small capital is menaced from above and below.

In recent years there has been an obvious shrinkage of the stratum of petty property holders. We can observe the decline of a social world and a moral economy, whose practices and institutions are being violated. What is being objected to is, in Thompson's phrase, 'an outrage to the moral assumptions quite as much as actual deprivation' (Thompson, 1971, p.79). Similar processes have been in train in most western societies but in Britain they seem to have gone further than elsewhere. As the Bolton Report (1971) showed, we now have a lower proportion of our manufacturing employment in small establishments than any other western country. The *Census of Distribution* (1975) documents a reduction in the overall number of retail outlets since World War II and private landlordism has declined dramatically. True, there are some very recent indications of counter-trends, with increases in the number of self-employed artisans and professional workers, but overall there can be little dispute about the contraction of small business and with it the kind of competitive capitalism of an earlier era.

How should we account for this? There seem to be four major factors worth considering.

First, and most obviously, there has been a long-term trend towards the concentration of capital. This was quite evident more than a hundred years ago, but in the past forty years or so the pace of mergers and agglomerations and the growth of huge corporations has accelerated. Big business has squeezed little business, buying out competitors, undercutting the profit margins of small producers, seeking 'vertical integration' of manufacturing and distributive processes. And by and large the small fry have done little to resist these incursions: they remained fragmented and unorganised. The shopkeepers we interviewed ten years ago (Bechhofer *et al.* 1974; Bechhofer and Elliott 1978) showed little inclination to get together to fight. They either failed to perceive any real threats or they simply refused to join any collective organisations.

Secondly, small business has been adversely affected by some actions of an increasingly interventionist state. Petty producers and distributors have complained bitterly about selective employment tax, value added tax, national insurance contributions, the invasion of their privacy by Customs and Excise inspectors searching for VAT irregularities and the licensing powers of central government or municipal authorities. Most recently they have bemoaned the legislation facilitating 'closed shop' agreements and the enactment of the Employment Protection Act which they argue restricts the legitimate rights of businessmen in the hiring and firing of workers. They have been outraged by capital transfer tax and horrified by the spectre of a wealth tax.

Small businessmen argue that most forms of state intervention have had deleterious effects, at least as far as they are concerned. They allege that taxation levels are 'penal' and have produced such a narrowing of income differentials between themselves and their workers that 'enterprise', 'risk-taking' and 'responsibility' no longer command just rewards. To add insult to injury they claim that while they act as unpaid tax collectors for the state (a reference usually to VAT) the recipients of largesse from these funds are not little men like themselves but the big industries, the multi-nationals in trouble, the 'lame duck' corporations. The collection of value added tax it is suggested is an arduous and expensive business and the costs are not easily absorbed by small-scale enterprise. How galling then to watch these public funds bailing out the very companies who already threaten them in purely commercial terms. It is not difficult to see why they so often portray the state as malevolent.

Nothing makes plainer the significance of state action on petty property than the history of legislation on private landlordism in Britain. The first Rent Restriction Act was passed in 1915 against a background of a Glasgow rent strike which threatened to spill over into a much wider confrontation linked to industrial unrest in the West of Scotland. In the middle of a war, industrial and social peace was bought by the promise of low and controlled rents. To the many small landlords it looked as though their interests had been 'sacrificed'. The rentiers received little support from industrial capital perhaps because few major industrial enterprises were involved in the ownership of domestic property but mostly because tackling the rent issue 'uncoupled' this source of discontent from the struggles of the workplace. The interests of big business and of the state were served: those of the landlord were not. The decline of private landlordism can be dated from this Act. Since then though there have been brief periods of 'decontrol', the state has greatly limited the rights of these property owners. And it is the abrogation of what are construed as 'traditional' and legitimate' property rights which really rankles. Under Labour governments landlords have not only faced restrictions on the rents they can charge and the manner in which they may periodically be increased, but there have been considerable concessions to tenants over the issue of security of tenure. The effect has been to make many privately rented properties thoroughly uneconomic. Our own study has produced many instances of housing which is still rented at levels appropriate to the 1920s. Thus the rights to profits have been circumscribed, the rights of usage in terms of repossession have been limited and the right to admit or exclude others from the use have been curtailed. The *relationships* based on the owning and renting of property have been markedly changed. The result is evident. In every British city there are stocks of dilapidated, neglected property, flats and houses which have simply not been maintained. And especially since the 1950s there has been a massive flight from landlordism on the part of those who were able to sell their property. In this way the world of petty property has certainly contracted.

But neither the actions of the state nor the secular growth of large concerns tells the whole story, for behind these 'structural' explanations for the decline of petty property there are 'ideological' elements to be considered. State action so obviously aimed at restricting landlordism was called out by specific protests or grievances but it was made possible and sustained by that generalised image of the landlord as an avaricious oppressor. The fact that he had become a 'folk-devil' meant that there would often be highly emotive responses to the periodic rediscovery of exploitative practices and all too often the passing of general, nationwide legislation to tackle problems which were real enough but often highly concentrated in particular cities or particular areas of the housing market. The ruthless practices of Mr Rachman in London in the early 1960s awakened old memories of the landlord's power and revitalised left wing critiques of such forms of property ownership. Even among those who are the owners of rented property we found partial acceptance of the imagery. There were landlords who told us they were 'ashamed' that they owned rented property, that even though they did not grind the faces of the poor, still there was something 'dirty' about being a landlord. It is these generalised beliefs which legitimate many forms of government action and which encourage the disposal of rented property. It has contributed much to the decline of this particular form of small business enterprise in Britain.

Another 'ideological' element to be considered is the widespread disdain for small business which attended many of these attempts by politicians to modernise the British economy, to streamline it and make it technologically much more sophisticated. 'Small' connoted 'archaic', 'inefficient', 'unprofitable'. The hopes for growth were pinned on large companies, the wielders of modern technology the real wealth producers. So, multinational corporations were given every inducement to set up shop and the state undertook to encourage mergers and to promote technological development. Colleges and universities were exhorted to expand their science and technology programmes; a second industrial revolution was on the horizon. Graduates looking for jobs rarely expressed any desire to enter small businesses. The real excitement, the chance of a career and the prospects of a fat salary were to be found with the big concerns. Small business then found few champions; it enjoyed little ideological support.

Indeed, through the 1960s and early 1970s the sense of powerlessness grew. The Labour Party was in office throughout most of the period and it seemed to many as though the traditional trade associations and chambers of commerce were becoming more and more ineffectual in their dealings with indifferent or even hostile governments. The election of the Heath administration in 1970 raised some hopes that the Tory party would treat small business rather more sympathetically – after all it was the party which the vast majority of petty property owners supported. The optimism soon proved ill-founded. The Right Progressives, as the Heath faction has been called, soon showed themselves just as committed as their Labour counterparts to the promotion of big business, to technological progress and technocratic management of the economy and the polity. The Heath government was concerned with the 'politics of power' and it neglected, if we accept Gamble's judgement (1974) the 'politics of support'. Specifically it neglected the sizeable constituency of small business, and what was even worse – it introduced the value added tax and raised the national insurance contributions of the self-employed in what was perceived as an unjust way. Coupled with the reversal of declared policies on statutory wage and price controls this appeared to many small businessmen as betrayal. The response was immediate. Within a few months a crop of new organisations appeared. Some, like John Gorst's Middle Class Association, were deliberate attempts to co-ordinate grass roots middle class discontent with internal dissent in the Tory party. The purpose was to oust Heath and his faction and return the party to more traditional forms of conservatism – which would mean more support for those 'who are disposed to self-provide'[2] and less state intervention in the economy. Other organisations like the National Federation of the Self-Employed simply sought a more effective voice for small property holders than that supplied by the host of small trade associations. In their more expansive moments some small business leaders talked of creating a 'third force' alongside the TUC and the CBI. From the defeat of Heath to the election of Margaret Thatcher the sound of middle class and especially *petit bourgeois* discontent grew louder and louder.

Lament for a World They Have Lost

The interviewing of our sample of Edinburgh landlords took place in this period, and provided extensive evidence of the sense of resentment and bewilderment which affected many small property holders. Most of our sample of two hundred landlords were small manufacturers or merchants, shopkeepers, self-employed businessmen or traditional professionals – lawyers and doctors and the occasional professor. There were widows living on the income from some mixture of property, shares and pensions – most of them had been the wives of local businessmen. There were no major employers of labour, very few white collar workers and hardly any manual workers represented. The landlords were drawn overwhelmingly from the local – mostly small – bourgeoisie.

From the interviews there emerged a powerful sense of those intimate ties between property and the 'self' on which other writers have commented:

> In making the object my own, I stamp it with the mark of my own person; whoever attacks it, attacks me; the blow struck it, strikes me, for I am present in it. Property is but the periphery of my person extended to things.
>
> (Beaglehole 1931, p.302)

The state, big business and organised labour had all, in different ways, 'struck' their property and hence them.

Among a number of landlords, especially those who were artisans who had started up their own businesses, we found a Lockean view of property. A man established rights to property because he worked on it, mixed his labour with it. At the time of the interviews there was discussion of increasing worker control of industry. A self-employed joiner asked the rhetorical question:

> Is it fair that the boss can invest thousands of pounds and work his fingers to the bone, then the workers come along and say they want a share?

There was much bitterness that what they saw as the rights of the property holders were being challenged: the rights of a shopkeeper or a tradesman to hire and fire workers, the right of landlords to evict unwanted tenants. What they own is *theirs*, is the view, and neither the state nor organised workers should challenge that. But they did. The state, through the local authorities, could impose severe restrictions on their rights to profits, to the use and the control of their property. One landlord provided the following illustration: Edinburgh Corporation demanded that in the course of roof repairs on a block of fifty small flats the chimney stacks should be rebuilt with local stone. The additional cost of this material, together with the delay produced by discussions of its necessity, led to an inflation of the original estimate of £3500 to a final bill of £14,700. And this on an old tenement block producing extremely low rents.

It is clear though that the indignation is not just about the material costs that are incurred. As with a great many of the small businessmen we have interviewed in the last year or so – the spokesmen or members of the new associations of the self-employed – there are social and moral changes which also underlie their discontent. The changes in social relations experienced directly through landlordism or through running their own businesses were seen as part of a wider alteration of class relations. Thus, the past twenty or thirty years have seen the rise of an organised working class in Britain, which has gained political power and which has been the major beneficiary of post-war affluence. That, at least, is their interpretation. A retired hotelier among our landlords observed:

> Today the workers have much more money. They come in asking for 'Chateau Neuf du Pape' where before the war they wouldn't have known about that, only the gentry did. Now they go back to the factory and discuss wines. The working class is living above its means.

And a general practitioner who was also a landlord drew on his house-call experience:

> The working class have done awfully well from what I see – they've got everything. One has to mind how one walks on their fitted carpets. They have cars outside and holidays abroad. They get everything.

There is much resentment at what is seen as the wealth, security and power of the working class and a widespread belief that these have been gained 'illegitimately' by the strength of trades unions. Ultimately the cause of Britain's economic and political decline is traced back to the working class and to the collapse of an old system of social relations that guaranteed stability and discipline. The widow of a grocer encapsulated several of the themes that recurred in these interviews:

> The whole problem is that people don't work hard enough. There is too much mollycoddling by the state and employers because of the power of the unions. My father (a builder) used to fire people on the spot if he thought they were not working hard enough.

Today, the bourgeois elements are no longer able to impose those values of diligence, thrift and discipline which allegedly had underpinned our success in the world. Time and again Britain was portrayed as sliding towards anarchy:

> . . . on one level, the problems are economic but more fundamentally they are moral. (Its) the releasing of destructive forces, a lack of discipline and greed which exists in all of us but are not controlled now.

A few resisted. The entrepreneurial middle class, our respondent went on, were

> . . . people who are frugal in their spending habits, the savers who put some money away for themselves and the country.

But a lawyer was less certain about that:

> A hundred years ago, people put their money into something such as property, it was a social investment. Now they just spend it. The wealth of society is being consumed.

The result was that local bourgeois groups had declined. Indeed some saw the destruction of that stratum that used to 'invest' in their local communities. Some of the old ladies, reminiscing about the Edinburgh they had known as girls, described a social world in which secure, affluent families like theirs enjoyed a great deal of political power and social influence. They were deferred to by a working class which 'knew its place'. And it was kept there by the property relations of competitive capitalism.

Our respondents were often quite forthcoming about what was needed to restore some of the old order:

> We need moral regeneration. Keith Joseph said it. We shouldn't have indiscriminate breeding of people, especially those who are the unfittest and who have large families.

a pig farmer told us. We were informed that what the country needed was greater freedom for those like themselves and less freedom for those who do not require or know how to use it – the working class. Most frequently we learned that the principal requirement was:

> strong government to force people to work, no security benefits for not working, no strikes, a wage freeze and strict controls over prices.

A plumber, brought up in East Germany, believed that their political means married to the west's economic goals would benefit us greatly.

The assessment of recent changes in Britain were overwhelmingly negative, their most common motif being a lament for a social world and a system of social relationships which had been lost, bringing a very real hurt to them.

The Making of a Retrospect

In the past five or six years a large number of new organisations to represent diverse petty property owners have been set up. There have been 'small landlords' associations, groups to represent 'independent' business people and associations and federations for the self-employed. Some are very small, others have proved short-lived but a number have grown and become firmly established. The National Federation of the Self-Employed, for instance, claims to have between forty and fifty thousand members and can mobilise a great deal of money in efforts to have its voice heard. Alongside the organisations representing particular occupational and economic interests there have also appeared other bodies such as GB75 or Civil Assistance whose members anticipated the need for middle class 'vigilantes' to maintain essential services and social order in the event of a national strike. And there are yet other groups – leagues might be the appropriate term – such as the National Association for Freedom committed principally to the 're-education' of the middle class and the re-establishment of traditional bourgeois values. These new associations articulate many of those discontents and resentments that we found among our Edinburgh landlords. It looks as though the 'unorganisable' sectors of the middle class, the independent, individualistic entrepreneurs, and the people of petty property, are beginning to collaborate and gain some common voice. They are not just identifying economic grievances and pressing to redress these; they are constructing a 'representation' of an economic and moral order which they want to re-establish. In Britain such attempts to mobilise a sector of the middle class are not without historical precedent – but they are rare. So how should we explain agitations?

We can begin by recognising that the place of small business in public consciousness has altered a good deal in recent years. 'Small' has been rehabilitated. We now find politicians of all persuasions finding kind words for small business. Where once it was deemed old-fashioned and doomed to extinction it now appears as the means of revitalising the inner city districts, stimulating local economies, re-kindling the entrepreneurial spirit, encouraging innovation and reducing unemployment. Small has become beautiful. By contrast 'big', that is to say, big business, has in many ways fallen from grace. In the 1960s the massive corporations held the promise of growth and modernisation. Today a number of them are holding out begging bowls.

Big business, it is argued, has brought all forms of capitalist enterprise into disrepute. There have been too many scandals over the role of multinational corporations backing repressive regimes, or selling with the aid of bribes, or concealing profits and evading taxes, for them to be viewed with uncritical approval in the 1970s. Indeed, say the proponents of small enterprises, big business has violated the codes of that 'moral economy' which they represent. Big concerns do not always honour their obligations. They deliberately refuse to settle accounts on time; they cut off orders or supplies to small firms without warning; they act to suppress small business innovation. The small business lobby has been orchestrating the critique of the corporations (and a critique of 'big government' too) with some skill. There is much in their attack on the corporations and their protest about 'bureaucracy' which earns them popular sympathy.

Somewhat surprisingly we find that some of the big enterprises actually appear to be adding their weight to these efforts to regenerate small business. Shell, for instance is providing money for research on small business. And why should it be in their interest to modify if not reverse the historical trend towards capital concentration? The answers can still be found in terms of the profit motive. It can pay large companies to subcontract some of their activities to small businesses, especially those making most use of cheap immigrant labour or relying on the exploitation of family labour to produce their goods. In some instances smaller firms appear more efficient than large ones; not only do they have lower labour costs, they also have lower levels of unionisation and lower strike rates than big concerns. Encouraging small business may also mean weakening or slowing the advance of unionism. For these reasons we may well see considerable encouragement of small firms by the large enterprises – especially in the form of subcontracting and franchising.

The 'rehabilitation' of small business though is also a matter of political expediency. The growth of small business groups agitating for the creation of free market conditions, less government interference and the like, coincided with the election of Margaret Thatcher and the so-called 'radical' right to the leadership of the Tory party. Not only were there some obvious ideological affinities between the *petit bourgeois* groups and Thatcher's ideas about 'rolling back the state' and encouraging free enterprise, but the increasingly organised small business stratum represented a valuable constituency, one that had to be placated after the Heath years if it were to return to its 'natural' political home – the Conservative party. In order to achieve this the Tory party has encouraged and contributed to the creation of what, following Raymond Williams, we can call a 'retrospect', an image of an idealised 'traditional' society against which contemporary changes can be measured.

The *petit bourgeois* in the West have from time to time helped create 'retrospects' of 'traditional' capitalist societies in which free and independent men competed in the market place, where monopolies were held at bay and the invisible hand steered individual competition along paths of efficiency, prosperity and freedom. Such a 'retrospect' was an integral part of the '*mittelstand*' agitations in Germany at the turn of the century, and it appeared in Britain in the 1930s and in a weak form in the Freedom Group established by Edward Martell in the early 1960s. What makes the present manifestation remarkable is partly the size and diversity of the groups involved but mostly the fact that the images it conveys, the policies it wants pursued have been taken up by the leadership of a major party whose recent electoral victory seemed to owe a good deal to their manipulation of this 'retrospect'.

The small businessman has become a symbol for the 'new right' in Britain, representing, it is claimed, the virtues of an old order in which small property played an important and valued part in the life of the community and society. The government promises attempts to restore the moral economy of the *petit bourgeoisie* but they are unlikely to be very successful for the 'retrospect' of the old order provides a poor analysis of the real changes that have accompanied the growth of monopoly capitalism. Retrospects are called out by fear: they offer a basis for a critique; they may offer comfort and hope to those who have lost power and honour, but they contain no historical comprehension of the framework of structural relations that supported those selectively recalled social worlds. No rolling back of the state, in a 'social market economy' can restore the world for which our shopkeepers and landlords and other small property owners are grieving. The giant corporations cannot be wished away and the British working class even though it has now won some protection from the worst forms of exploitation will not quickly forget the folk images shaped when the world of small property was young.

Notes

1. The first of these was a project 'Small Shopkeepers and the Class Structure', directed by F. Bechhofer and B. Elliott; the second 'The Property Owners: the Sociological Significance of Landlordism' involved B. Elliott and D. McCrone; and the third and still ongoing study 'Mobilising the Middle Class: A study of Bourgeois Social Movements' brought together all three of us. Consequently our colleague Frank Bechhofer deserves credit for some of the information and ideas contained here. He has no responsibility for the weaknesses.

   All the projects were funded by the Social Science Research Council.
2. The phrase comes from an interview with John Gorst. The general interpretation of the links between the new associations and the unrest inside the Tory party is based on a series of interviews with members of parliament and leaders of the main middle class or small business leagues and associations carried out in 1978 and 1979.

References

Beaglehole, E., *Property: a Study in Social Psychology*, London, Allen and Unwin, 1931.

Bechhofer, F. and Elliott, B., 'The Voice of Small Business and the Politics of Survival', *Sociological Review*, February 1978.

Bechhofer,, F., Elliott, B., Rushforth, M. and Bland, R., 'The Petit Bourgeois in the Class Structure', in F. Parkin (ed.), *The Social Analysis of Class Structure*, London, Tavistock, 1974.

Booth, C., *Life and Labour of the People of London*, London, 1897, (Penguin edition 1971).

Butt, J., 'Working Class Housing in Glasgow 1851–1914', in S. D. Chapman (ed.), *The History of Working Class Housing*, Newton Abbot, David and Charles, 1971.

Census of Distribution and other Services, Department of Industry, HMSO, 1975.

Elliott, B. McCrone, D. and Skelton, V., 'Property and Politics: Edinburgh 1875–1975', in J. Garrard *et al.* (eds.), *The Middle Class in Politics*, London, Teakfield, 1978.

Fraser, D., *Urban Politics in Victorian England*, Leicester, Leicester University Press, 1976.

Gamble, A., *The Conservative Nation*, London, Routledge and Kegan Paul, 1974.

Garrard, J., 'Leaders and Politics in Nineteenth Century Salford', Research Paper, Department of Sociological and Political Studies, University of Salford, 1977.

Gauldie, E., *Cruel Habitations: A History of Working Class Housing*, London, Allen and Unwin, 1974.

Gramsci, A., *Selections from the Prison Notebooks*, London, Lawrence and Wishart, 1976.

Guthrie report, *Report of Committee on Letting of Working Men's Dwellings in Scotland*, London, HMSO (ed. 3715), 1907.

Hennock, E. P., *Fit and Proper Persons*, London, Edward Arnold, 1973.

Jones, G. S., *Outcast London*, Oxford, Clarendon Press, 1971.

Kaufman, M., *The Housing of the Working Classes and the Poor*, London, T. C. and E. C. Jack, 1907 (new edition 1975).

Lazarus, H., *Landlordism*, London, General Publishing Co. Ltd., 1892.

MacPherson, C. B. (ed.), *Property: mainstream and critical positions*, Toronto Press, 1978.

Mearns, A., *The Bitter Cry of Outcast London*, first published 1893, Leicester, University of Leicester Press, 1970 edition.

Molotch, H., 'The City as a Growth Machine: Towards a Political Economy of Place', *American Journal of Sociology*, **82**, no.2, 1976.

Report of the Committee of Enquiry on Small Firms (Bolton Report) Cmnd 4811, HMSO 1971.

Roberts, R., *The Classic Slum*, Harmondsworth, Pelican, 1973.

Shaw, G. B., *Widowers' Houses* (1927) Oxford, The Bodley Head, 1970 edition.

Thompson, E. P., 'The Moral Economy of the English Crowd in the Eighteenth Century', *Past and Present*, **50**, 1971, pp.76–136.

Tressell, R., *The Ragged Trousered Philanthropists*, London, Lawrence and Wishart, 1955.

7 Some Aspects of Property Distribution and Class Structure

Gordon Causer

Property and Class Theory

The institution of property and the relationships associated with it have traditionally occupied a central place in the analysis of class structure in capitalist societies. Despite periodic attempts to deny the continuing relevance of property to class formation or to treat it as a residual factor relations of ownership and control remain of critical importance to class analysis. The reasons for this continuing importance are not difficult to identify. Not only does property ownership remain heavily concentrated, but the distribution of certain types of property (notably land, shareholdings and government securities) is markedly skewed towards the upper end of the wealth distribution (see Table 7.1). Thus the top 2.5 per cent of wealth-holders own just over 25 per cent of all wealth, but around 70 per cent of land and listed shareholdings, and over 60 per cent of government securities.

The significance of property lies, however, not in its concentration alone, but in the relationships that are constituted by, and in their turn reproduce, the unequal distribution of wealth. Analysts of class relations have distinguished those forms of property that are held for purposes of personal consumption from those that are held as a means to the acquisition of revenues or that establish relations of power and dependence between their holders and others (Lafargue 1975, pp.3–9; Newby *et al.* 1978, p.334; Hobhouse 1915, pp.21–3; Parkin 1979, p.49). Although, as Saunders has demonstrated in the case of owner-occupied housing (Saunders 1979, Chapter 2) the line between these two categories is not always clear-cut, it is clearly the latter type of property (in particular where it is located in the system of production and distribution of goods and services) which is of principal significance to class analysis.

Property, as several writers have indicated, is not a thing, but a set of rights in an object or asset, in particular the right to control its use (including its disposal) and to benefit from its utilisation. Where property takes the form of land, or industrial or commercial capital, where its utilisation requires the use of the labour of others, a further set of rights involving the exercise of authority over labour, is entailed by the more general rights of control (cf. Wright 1976). The peculiar

Table 7.1 Distribution of the total value of holdings of individual assets by range of net wealth, United Kingdom, 1976[a]

	Range of Net Wealth (Lower Limit)							
	Nil	*£5000*	*£10 000*	*£20 000*	*£50 000*	*£100 000*	*£200 000*	*Total*
Asset/Liability	%	%	%	%	%	%	%	%
Physical assets								
Dwellings (gross)	5.6	19.7	35.6	25.1	8.1	3.4	2.5	100
Land	0.4	2.2	6.8	20.8	15.3	12.4	42.1	100
Other buildings	1.7	5.9	17.6	28.7	21.8	15.3	9.0	100
Household goods	14.5	18.1	22.8	20.7	8.9	6.1	8.9	100
Trade assets	2.1	7.7	12.7	36.1	21.0	12.1	8.3	100
Financial assets								
Listed ordinary shares[b]	1.3	2.2	5.4	20.9	24.4	20.8	25.0	100
Other company securities	1.0	1.1	4.4	16.6	24.5	21.4	31.0	100
Life policies	14.1	21.7	30.0	25.7	5.2	1.9	1.4	100
Building society deposits	10.5	16.6	26.2	32.0	10.1	3.5	1.1	100
Listed UK government securities	5.5	5.0	6.3	21.2	17.1	16.2	28.7	100
Cash and bank deposits	13.9	14.4	18.4	21.3	12.6	9.6	9.8	100
National savings	23.5	23.0	27.5	18.9	4.9	1.6	0.7	100
Other	15.6	21.1	21.5	22.3	8.4	4.8	6.2	100
Liabilities								
Personal debts	17.9	13.4	16.8	23.1	10.7	8.0	10.1	100
Property debts	17.2	27.0	31.7	19.5	3.1	0.9	0.6	100
Net wealth	7.9	16.1	25.8	24.8	10.9	6.6	7.9	100
No. in range as % of estimated total of wealth owners	42.9	24.4	20.8	9.4	1.8	0.5	0.2	100

Notes: a This table relates only to those individuals whose estates would require probate or be liable to capital transfer tax.
b Including unit trusts.

Source: Royal Commission on the Distribution of Income and Wealth, 1979a, Table 4.7, p.102

significance of property therefore lies in its constitution of both economic and authority relations. On the one hand it permits the accumulation of further capital through the generation of revenue; on the other it establishes relations of authority between its possessors (or their agents) and certain categories of non-owners (or, in the case of those utilising their property to work independently without the employment of labour, frees them from such relations). The remainder of this paper seeks to explore the implications of property rights for class formation in the sphere of production and distribution.

Corporate Property and Class Formation[1]

The increasingly corporate nature of industrial and commercial property ownership, and the growing role of financial institutions, have been widely debated. Not only do corporate enterprises dominate the economy, but shares in such enterprises are increasingly held by institutional investors – unit and investment trusts, pension funds and insurance companies. By 1975 these institutions were beneficial holders of some 43 per cent of ordinary shares (Erritt and Alexander 1977, p.100). While individual institutions rarely hold a major proportion of the shares in any one company, they collectively hold between one-third and one-half of the shares in many large companies (Nyman and Silberston 1978, pp.85–6; Midgeley and Burns 1977, p.16; Dobbins and McRae 1975, pp.381–5). The consequence of these trends has been twofold. Firstly, there has been some disjunction, if not a complete fragmentation, of property rights, and secondly, the linkage between corporate property and class formation has become less direct, leading one commentator to remark that

> the property-owning bourgeoisie appears today to be a small and somewhat select class; indeed it can be argued that capital now refers more to an abstract category than to an identifiable class of people.
>
> (Saunders 1979, p.66)

As argued above, what gives to property its particular significance is its embodiment of both rights to benefit and rights to control. What characterises the corporate enterprise today is the partial disjunction of these rights. The 'separation of ownership and control' is in reality a separation of different rights of ownership. Ownership of the income-producing asset (land, machinery, etc.) is vested in the company itself, while ownership of the company is variously distributed among individuals and institutions. The right to benefit is thus diffused among a relatively wide range of individual shareholders and, indirectly, to the investors in insurance companies and unit trusts and the members of pension schemes. At the same time as the right to benefit is distributed more widely in these ways, rights of control, at least on a day-to-day basis, are exercised by full-time management who may lack any formal rights of ownership.

The effect of these trends on the nature of the enterprise has been widely debated (Scott 1979), though usually on the basis of inference from data on shareholdings rather than direct study of processes of decision-making. There remain many large companies in which a single individual or group retains a significant proportion of shareholdings, with the consequent possibility of domination or preponderant influence on the board (Nyman and Silberston 1978). In other cases a relatively small group of shareholders may be able to exercise ultimate control through a coalition (Scott 1979, p.41). In addition institutional investors have moved in the direction of intervention in major policy decisions and the exercise of a more regular informal influence (Midgeley 1975, pp.77–8; Hadden 1977, pp.332–4). While this represents a form of shareholder control, the rights of control and the right to benefit remain separated, with the former being vested in the management of the institutions, not in the providers of the funds.

The persistence of traditional forms of shareholder control and the development of new ones indicate that rights of control are not vested unequivocally in professional management. But nor are they vested unequivocally in large shareholders. Pahl and Winkler point out that the control of information and the expertise possessed by full-time management allows the possibility of the manipulation of those not involved in the running of the business on a full-time basis (Pahl and Winkler 1974). Outside shareholders (especially institutions) have their own sources of expertise and information, but the quality of these varies from area to area. A feeling that they lack the necessary expertise has inhibited institutional interventions in the past (Dobbins and McRae 1975, pp.386–7). In addition there will be companies, even if a minority, where control by professional management will be a reality. Using fairly generous criteria of owner control[2] Nyman and Silberston identified slightly over a half of 224 large firms as being owner-controlled. While this figure may understate the degree of owner-control as defined (Nyman and Silberston 1978, pp.85–6), it still leaves scope for a significant number of management controlled firms. Perhaps the most reasonable conclusion, looking at the corporate sector as a whole, is that ultimate control is variably distributed between large individual and family shareholders, leading executives and representatives of the investment institutions. Whatever the pattern of control, it remains the case that a substantial number of beneficiaries (small shareholders, investors in institutions) exercise no conceivable rights over the use to which their investment is put.

The diffusion of rights to benefit and the partial dissociation of different rights in property, while they have reduced the connection between specific enterprises and large holdings of wealth, have not led to the disappearance of a propertied class with its roots in the corporate enterprise. Despite some diffusion the ownership of shares and other company securities remains heavily concentrated at the upper end of the wealth distribution. That those with substantial property holdings are also concentrated at the upper end of the income distribution is indicated in Table 7.2, which shows the distribution of dividends and interest to those at different income levels.

Table 7.2 *Dividends and interest taxed at source*[a] *received by tax units at different statutory income levels,*[b] *1972/3*

Total statutory income (£)	*% of recipients*	*% received*	*Average per recipient (£)*
Under 1000	24.1	6.9	162
1000–2999	43.9	23.5	329
3000–5999	21.8	26.3	830
6000–9999	6.5	17.1	1 667
10 000–19 999	3.2	16.6	3 179
20 000+	0.5	10.1	11 884

Notes: [a] Interest taxed at source includes interest on most government securities quoted on the stock exchange, on local authority loan stocks and on company loan stocks, but excludes interest on bank deposits, savings bank accounts, building society shares and deposits, and national savings securities.
[b] Total statutory income refers to taxable income (before tax) from all sources after allowable deductions but before reliefs and allowances for tax.
Source: Adapted from Royal Commission on the Distribution of Income and Wealth, 1975, Table 12, p.23

As Table 7.2 suggests, the greater the income received the greater is the proportion of it likely to be derived from property, and whilst not all those in the highest income bracket receive their income primarily from property, it is reasonable to infer that a significant group do so. In this connection we may note Noble's estimate that in 1970/1 there were some 12 600 individuals owning property which produced £10 000 or more per year before tax (Noble 1975, p.182). Thus the linkage between corporate property and private wealth may take less direct forms, but has not been broken.

At the same time, Table 7.2 also indicates that the great majority of recipients of dividends and interest are to be found in lower income ranges, with nearly 70 per cent having total incomes of £3000 or less. To these small property-holders we should add the 11.5 million covered by occupational pension schemes and the 13 million tax units paying life assurance premiums (Government Actuary 1978; Royal

Commission on the Distribution of Income and Wealth, 1975, p.46). In none of these cases does the right to receive benefits of property ownership make the recipients members of a propertied stratum. Both groups lack any effective control over the utilisation or disposal of the property from which they receive benefits, and contributors to pension funds and life assurance lack even control over the way in which their money is invested (Midgeley 1975, pts. B and C; Newby *et al.* 1978, p.385).

The per capita income derived from dividends and taxed interest is, on average, very small in the lower income ranges, and provides little basis for social differentiation. The situation with regard to members of pension funds and insurance policyholders is slightly more complex. Only about 50 per cent of workers are covered by occupational pension schemes, and these are disproportionately concentrated in non-manual occupations, in larger firms and in the public sector (Government Actuary 1978). The linking of pensions to income during some period of working life means that a larger share of the funds generated is received by those who, during their working life, were higher-paid employees. The right to benefit is thus distributed in ways that reflect and reinforce the inequalities of the labour market – i.e. it is distributed disproportionately to those in better-paid and more secure employment. As a consequence the inclusion of occupational pension rights in estimates of wealth distribution reduces the total share received by those in the highest decile, but leads to an increase in inequality in lower deciles (Royal Commission on the Distribution of Income and Wealth 1979a, p.109; Burghes 1979, p.27). A similar situation applies in the case of life insurance. The higher the income of a tax unit the higher (on average) its contribution to life insurance (Royal Commission on the Distribution of Income and Wealth 1975, Table 21, p.44). In addition households at lower income levels are more likely to be contributing to those forms of policy which have higher expense ratios and a smaller participation in profits (Counter Information Services 1973, pp.3–4). As with occupational pensions the relative benefit acquired reflects and reinforces existing inequalities.

The identification of a propertied class raises the question of its reproduction over time. The salience of property for class divisions is reflected not only in its capacity to reproduce itself in the short term through accumulated revenue, but also in its high potential for inter-generational transmission. Harbury and McMahon (1974) have shown that around two-thirds of men leaving at least £100 000 in the 1950s and 1960s were sons of fathers who left at least £25 000, and though more recent research (Harbury and Hitchens 1976) suggests a slight reduction in the 1970s, these figures indicate a significant level of transmission of class position from generation to generation, especially when the possibility of additional sources of inheritance is taken into account.[3] In addition transmission of social position may be effected via access to elite educational institutions, reinforced by ties of kinship and social association, a possibility which gives particular importance to the question of the relationship between the propertied and the managers of corporate property.

Managers and Social Class

The preceding discussion has treated the formal owners of corporate property and those who manage it on their behalf as distinct groups. In reality, of course, as critics of the thesis of the separation of ownership and control have emphasised, there is significant overlap between the two (Nichols 1969, pp.71–9). A number of studies have shown that top executives and directors are drawn from privileged social backgrounds (commonly measured by the index of public school education) and participate to a greater or lesser degree in the ownership of shares (Whitley 1973: Stanworth 1974; Stanworth and Giddens 1975; Thomas 1978). Whether this can be taken to imply that senior management are drawn from the propertied class (as argued, for example, in Scott 1979) is a different matter. The full-time manager in particular may have origins outside this group. In the United States executive directors have been found to come from a wider social background than non-executive directors, and British studies consistently indicate that top managers are drawn from a wider social background than directors alone (Soref 1976; Clark 1966, p.68; Leggatt 1978, p.816). Nor is the fact that a director holds some shares in itself proof of membership or origin in a significantly propertied group. Many companies require that directors hold a certain (usually small) number of shares in the company (Midgeley 1975, p.9). In Florence's study (now somewhat dated) of very large industrial and commercial companies just over a quarter of directors held no more than the qualifying minimum of shares (Florence 1961, p.99). More recent studies also point to limited shareholding by a substantial minority of directors. Stanworth's study of seventy-five leading companies found over one-third of directors with holdings of £3000 or less, and nearly one-fifth with holdings of no more than £1000 (Stanworth 1974, p.255).

Further, the linkage between property ownership and senior managerial status is a two-way one. While in some cases property ownership, or a background in the propertied class, undoubtedly facilitates access to top executive positions, in other cases occupancy of these positions may provide a means of access to property. In the first place shareholding may be made possible by company schemes for assisting share acquisition by senior management (though these are vulnerable to changes in tax laws), and in the second place the high level of managerial remuneration will provide the means for direct purchase of shares, at least on a modest scale (although, as Parkin [1979, p.58] points out, this means of access is shared by those at the top of other administrative and professional hierarchies). The implication of these processes of property acquisition is that, for a small minority, the managerial hierarchy may provide a channel of mobility into the class of property owners.

The level of managerial salaries (at both senior and subordinate levels) raises a further issue. Senior management, to a degree, and subordinate managers to a much greater extent, exercise certain of the functions of property ownership without participating formally in that ownership, and derive their rewards primarily from salaries. In the case of senior management these salaries alone are enough to place them among the most privileged groups in society, as full-time business executives account for the great majority of higher incomes from employment (Royal Commission on the Distribution of Income and Wealth 1976a, pp.33–4). Similarly, lower-level managers remain an economically advantaged group, despite claims of the erosion of managerial salaries in recent years (Pond 1979). How far does this position arise from their role as the agents of capital?

Recent neo-Marxist analyses have stressed this role, either to locate managers unambiguously in the bourgeoisie, or to see them as occupying a structurally ambiguous position, performing functions of both labour and capital (Poulantzas 1975, pp.175–82; Wright 1976; Carchedi 1977, p.13; Crompton and Gubbay 1977, pp.154–5). From the latter point of view the differentiated rewards of managers can be seen as reflecting the control (as opposed to coordination) aspects of their role, and as serving to symbolise and support the structure of authority based on capitalist property rights. As Crompton and Gubbay put it:

> . . . a degree of material advantage is required if the integrity of the dominant structure of capitalist authority is to be preserved. In the establishing of different incomes from employment there is no doubt that authority . . . is a key factor in justifying unequal rewards.
>
> (Crompton and Gubbay 1977, pp.155–6)

In addition, as Crompton and Gubbay (among others) note, senior managerial personnel play a role in determining their own remuneration. While this is not normally a direct determination of their own salaries (in most large companies the remuneration of executive directors is determined by their non-executive colleagues), senior executives may influence their own income by participation in the determination of the general salary structures by reference to which their own rewards will be determined (Westergaard and Resler 1975, p.53; Royal Commission on the Distribution of Income and Wealth 1976a, pp.113–4). In so far as this does occur the level of managerial remuneration will reflect the rights of control exercised by senior management, and hence not simply their position as agents of capital but also the partial dissociation of property rights discussed in the previous section. Far from being 'in considerable measure . . . a claim on profit', as Westergaard and Resler (1975, p.53) suggest, it is the priority of these claims over profit (determined after other costs are met) which gives the self-determination of managerial incomes its significance.

For the lower levels of management the claim that managerial remuneration both symbolises and sustains the hierarchy of authority is plausible. In most large organisations managerial rewards are established by a combination of internal grading (often based on job evaluations involving such factors as authority and responsibility) and reference to external relativities (Royal Commission on the Distribution of Income and Wealth 1976b). Thus, while labour market factors enter the calculation (comparison with rates elsewhere) they do so within the wider context of a general pattern of managerial rewards established by reference to the structure of authority and control in the organisation, and justified by the greater responsibilities of managerial positions and the concomitant stresses and uncertainties (Lydall 1968, pp.125–7; Merrett 1968, pp.8–9). What is less clear is how far this pattern of reward differentiation reflects the structure of *capitalist* authority, for, as Parkin points out, the right to deny others access to the means of life and labour which derives from control over productive property

> can obviously be vested in a variety of institutional forms, including the capitalist firm, a nationalised industry, or a Soviet enterprise.
>
> (Parkin 1979, p.53)[4]

The persistence of differentiated rewards for management even where the ownership of the enterprise is formally vested in the workforce itself[5] raises questions as to how far such rewards are a property of control hierarchies in general and not simply those associated with private capital.

The distinctiveness of the class position of the lower level managers is further called into question by the similarities in income, life-style and status of other positively privileged white-collar groups such as professionals and administrative personnel in the public sector and elsewhere. The specific function of the manager within the enterprise does not appear to differentiate this group in any highly significant way from certain other sections of the middle class. It is therefore not particularly surprising that, in contrast to the owners of substantial property, the lower levels of management display only limited generational reproduction of occupational position. Lacking the direct power to transmit social position which derives from legal ownership, managers can pass on their positions only through indirect and imperfect mechanisms such as influence on children's motivations and possibly the provision of contacts in the business world. The low level of occupational reproduction in the managerial group is indicated in Leggatt's study of managerial origins where (leaving aside directors) less than 10 per cent of managers were themselves the sons of managers (Leggatt 1978, p.821). So while there are several respects in which the class position of senior executives can be related to the distribution and exercise of property rights, for the lower levels of management the relationship is much more problematic.

Small Capital and the *Petite Bourgeoisie*

Despite the growing dominance of corporate forms of property, with its attendant disjunction of property rights, more traditional forms of ownership persist in many sectors of the economy. Indeed the past ten years have marked the 'rediscovery', both political and sociological, of small capital and the *petit bourgeoisie* (Bechofer and Elliott 1976; McHugh 1979). There has, however, been a tendency in recent literature to group together under the general heading of the '*petit bourgeoisie*' a somewhat diverse group of social positions, ranging from the corner shopkeeper to the owner of a business employing well over a hundred people. In terms of economic position and authority relations it seems more useful to distinguish two groups, although the line betwen them is necessarily blurred. On the one hand the entrepreneurial bourgeoisie both own and manage their own businesses, employing and directing labour, often on a substantial scale. On the other hand, the *petit bourgeoisie* own property primarily as a necessary condition of the performance of their own labour. The owner-managed business is thus distinguishable from the *petit bourgeois* enterprise by:

1. a degree of functional differentiation – the company is owner-managed rather than owner-operated, and the owner-manager's direct participation in production is limited;
2. a significant level of employment of labour other than that of the owner's immediate family;
3. economic returns from investment and entrepreneurship rather than primarily from the owner's own labour (Deeks 1976, pp.58–9; cf. Poulantzas 1975, pp.138–9; Wright 1976, p.31).

The owner-manager – the traditional entrepreneurial capitalist – is thus found typically in the smaller business enterprise in the commercial and industrial sector, while a similar class position is occupied in the agricultural sector by full-time working farmers employing hired labour to produce for the market.[6] The property rights of use, benefit and control which are partially dissociated in the corporate sector here remain in the hands of a single individual or small group. In Boswell's sample of firms in the hosiery and engineering industries employing fewer than 500 people, three-quarters had all or most of their shares held by working directors, and a broader survey by Merrett-Cyriax Associates of firms employing fewer than 200 people found chief executives holding over half the shares in nearly two-thirds of the sample (Boswell 1973, p.210; Merrett-Cyriax Associates 1971, p.34). Where shareholdings are more widely diffused it is typically among the families of those actively involved in the firm. However, while there is a fusion or near-fusion of rights of control and the right to benefit in the form of profit, the owner-manager does not directly supervise either the production process or the labour force; instead he delegates these tasks to subordinates.[7] But in contrast to the large corporation, with its clearly defined separation of responsibilities and functions, the scale of the smaller firm allows the owner-manager to intervene directly in these processes.

For the entrepreneurial capitalist the ownership of property provides a superordinate position in the structure of authority. Whether it also provides a privileged position in the structure of material reward is more controversial. Several studies have stressed the modest incomes of the group, in comparison with that of even subordinate managers in the large corporation (Merrett-Cyriax Associates 1971, p.14; Golby and Johns 1971, p.10; Deeks 1976, p.197), but the existence of economic returns in several different forms (directors' fees, executives' salaries and shareholders' dividends) and the balancing of these for tax advantage makes accurate assessment difficult, especially as there may be an overlap between personal and business finances (Boswell 1973, p.160; Newby *et al.* 1978, p.144). Recent studies by the Royal Commission on the Distribution of Income and Wealth suggest a more privileged position. In 1974/75 one-fifth of close company proprietors[8] were in the top 5 per cent of income recipients, and approximately one-third in the top 10 per cent, while the distribution of shareholdings in companies without a Stock Exchange listing (predominantly, though not exclusively, smaller owner-managed companies), suggested a distribution between wealth-holding groups almost identical to that of listed ordinary shares (Royal Commission on the Distribution of Income and Wealth 1979a, p.145;

1979b, p.148). Of course, the magnitude of owners' incomes does not say anything about the magnitude of capital accumulation within the enterprise itself. In early years profits may largely be ploughed back and personal drawings kept low with a view to higher incomes in the long term. Conversely, in stagnant or declining firms the enterprise may be subsidised from directors' remuneration or investments made elsewhere at times of greater prosperity (Boswell 1973, p.160). In this case, where family investment and employment is locked into the family firm, property ownership may become a source of steady impoverishment rather than accumulation.

The importance of the smaller firm resides not only in the basis it forms for the continuation of a traditional bourgeoisie, but also in the opportunities it provides for mobility into the propertied class via entrepreneurship. Studies of inheritance (Harbury and McMahon 1974, pp.133–6; Rubinstein 1974) find an important minority of 'self-made' men among the rich, and it seems probable that entrepreneurship and the realisation of capital gains provide the main alternative route to inheritance in securing substantial wealth. Given the greater growth rate of founder-managed firms relative to others in the small business sector (Boswell 1973, pp.64–75; Merrett-Cyriax Associates 1971, pp.36–7) it is through these firms that larger fortunes are most likely to be accumulated. This is of some importance, as the founders of such firms are drawn substantially from working class or lower white collar backgrounds, and often have limited educational attainments or a history of interrupted education (Boswell 1973, pp.230–1; Deeks 1976, pp.106; Economists' Advisory Group 1978, p.13; Stanworth and Curran 1973, pp.90–4). This suggests that the small business may provide a channel of mobility for at least a small minority of those whose opportunity of advancement by other routes is limited. (It should, though, be noted that the majority of small firms fail in their early years.) Harbury and McMahon's finding that 'self-made' men are more likely to be found in industries which allow scope for the entry of small firms with little initial capital appears to bear this out (Harbury and McMahon 1974, pp.133–6). However, in the small capital sector, as among those whose wealth derives from the corporate sector, inheritance predominates over external recruitment. Many small firms continue to be run by the descendant(s) of the founder, with inheritance playing a particularly important role in spheres such as agriculture (Boswell 1973, pp.125–37; Deeks 1976, p.81; Newby *et al.* 1978, p.61).

For those who are upwardly mobile through entrepreneurship, entry into the *petite bourgeoisie* in those sectors of the economy having low costs of entry is likely to be the first step. Like the small capitalist owner-manager the member of the *petite bourgeoisie* exercises control over economic resources by virtue of rights of ownership, but does so in a situation of low functional differentiation and limited control over labour. Of the small shopkeepers studied by Bechofer and his colleagues 84 per cent had fewer than three full-time (or six part-time) assistants, 44 per cent had no paid assistance, and 20 per cent had no assistance of any kind (Bechofer *et al.* 1974a, p.473). A similar pattern may no doubt be found among many of the self-employed, and in agriculture among those small farmers who utilise little or no hired labour and may not even be able to support additional family labour on any scale (Newby *et al.* 1978, pp.68-9). The limited employment of labour, and the low level of differentiation of work tasks, mean, as Bechofer and Elliott point out, that the *petit bourgeois* 'gets his living by mixing his own labour with his own capital' (Bechofer and Elliott 1976, p.78). Property is owned mainly as a means of engaging in the work process, rather than to employ others.

For a variety of reasons the position of the *petite bourgeoisie* is an ambiguous one. While its ownership of property confers only limited power over others it does provide an independence of the inequalities of the workplace which is denied to those in employment. But if this group is advantaged in respect of authority relations relative to those in employment its material advantage is less clear. Bechofer and his colleagues note that small shopkeepers receive incomes that are not appreciably superior to those of many manual workers, although the ability to accumulate capital in the business allows sporadic drawings for large expenditures (Bechofer *et al.* 1974b, pp.106–8). The recent survey by the Royal Commission on the Distribution of Income and Wealth suggests that, while the self-employed do, on average, enjoy superior incomes and consumption patterns to those of the employed population, it is typically the self-employed professionals who are the most prosperous, with those in such sectors as the retail trade and motor repairs enjoying a considerably more modest return (Royal Commission on the Distribution of Income and Wealth 1979b, p.183). Of course, such estimates exclude the benefits gained through capital accumulation, but they also exclude the effects of capital losses. Once again it is in those sectors where entry requires relatively little in the way of capital or qualifications (e.g. road haulage, retailing and construction) that bankruptcy is at its greatest, stressing once again the precarious position of the archetypal *petit bourgeois*.

This somewhat marginal position is reinforced (at least in Britain) by the position of the *petite bourgeoisie* in the structure of social mobility. The *petite bourgoisie* have the rights of disposal in the property they own, thereby creating the conditions for inter-generational transmission of social position via inheritance. However, the limited scale and profitability of many enterprises will tend to preclude the provision of jobs for family members on their first entry into the labour market. Bechofer and Elliott (1978, pp.78–9) suggest that the children of small shopkeepers tend to enter the more central middle class occupations (professional, administrative, etc.), in which case the relative stability and security of such employment may make children unwilling to leave it to take over little businesses on the retirement or death of parents. Whatever the reason the low level of inter-generational transmission of positions in this group is borne out by the results of the 1972 survey of social mobility in England and Wales, in which the children of proprietors (especially of proprietors without employees) showed a degre of inheritance of social position below that of almost any other group (Erikson *et al.* 1979, p.432).

The dividing line between the *petite bourgeoisie* and the entrepreneurial bourgeoisie is not a clear-cut one. Through the expansion of business, the hiring of labour on a larger scale and the introduction of differentiated work organisation the *petit bourgeois* may expand his business and join the class of capitalist entrepreneurs. For the majority, however, their natural position will remain on the margins of the propertied classes.

Conclusion

In this paper I have suggested some of the ways in which the ownership of property, and the rights attendant upon it, enter into the constitution of class positions. The owners and managers of corporate wealth, the entrepreneurial capitalists and the *petite bourgeoisie* each embody a particular combination of the rights of property. While the steady extension of the corporate form of industrial and commercial property has entailed some separation between the possession or exercise of these rights, it has not depersonalised capital to the point where it may be regarded simply as a disembodied social category. Not only do the entrepreneurial bourgeoisie and (in an attenuated fashion) the *petite bourgeoisie* continue to embody the fusion of property rights in an individual or small group, but the continuing concentration of private shareholdings and the linkage between senior executives and property ownership enables us to identify a class of corporate capital, albeit with a partial diversion into rentier and managerial elements, and with a significant measure of ownership extended (directly or indirectly) beyond this limited group.

Inasmuch as it is possible to make comparisons over time, it appears that the concentration of wealth has been in steady decline during the twentieth century, although it is difficult to disentangle the relative contribution to this process of capital taxation, differential accumulation, redistribution within families and the growth of 'popular' wealth (Atkinson and Harrison 1978, pp.235–40). Despite this trend, and the development of financial institutions deploying a large number of relatively small savings, capital ownership remains highly concentrated and central to the process of class formation.

Notes

1. In this section, as in those that follow, I have confined discussion in the main to the contemporary British situation.
2. A holding of 5 per cent or more of voting shares by a single institution or by directors and their families, or the presence of a family Chairman/Managing Director where the former criterion was not met.
3. Parkin's argument (1979, p.61) that inter-generational transmission of property-based class positions is relatively low depends on identifying such positions with occupational rather than ownership status. Inheritance of wealth rather than inheritance of occupational position would seem to be the relevant criterion.
4. It may be rejoined that all of these entail the control over capital of a differentiated or privileged minority, but this in itself is inadequate to reduce diverse institutional forms to a single common type.
5. See, for example, the discussion of Adizes (1971, pp.49–60) on the reward structure in self-managing Yugoslav enterprises.
6. The situation in the agricultural sector is complicated by the fact that one of the essential factors of production, land, may be held in various forms of tenancy arrangement. Historically this led in certain areas to a three-class system of large landowners, tenant farmers and hired labour. The trend in the twentieth century has been strongly in the direction of owner-occupation, but the intervention of financial institutions has led to the development of new forms of tenancy. While tenancy is of importance elsewhere, it is of special significance in the agricultural sector because of the finite availability of land and its centrality to certain forms of production. On the development of tenancy and ownership in agriculture see Newby *et al.* 1978, pp.95–115; Massey and Catalano 1978, chapters 4–6.
7. In practice there is obviously a continuum, with the degree of separation depending on the size of the enterprise and the labour force, the nature of the product and the technology involved, and so on. In farming, with its small labour force relative to output, there is more of a direct involvement in production and supervision, but here too the amount of time spent away from the production process increases with the size of the farm (Newby *et al.* 1978, pp.49–50).
8. A 'close company' is defined in a complex fashion by the Income and Corporation Taxes Act 1970, but is essentially a company controlled by five or fewer people, or by its director shareholders.

References

Adizes, I., *Industrial Democracy: Yugoslav Style,* New York, Free Press, 1971.

Atkinson, A. B., and Harrison, A. J., *The Distribution of Personal Wealth in Britain,* Cambridge, Cambridge University Press, 1978.

Bechofer, F., and Elliott, B., 'Persistence and change: the petite bourgeoisie in industrial society', *Archives europeéennes de sociologie,* **17**, no. 1, 1976.

Bechofer, F., and Elliott, B., 'The voice of small business and the politics of

survival', *Sociological Review*, **26**, no. 1, 1978.
Bechofer, F., Elliott, B., Rushforth, M. and Bland, R., 'Small shopkeepers: matters of money and meaning', *Sociological Review*, **22**, no. 4, 1974a.
Bechofer, F., Elliott, B., Rushforth, M. and Bland, R., 'The petits bourgeois in the class structure: the case of the small shopkeepers', in F. Parkin (ed.), *The Social Analysis of Class Structure*, London, Tavistock, 1974b.
Boswell, J., *The Rise and Decline of Small Firms,* London, Allen and Unwin, 1973.
Burghes, L., 'The old order', in F. Field (ed.), *The Wealth Report,* London, 1979.
Carchedi, G., *On the Economic Identification of Social Classes*, London, Routledge and Kegan Paul, 1977.
Clark, D. G., *The Industrial Manager, his Background and Career Pattern,* London, Business Publications Ltd., 1966.
Counter Information Services, *Your Money and Your Life: Insurance Companies and Pension Funds*, London, Counter Information Services, 1973.
Crompton, R. and Gubbay, J., *Economy and Class Structure*, London, Macmillan, 1977.
Deeks, J., *The Small Firm Owner-Manager: Entrepreneurial Behaviour and Management Practice,* New York, Praeger, 1976.
Dobbins, R., and McRae, T. W., *Institutional Shareholders and Corporate Management,* Bradford, M.C.B. Journals, 1975.
Economists' Advisory Group, *Small Firms in Cities,* London, Shell U.K. Ltd., 1978.
Erikson, R., Goldthorpe, J. H. and Portocarero, L., 'Intergenerational class mobility in three Western European societies', *British Journal of Sociology,* **30**, no. 4, 1979.
Erritt, M. J. and Alexander, J. C. D., 'Ownership of company shares', *Economic Trends*, September 1977.
Florence, P. S., *Ownership, Contol and Success of Large Companies,* London, Sweet and Maxwell, 1961.
Golby, C. W., and Johns, G., *Attitude and Motivation* (Committee of Inquiry on Small Firms, Research Report 7), London, HMSO, 1971.
Government Actuary, *Occupational Pension Schemes 1975: Fifth Survey by the Government Actuary,* London, HMSO, 1978.
Hadden, T., *Company Law and Capitalism*, 2nd ed., London, Weidenfeld and Nicholson, 1977.
Harbury, C. D. and Hitchens, D. M., 'The inheritance of top wealth leavers: some further evidence', *Economic Journal,* **86**, 1976.
Harbury, C. D. and McMahon, P. C., 'Intergenerational wealth transmission and the characteristics of top wealth leavers in Britain', in P. Stanworth and A. Giddens (eds.), *Elites and Power in British Society,* Cambridge, Cambridge University Press, 1974.
Hobhouse, L. T., 'The historical evolution of property, in fact and in idea', in *Property: its Duties and Rights*, London, Macmillan, 1915.
Lafargue, P., *The Evolution of Property*, London, New Park Publications (originally published 1891), 1975.
Leggatt, T., 'Managers in industry: their background and education', *Sociological Review,* **26**, no. 4, 1978.

Lydall, H., *The Structure of Earnings*, Oxford, Oxford University Press, 1968.
McHugh, J., 'The self-employed and the small independent entrepreneur', in R. King and N. Nugent (eds.), *Respectable Rebels*, London, Hodder and Stoughton, 1979.
Massey, D. and Catalano, A., *Capital and Land*, London, Edward Arnold, 1978.
Merrett, A. J., *Executive Remuneration in the United Kingdom*, London, Longmans, 1968.
Merrett-Cyriax Associates, *Dynamics of Small Firms* (Committee of Inquiry on Small Firms, Research Report 12), London, HMSO, 1971.
Midgeley, K., *Companies and Their Shareholders: The Uneasy Relationship*, London, Institute of Chartered Secretaries and Administrators, 1975.
Midgeley, K. and Burns, R., *The Capital Market: its Nature and Significance*, London, Macmillan, 1977.
Newby, H., Bell, C., Rose, D. and Saunders, P., *Property, Paternalism and Power*, London, Hutchinson, 1978.
Nichols, T., *Ownership, Control and ideology*, London, Allen and Unwin, 1969.
Noble, T., *Modern Britain: Structure and Change*, London, Batsford, 1975.
Nyman, S., and Silberston, A., 'The ownership and control of industry', *Oxford Economic Papers*, **30**, no. 1, 1978.
Pahl, R. E. and Winkler, J. T., 'The economic elite: theory and practice', in P. Stanworth and A. Giddens (eds.), *Elites and and Power in British Society*, Cambridge, Cambridge University Press, 1974.
Parkin, F., *Marxism and Class Theory*, London, Tavistock, 1979.
Pond, C., 'The higher paid and the crisis of living standards', in F. Field (ed.), *The Wealth Report*, London, Routledge and Kegan Paul, 1979.
Poulantzas, N., *Classes in Contemporary Capitalism*, London, New Left Books, 1975 (originally published 1974 as *Les classes sociales dans le capitalisme aujourd'hui*, Paris, Editions du Seuil).
Royal Commission on the Distribution of Income and Wealth, *Report No. 2: Income from Companies and its Distribution*, Cmnd 6172, London, HMSO, 1975.
Royal Commission on the Distribution of Income and Wealth, *Report No. 3: Higher Incomes from Employment*, Cmnd 6383, London, HMSO, 1976a.
Royal Commission on the Distribution of Income and Wealth, *Selected Evidence submitted to the Royal Commission for Report No. 3*, London, HMSO, 1976b.
Royal Commission on the Distribution of Income and Wealth, *Report No. 7: Fourth Report on the Standing Reference*, Cmnd 7595, London, HMSO, 1979a.
Royal Commission on the Distribution of Income and Wealth, *Report No. 8: Fifth Report on the Standing Reference*, Cmnd 7679, London, HMSO, 1979b.
Rubinstein, W. D., 'Men of property', in P. Stanworth and A. Giddens (eds.), *Elites and Power in British Society*, Cambridge, Cambridge University Press, 1974.
Saunders, P., *Urban Politics*, London, Hutchinson, 1979.
Scott, J., *Corporations, Classes and Capitalism*, London, Hutchinson, 1979.
Soref, M., 'Social class and a division of labour within the corporate elite', *Sociological Quarterly*, **17**, no. 3, 1976.

Stanworth, M. J. K. and Curran, J., *Management Motivation in the Smaller Business,* London, Gower Press, 1973.

Stanworth, P., 'Property, class and the corporate elite', in I. Crewe (ed.), *British Political Sociology Yearbook, vol. 1,* London, Croom Helm, 1974.

Stanworth, P. and Giddens, A., 'The modern corporate economy', *Sociological Review,* **23**, no. 1, 1975.

Thomas, A. B., 'The British business elite: the case of the retail sector', *Sociological Review,* **26**, no. 2, 1978.

Westergaard, J. and Resler, H., *Class in a Capitalist Society,* London, Heinemann, 1975.

Whitley, R., 'Commonalities and connections among directors of large financial institutions', *Sociological Review,* **21**, no. 4, 1973.

Wright, E. O., 'Class boundaries in advanced capitalist societies', *New Left Review,* **98**, 1976.

8 The Bureaucratic Collection of Small Consumer Debts[1]

Paul Rock

Introduction

It is evident that the provision and management of consumer credit extend into most areas of social and economic life. It is a process without neat boundaries and any description must therefore be a little arbitrary. In this chapter, I shall simply ignore much of the context and organisation of debt-collection in England and Wales, turning my analysis towards one distinct and reasonably interesting theme. I shall focus on the enforcement of debts as the foundation of a kind of status passage, an ordered career which propels defaulters through a sequence of prepared stages in an attempt to coerce repayment. The collection of debts owed to large, bureaucratic creditors can be pursued for long periods of time. Its structure and style are carefully devised to impart an impression of significant change and development. It fosters the belief that the defaulter's intransigence is about to become ever more consequential. In turn, those who collect debts work with an elaborate symbolism which is built into the spacing, pacing and content of their approaches. Enforcement is represented as an unambiguous progression towards an unpalatable fate. As debtors near that fate, they are encouraged to review the meanings of their actions and their implication in the collection system. The bureaucratic control of default therefore hinges on the manipulation of debtors' identities. It routinely plans moral careers for hundreds of thousands of people. But it is also subject to unusual constraints which merit particular attention.

The Ends of Debt-Collection

> The three basic principles of collection procedure that every credit manager should always bear in mind are: 1. GET YOUR MONEY. 2. GET IT PROMPTLY. 3. RETAIN YOUR CUSTOMER'S GOOD WILL WHILE COLLECTING FROM HIM. Another consideration . . . is 4. SEEK EVERY OPPORTUNITY TO MAKE YOUR COLLECTION PROCEDURE CONTRIBUTE TO YOUR CONCERN'S SALES POLICY. It may seem contradictory to say that a collection procedure should both be efficient in obtaining customers'

> payments and yet maintain their good will. It may seem even more impossible that an effective collection system should contribute to sales policy. Yet as all credit managers learn sooner or later, these two objectives of collection policy are categorical *musts*.[2]

When someone has been extended credit, he may take any one of a number of established routes before he becomes of no further interest to his creditor. A creditor would maintain that the ideal route is a strict adherence to the terms contained in the contract. A debtor who commits himself to paying eighteen monthly instalments will pay those instalments in eighteen months without any intervention from the creditor. The most common path, however, combines eventual repayment with a series of minor forays into the enforcement career. Every time a person receives a notice from a gas board, a rating authority or a commercial concern, he enters an artfully contrived system of social control. Most creditors expect that the majority of their agreements will go into default on at least one occasion, and, at any single time, their enforcement will be directed at some 10 per cent of their customers.

The organised response to default is superficially simple but analytically complex. It maps out alternative sequences of action which can be applied to different 'types' of default. The sequences are all variants of one basic model: a stream of increasingly threatening letters, a personal confrontation between debtor and creditor, and, finally, enforcement pursued by specialist debt-collectors and the courts. This process conforms to Roth's definition of the career as 'a series of related and definable stages or phases of a given sphere of activity that a person goes through on the way to a more or less definite and recognizable end-point or goal'.[3] Careers can be described by their key structural characteristics: their intricacy, duration, intensity, direction, tempo and prevailing rationality. These features are all interrelated and their interaction becomes especially complicated when a career is as protracted and devious as an enforcement sequence.

Any deliberately constructed career is shaped primarily by the purposes which it is supposed to achieve. Enforcement has no single end. It is not only aimed at the rapid recovery of debts, it also performs ancillary functions and is subordinated to other institutional goals. It is apparent that credit managers are required to be chiefly preoccupied with finance, and financial criteria are expected to dominate their handling of default. Enforcement cannot be conducted in a manner that conflicts with the companion demand for economy. Creditors will be reluctant debt-collectors if enforcement costs more than the amounts that can be recouped. They may even resort to a token display of vigilance and abandon any pretence of serious action.

Creditors must arrange their whole enforcement system so that it is not unduly expensive. Although all social control agencies are affected by economic constraints, debt-collecting institutions are uniquely restrained. Murder, rape and drug addiction cannot be nicely measured in monetary terms and their prosecution is impelled by moral pressures which defy such measurement. Collection, however, is peculiarly susceptible to costing. It is also taken by some to be unconcerned with the regulation of immoral conduct. The ostensible aim of enforcement is the reduction of economic loss, and collection is governed by considerations of how cheaply an efficient system can be administered and how financially advantageous each step is likely to be. There can be no certainty that the costs of enforcement will be recovered from a reluctant debtor. Some debts are discharged by those who do not contribute to the costs of action, whilst others are abandoned as irretrievable. Every large creditor is capable of losing a substantial amount each year because he may have to pursue several thousand accounts. The search for inexpensive remedies influences all collection policy.

That search may nevertheless permit enforcement to take the guise of punitive action against certain 'types' of defaulter. Punishment of the 'professional' debtor may be defined as economically valuable but it sometimes appears to displace dispassionate monetary calculation. Straightforward enforcement may also be upset by a recognition of the need to ward off potential defaulters. On occasions, enforcement can become a gigantic exercise in deterrence. Most creditors budget for bad debts but their losses may grow to a bankrupting size if they do not ostentatiously collect debts. Successful deterrence is thought to centre on forcing harassed defaulters to perform roles in a drama enacted for an audience of 'professional' and 'feckless' debtors. Enforcement must be visible, frightening and seemingly inexorable.

A creditor who emphasises the deterrent function commits himself to a special presentation of the institution which he serves. Such a presentation can pose acute organisational problems. Creditors play a number of parts which place disparate demands on the construction of their institutional identity. Enforcement is an aspect of what Hughes has called 'dirty work': it is regarded as squalid and unattractive. It is in competition with another impression which creditors try to promote. Firms are usually advertised as the co-operative and responsive suppliers of a desired service. The dirty work of collection cannot readily be disentangled from a creditor's other activities. A precarious solution may be accomplished by delegating the damaging conduct of enforcement to another institution with another name.

Indeed, the assumption of disreputability is one of the principal functions of specialist debt-collectors: they have come to occupy a stigmatised position in the moral division of commercial labour. But a creditor who would impress his respectability on the larger world may well curtail all collection tactics that might tarnish it. Frequently, therefore, creditors eschew all vulnerable modes of enforcement.

Creditors not only confront a universe of external critics and potential customers. There are many debtors amongst the wider population of defaulters whose reactions to vigorous enforcement are as significant as those of the uninvolved outsider. Most defaulters are held to be 'normal' consumers whose payments have temporarily lapsed. By extension, it is thought that they will resume payments if their management is tactful. A creditor cannot afford to estrange one whom he defines as an 'unfortunate' or 'feckless' debtor and transform him into an embryo 'professional'. As I shall argue, all enforcement attempts to prevent the translation of mere rule-breaking into an existentially-committed secondary deviance. That caution pervades the production of the first stages of an enforcement career. It is one of the reasons why debt-collection is stratified into stages.

In all these ways, the enforcement career is turned away from the elementary collection of debts. A proliferation of ends complicates the manufacture of an enforcement system. Contradictory ambitions are subjected to a limited reconciliation in a multi-tiered process. A creditor can resolve some of the problems of estrangement, publicity, deterrence, punishment and selection by instituting a system of serial tests. Each stage of a career encapsulates one or more tests of hypotheses about a debtor's situation and motives. The results of the tests become automatic guides to action in succeeding stages.

Results take the form of a 'reasonable' or an 'unreasonable' response from a debtor. A reasonable response will lead to a temporary abatement of enforcement whilst a debtor's behaviour is monitored. The unreasonable response is most often no response at all, and it mechanically suggests the need to pass the debtor on to a more severe stage. That is, if a desired reaction is not forthcoming, a creditor's situated reasoning requires him to assume that the debtor does not fall into the class of possibilities covered by the actions of that stage. The defaulter may be appropriately managed by more unpleasant techniques and the apposite stage will eventually be found after sufficient tests have been applied. Thus one creditor observed, 'if you don't get any sense out of the debtor, you've got to put him into the machine'.

In the main, therefore, a career is constituted to generate its own understandings about default. The typical information upon which a creditor acts is an absence of information. The default which becomes typified as deviant is often the sheer inaction of debtors. But it is not solely the absence of a response which allows default to acquire an increasingly sinister meaning, it is also the growing magnitude of that absence. Structured by time, the passage of stages produces benchmarks which signify the course and quality of default. Time itself is a valuable measure of what a debtor is 'really' like and what should be done to him. As consecutive instalments remain unpaid, the default becomes enlarged and the debtor's deviance swells.

Roth has argued 'those who control the careers of others to some degree must decide upon appropriate times for making changes in those careers, and if they deal with many such careers, they are under pressure to regularise this process of definition'.[4] The larger creditors are forced to organise their enforcement in minute detail, frequently turning it into a process which can be transferred to computer. They are armed with only the sparsest data, and those data are manufactured by debt-collection itself. In most cases, they know what debtors told them when applications were first made for credit. They also know that those debtors are not replying to their overtures. They might hazard guesses about the reasons and settings of default, the risks presented by any instance of default, and the most successful method of controlling it. Yet a haphazard and individualised system is extraordinarily expensive and cumbersome to manage. It has been replaced by a scheme that is designed automatically to cover all possible contingencies, starting with the most sympathetic explanation of the cause of default and ending with the least. The whole gamut of institutional conceptions of indebtedness is mechanically incorporated in the career. Problems of selection are dwarfed. The process furnishes all the answers necessary for action.

The Nature of Sanctions

Economy, a reliance upon the serial testing system, a shunning of dirty work and trepidation about alienating the 'normal' consumer conspire together to halt the ready use of sanctions. By far the most important constraint is the financial cost of doing anything concrete. Unless a career is intended to be punitive or deterrent in nature, a creditor will be loath to lose money in the pursuit of a debtor. He may sham activity but he will usually avoid it. The bulk of petty debts will be chased in a seemingly strenuous manner but no palpable action will be taken. The fear caused by words and symbols becomes a substitute for the reactions evoked by a physical confrontation with social control. Indeed, there appears to be a clear relationship between the belligerence of the sentiments expressed in a sequence of letters and the creditor's reluctance to replace the letters with activity of any sort. This relationship may also be discovered in the timing of the career. A small debt will be enforced with more bellicose letters which will be sent over a longer period. The cost of flourishing threats is the same whatever the size of a default.

So dominant is the serial testing system that it is held to underwrite the inefficacy of expensive coercion. Of course, many debts *are* pursued in the courts, executions and attachment orders *are* imposed, but the vast majority of defaults are countered by feints and threats. It is argued that a debtor who is unperturbed by the prospect of action must 'necessarily' be a person who will be unmoved by the realisation of that action. He has been tested, has failed, has passed a bench-mark and become even more demonstrably incorrigible. That failure increases a creditor's hesitancy because it is believed that such a debtor will be untouched by his weak and expensive techniques of intimidation. Threats thus become of greater moment than sanctions, and one creditor remarked:

> The threat of court is *efficient*. If a person's willing for it to go as far as there, then I don't think it really matters. The *hint* of taking someone to court is much better than having to take someone to court . . . obviously, if it's gone as far as actually proceeding in court, then he *must* be a bad egg and he's not perturbed about it.

Curiously, then, the need to use force frequently implies that force will be useless. Courts, professional debt-collectors and so on exist to provide symbolic ammunition for the creditor. The threat of action at all times is more important than action itself. Action is held to be impotent, costly, a test of its own lack of value, and capable of engendering secondary deviation. It has generally been displaced by the deliberate management of apprehension. Creditors try to create a controlled anxiety by building an abundance and variety of threats into the career. They may do so by fabricating possible consequences, inventing dummy firms of debt-collectors which are no more than a department of the creditor's own organisation, and exploiting ambiguity. An illustration of this symbolic work is provided by the sequence of weekly letters which were issued by one creditor. The first four letters are comparatively mild:

> Letter 1: 'We have recently sent you a statement of account showing an amount outstanding of. . . . We hope you found our statement to be in order and that we may look forward to receiving your remittance in course of post.'

> Letter 2: 'We wish to remind you that we have outstanding on our books an amount of £ . . . . As this amount is overdue for payment we shall be grateful if you will let us have a cheque in settlement by return.'

Letter 3: 'When sending you a statement of your credit account with us earlier this month and also in the preceding month we asked if you favour us with a settlement payment, but we cannot trace that this has been received. We are very anxious indeed to meet your wishes about this account, but the position is that our credit policy is based upon the expectation that all accounts will be paid monthly, and we therefore respectfully request that you will send us a settlement of the account within the next few days.'

Letter 4: 'Although we have addressed a number of applications to you for payment of your overdue account, we cannot trace that you have yet made settlement. In order to avoid further difficulties arising we must ask you to be good enough to send us your payment for the full amount due. Failing receipt of such payment from you within the next few days we shall have to consider taking other steps for the collection of this debt.'

The sequence was then taken over by a dummy debt-collector:[5]

Letter 5: '____________ present their compliments and would point out that the instalment due under your Hire Purchase Agreement has not yet been received.'

Letter 6: '____________ regret that the instalment due under your Hire Purchase Agreement remains unpaid. If payment to cover this instalment in full is not received at once we shall have to take such steps as we feel to be best without further notice to you.'

Letter 7: 'We are unable to trace a reply to our previous application to you for payment of instalments due under your Hire Purchase Agreement. In order that you shall continue to enjoy unhindered the benefits of this hiring, we must ask you to make immediate payment of the amount due. Failing receipt of such payment within the next few days we shall have to consider taking other action in this matter.'

This enforcement programme clearly illuminates a number of critical aspects of the career system. First, tests are applied successively to ascertain what the most appropriate collection style should be. By Letter 4, it seems to be apparent to the creditor that the debtor must be somewhat recalcitrant. The first three letters completed one movement of the career and the fourth introduced the second movement. The idea of process is intrinsic to the sequence. Roth has argued 'long stretches of time may be made more 'psychologically manageable' by being broken up into small segments. When the markers used to divide periods of time into segments are also signposts of progress in a given direction, we have the foundation of a career timetable.'[6] When a debtor refuses to respond to three letters, he passes a marker and deserves some coercion. The 'reasonable man' would have replied: the debtor did not do so and cannot be structurally defined as reasonable.

The coercion to which he will be exposed in the second movement is unspecified; a threat is often more uncongenial if the sanction is unknown. Ambiguity is then a second feature of collection. Enforcement would be discredited if it rested on falsifiable predictions of action. Thus the threats offered by the debt-collector in Letters 7 and 8 are also vague. They hint at 'such steps as we feel to be best' and 'other action' but nothing more. Later phases of the career are likely to be similarly indefinite. Debt-collectors can be superseded by solicitors' letters and solicitors by threats emanating from the courts. No action may be taken for several months after the seventh letter, but there is an illusion continually being fostered that sanctions are in the offing.

A third feature is a perpetual alteration of the tempo and significance of the career by the introduction of changes of actor and mood. One creditor argued:

> If he's unco-operative, then, of course, you may do something more strong about it. A lot of people respond quite sharply to solicitor's letters where they don't respond to reminders and routine letters from us. You get something with a solicitor's name and address at the top stating this, that and the other in seven days, then all of a sudden find the money.

The symbolic value of names, words and tone are exploited to the full in an attempt to discover the level of anxiety which will make a debtor pay what he owes. In the main, the next stage is always depicted as the movement when action will be taken, and it usually turns out to be a means of foretelling the awfulness of the stage that is to come. This process may be elaborated to a fine degree: creditors' letters will be followed by a dummy collector; the dummy will be replaced by a real collector; the second collector by a solicitor and so on. The logic of threats prolongs and multiplies the career's movements. It is another of the chief reasons why collection *is* constituted as a career.

The Animating Assumptions of Debt-Collection

An enforcement apparatus of this kind tends to create deviants through self-fulfilling prophecies. When the apparatus is in operation, a great variety of data assumes increasingly sinister meanings. The meanings lend momentum to enforcement and the progress of enforcement colours the meanings. The autonomy of the collection system leads to the production of deviant defaulters despite a paucity of knowledge. Someone who is illiterate, perplexed or absent will be automatically treated as if he were a recalcitrant or evasive professional debtor. Many creditors recognise that there is a disparity between the reality conveyed by their process and the reality which they are trying to organise. One stated, for instance:

> My assumption is that the majority of those (transferred to specialist debt-collectors) don't start out with the intention of defrauding. They have fallen on bad times and they haven't been sufficiently well educated to discuss it to bridge the gap. It's resulted in them going in so deep, and these tougher and tougher letters coming in, they feel they can't face the collection.

Nonetheless, few organisations can respond to defaulters as if they were the inert victims of confusion. They are offered nothing but the perspectives furnished by their own enforcement system. Unless debtors negotiate, they are inevitably branded as deviant. Creditors who appreciate the existence of disparate realities receive some reassurance from the observation that each movement of the career filters out a substantial portion of debtors. The career, starting at default and ending with the courts, resembles a pyramid. Such a structure persuades the creditors that every successive stage is occupied by debtors who are less and less typical of the general population of normal, moral consumers. It is a structure which defines all the participants in enforcement. Not only are defaulters awarded a situated identity, collection agencies themselves acquire meaning from their place in the evolution of the career. Professional debt-collectors, for example, are structurally intimidating because of their appearance at a particular and late phase of enforcement. They are the culmination of all that occurred before them, and they are described by those other stages. As creatures of the machine, they have little influence over the action which they can take and the interpretations which are made of that action. They are the manufactured villains of a dramatic presentation and efforts to make a more heroic role are inevitably frustrated.

I have alluded to the creditors' master typifications of defaulters. Those typifications underpin the rationality and construction of debt-collection, and they require some analytic amplification. The Feckless, Unfortunate and Professional Debtors dominate most critical decision-making. They are bureaucratic artifacts, generated by the conventional workings of institutions which manage millions of people.

Any bureaucracy is based on a division of labour which cannot be viable unless it offers its members a coherent paradigm for interpreting and co-ordinating the tasks which they perform. The world must be made orderly and intelligible before it can be manipulated. Concerted action demands a common vocabulary so that people can co-operate in their dealings with important objects. A bureaucratic vocabulary represents a store of stock solutions to stock problems. It will reduce the recalcitrant and complex to a series of repetitive operations. The greater the scale of the bureaucratic enterprise, the greater will be the dependence upon a simplifying paradigm. In the case of debt collection, economy and speed of response combine with scale to raise the paradigm to a position of paramount importance.

One crucial facet of such vocabularies is the transformation of an uncertain world into a series of predictable occurrences. It is the business of bureaucratic rules to stabilise work material and delineate characteristic ways of managing it. No system of rules can ever be exhaustive. The structure and vocabulary of an organisation will necessarily impose a selective grid on the cases which it can handle. Only a few features of those cases will be recognised by that grid, and those features will be systematically ordered so that they become susceptible to processing. The typical bureaucratic operation is conducted on phenomena which have been made serviceable by the pre-structuring work of the grid. When an organisation has considerable control over its material, ambiguous or anomalous events are likely to be forced into a familiar cast. Such recasting is made even more likely when the organisation has little information about those phenomena and when it is structurally ill-equipped to prepare more than a few standard responses to them. In the case of debt-collection, again, the richly textured world of default is stripped down to a skeletal set of paradigmatic types.

Enforcement can be visualised as a series of action and reactions: it is a progressive interaction which mechanically builds up a composite portrait of the defaulter. It is only through this interaction that the defaulter emerges as a knowable figure. What is bureaucratically identified as a debtor is no more than what the enforcement process itself can create. Typifications of debtors are constructed out of the knowledge generated by enforcement tasks.

Enforcement work, in turn, can be described as a system of coercive probes which elicit information-bearing responses. The organisation of those probes determines the resulting image of the defaulter. By examining those probes, I shall be able to explain how the collectors' master typifications are constituted.

Most collection is mediated entirely by letters. Personal confrontation between creditor and debtor is an uncommon event. Interaction which is conducted across a wide area of social space is grounded in a form of knowledge which is qualitatively different from that available to people in face-to-face settings. There is a wealth of detail which is simply unavailable to the participants. Responses cannot be made to facial expression, body gestures and the positioning of the self in its significant environments. Language and symbolic communication acquire highly conventional and generalised forms. There is certainly little scope for complex elaborations of meaning in the letter exchanges that take place in collection. On the contrary, interaction is reduced to a few standard formulae which are incapable of conveying much information. Ideas of the other person in such mediated transactions tend to become correspondingly featureless. The other becomes relatively anonymous and unchanging. He is seen as predictable and as saturated by a few definitive characteristics. He may be readily classed as a member of a comparatively homogeneous category of people.

The mediated relations of collection are generally no more than sequences of action without reaction from the defaulter. The knowledge conveyed by the process then becomes merely that the debtor is inactive. Enforcement must proceed with no sure data about the deviant. Its stages follow upon one another in hierarchical fashion; each evoking no response. When action translates inertness as meaningful, scope is provided for an organisational solipsism which defines the debtors solely in terms of organisationally-derived understandings. The structural influence of the career is then sovereign. The defaulter is simply a phantasm of the collection machine, responsive to any procedural changes introduced in the machine, slavishly reflecting the assumptions that are automatically injected into the machine.

Collection conducted by the large commercial bureaucracies allows little opportunity for debtors to negotiate identities for themselves. Typically, the paucity of the debtors' replies prepares the ground for the exercise of a total mastery over the definition of debtors. When there is little legitimate authority or power behind debtors' reactions, the possibility of negotiation is yet further reduced.

Debt collection in England and Wales is a massive enterprise which is regulated by minute calculations of cost. It is an enterprise which is intended to respond promptly and effectively to default. None of its constituent probes can be designed to convey a properly-rounded portrait of the defaulter. The expense and time devoted to such work would militate against the smooth functioning of a cheap control system. Rather, the informational poverty that distinguishes the system imposes its mark on the typifications which are in use. Judgements must be rapid, simple and decisive. The debtor is forced through one of the career routes that have been mapped out for the limited number of cases which the system can manage.

The pre-eminent goal of collection is the restoration of money or the resumption of payments, but that goal rests on the companion task of organising an adequate interpretation of default. Enforcement is unusual because it does not simply represent an attempt to control the consequences of an accomplished act. The deviance of defaulters remains persistently problematic. Future intention is as significant as past conduct. The interpretative procedures of enforcement are thus necessarily organized around the development of default in time. The emergent qualities of default are reinforced by the nature of collection work. Debt-collectors are unwilling and unable to employ sanctions which will bring the course of a default to an abrupt conclusion. They rely instead on threat and the symbolic work performed by the changing sequence of the collection career. Their operations are also extended over time. The typifications that flow from debt-collection necessarily reflect its temporal structure.

It is plausible that these influences conjointly bring about the tripartite classification of debtors into the Feckless, the Unfortunates and the Professionals. Restricted information leads to a simplified typing of debtors as static and discrete entities. The economy and scale of collection engender a limited number of typifications. A pre-occupation with the unfinished act and intention supplies the content of typifications with qualities relating to motivation. The temporal structure of default explains both the threefold classification and the procedures which are employed to place debtors.

Extending his judgement along a temporal continuum, a collector will know whether default was made at the beginning of an agreement (a professional), in the middle (feckless) or at the end (unfortunate). He will find that some debtors always reply to his overtures and are always accessible to his representatives (unfortunate); others reply erratically and are not always available (feckless); whilst others never respond and are elusive (the professionals). The debtor might pay as soon as any pressure is applied (unfortunate); he might repay after some time (feckless); or he might never repay (professional). One group of debtors will demand almost no enforcement effort (unfortunates); another will require more sustained effort (the feckless); and another considerable effort (professionals). Some will default on small sums (unfortunates), some on larger sums (feckless) and some on sizeable sums (professional).

Fecklessness, misfortune and deceit are the inevitable concomitants of a process which is engineered to disclose a defaulter's plans about future action. They are qualities which are related to the timing of activity, and they are qualities which are unearthed by the timing of activity. The probes put out by collection are staggered over time, and the typifications they generate reflect that staggering.

These typifications are most functional to enforcement. A collection strategy must recognise that some debtors default for 'innocent' reasons and that they would be alienated by tactics that impute dishonesty to them. Other debtors are considered too insensitive to appreciate the significance of what is done to them. A third group is defined as evasive and dishonest. It is not disturbed by a creditor's attribution of deviant motives. A parsimonious typology must cater for at least these three contingencies. Failure to do so would introduce possibilities of unwanted secondary deviation, allegations of improper coercion, and excessive leniency.

Because the threefold classification has solipsistic features, and because it stems from routine collection work, the scheme is applied throughout the career. At every stage of enforcement, three types of debtor are regulated. At every stage, the unfortunates are eliminated and professional and feckless debtors will be passed on to the personnel who man the next phase. A creditor will maintain that there are no unfortunates amongst the cases which he dispatches to a debt-collector. the debt-collector, in his turn, will invariably encounter unfortunate debtors and puzzle at the incompetence of his predecessor. The unfortunate defaulter is resurrected anew with each movement. His endless rebirth might evoke very different explanations. Successive collectors could be increasingly sensitive and discriminating in their filtering work, or they could be identifying those who are progressively less unfortunate. Yet it is more plausible that the collectors' actions are always designed to have three outcomes. Each enforcement phase has a beginning, a middle and an end. Debtors are classified by the staging of their reply.

Of course, once such a system of classification becomes institutionalised, its constituents do not need constant rediscovery every time a collector undertakes enforcement. Although the validity of a system requires reinforcement through feedback, the system itself will acquire a quality of objectivity and common sense which make it highly resistant to change. The professional, unfortunate and feckless debtors will become parts of the natural world, independent of the collector's will.

I have observed that every enforcement action can have three broad outcomes. It is tied to a bounded set of reactions. Collectors claim that the sets overlap to such an extent that they can be welded together. The man who defaults as soon as he receives credit, for instance, will not reply to letters or pay unless he is under extreme duress. The professional, feckless and unfortunate debtors are compositions based on information which emerges from enforcement activity. The professional is an artful, predatory person who shuns any links with the creditor; the feckless debtor is too disorganised and irresponsible to make sensible decisions; and the unfortunate is a co-operative, guilt-ridden individual who will pay whatever he can afford. It is transparent that a creditor can never 'really' know why a debtor defaulted. His typifications are pragmatic and emergent.

This kind of labelling machinery has profound effects on enforcement. The debtor who is least known to collectors is the most eligible candidate for the role of professional defaulter. Nothing may be known about him except his passivity. Passivity can arise from many sources: the debtor might be indignant about some injustice;[7] he might be illiterate, ashamed or so intimidated that he is unable to react. All the same, the inactive debtor will be heaped with disreputable traits if enforcement continues for any length of time.

Typification, Indeterminacy and Competition

Default possesses a peculiarity which distinguishes it from many other forms of deviance. Creditors and collectors suffer from their inability to classify a debtor accurately whilst enforcement is going on. Any early classification may have to be revised or discarded because there is always the risk that behaviour which *appears* deviant is 'really' something else. That is, default involves not one, but two separate instances of rule-breaking: there is an initial refusal or inability to comply with the terms of a contract, and there is also the possibility of a final refusal to discharge the debt. The problematic nature of default resides in the difficulty of determining when a 'final' time has been achieved. Whilst most borrowers become rule-breakers in the first sense, few become deviant in the second. Any defaulter *may* repay his debt in the end and, if he does so, his actions will inevitably acquire a radically different significance from those of a permanent defaulter. A seeming professional may, in fact, be otherwise. Indeed, newspapers sometimes contain reports about anguished debtors who return sums after decades of default.

Judgements made during the enforcement process must always be provisional because the defaulter's last action or inaction will alone decide what kind of person he has been all the time. However, whilst creditors cannot suspend their judgement indefinitely, they can never be sure that a debtor's action *is* his last. The unfortunate debtor might always make one more response which will reveal him as a fraud. Similarly, the professional might unexpectedly make a payment or demonstrate his probity.

Enforcement is not the only control system which is plagued by such indeterminacy. What might be the onset of alcoholism could also be nothing more than a 'binge'. Again, what might be the first stage of a mental breakdown could also be a 'temporary depression'. But most control agents are also able to make the comfortable assumption that deviant processes have natural histories, that in time it will become clear whether a person's drinking was an isolated episode or something more sinister. Collectors cannot make that assumption because default is an inactivity which lacks its own natural history. They cannot discern neat frontiers which divide one phase from another, neither can they predict the direction which phases might take. Indeed, most changes in the debtor's condition are imposed by the collectors themselves.

Collection can be made manageable only when default is defined in a certain way. After all, enforcement would be most taxing if there was no 'natural' point at which the harassment of a seemingly intractable debtor must cease. At some point, a collector is obliged to decide that no more can or should be done. In consequence, each enforcement career has to be artificially transformed into a distinct episode with a recognisable beginning, middle and end. When the episode draws to a close, the collector will believe himself competent to perform the decisive, authoritative act of categorisation. He will then proclaim that, further evidence notwithstanding, the debtor is *really* professional, feckless or unfortunate and, furthermore, he has been so all along. The episode will then be complete.

A viable collection system must also divide its enforcement episodes into small stages, each stage being followed by its own tentative review of what has occurred. As Greig argued, 'every efficient system must provide that at a certain stage . . . a slow account shall be brought to the manager's notice so that his skill and experience may be utilised and trouble saved'.[8] Having decided that a certain period of time is critical, collectors must project themselves forward in time and imagine what the debtor's behaviour in that period has signified. They search for a theme in the debtor's known past which will make sense of what has happened. Such reviews will often be rudely contradicted by unpredicted behaviour. It would be ill-advised to take precipitate coercive action on the foundation of those reviews alone. Expensive sanctions can be implemented only when a rare state of certainty is attained.

Debt collection is accordingly shaped by the problem of deciding how force should be applied. Defaulters are not cowed deviants who are constrained to comply with agents of social control. They are more akin to contestants who can punish a collector who makes a foolish move. Moreover, a collection system with weak sanctions cannot afford to estrange debtors who might still be amenable to persuasion or restrained methods. Thus Casson states that restraint is politic even at the debt-collectors' stage:

> It is wiser to employ a . . . Collection Agency than a lawyer. . . . [Lawyers] do not use tact. They do not try to educate debtors. They use the hammer. They write war letters. They do not endeavour to protect [the] goodwill of a firm. They do not consider future business. They use threats and peremptory demands. They deal in ultimatums. Once a debtor's account goes to a Solicitor he is destroyed as a customer.[9]

It is this risk of 'destroying a debtor as a customer' (or fostering secondary deviation) that thwarts the use of coercion. When a control agency is not powerful, its few weapons are liable to be as harmful to itself as to its subjects. Debt-collection is translated into an attenuated process of game-like feints, grounded in ambiguity, postponing activity, and supplying an elaborate impression-management.

Notes

1. This chapter is based on an earlier work, *Making People Pay*, London, Routledge and Kegan Paul, 1973. Little analytic work on collection has appeared since the publication of that book. Apart from an unpublished Ph.D. dissertation by Jacqueline Bass of Michigan State University and studies of defaulters by David Caplovitz, the major exception has been J. Hesketh, *Inside the System: How an Electricity Board deals with Fuel Debtors*, Family Welfare Association, Manchester, 1978. Fortunately, Hesketh's arguments seem consistent with my own.
2. W. Shultz and H. Reinhardt, *Credit and Collection Management*, New Jersey, Prentice Hall, 1962, p.250.
3. J. Roth, *Timetables*, Indianapolis, Bobbs-Merrill, 1963, p.xviii.
4. Roth, op. cit., p.xvii.
5. The creditor's sequence pursued a credit account debt whilst the debt-collector's letters refer to a hire purchase debt. They are parts of different careers. Nevertheless, the two movements are formally similar to a continuous series.
6. Roth, op. cit., p.115.
7. c.f. D. Caplovitz, *The Poor Pay More*, New York, Free Press, 1963.
8. C. Greig, *Commercial Credits and Accounts Collection*, London, Institute of Credit Management, 1964, p.141.
9. Quoted in Greig, op. cit., p.160.

9 Property and Family Solidarity[1]

Graham Allan

This paper is concerned with analysing the importance of certain aspects of property for the structuring of family and kin relationships in present day Britain. I have written here 'certain aspects of property' deliberately, for in a short essay it is quite impossible to elucidate more than a few of the ways in which family life is influenced by property – or the lack of it. Thus I shall not dwell on the inequalities that occur between families who are located at different points in the housing and labour markets. Numerous analyses of the consequences for family members of poor housing, insecure tenure and inadequate finances exist already in the literature.[2] Similarly I shall have little to say on changes in the distribution of property and income after marital separation and family breakdown. An account of the effects of recent modifications to laws concerning women's and men's rights over their collective property warrants a separate paper. Instead my focus tends towards anthropology and is concerned primarily with the way in which command of property influences the social control that family and kin exercise over one another. The first part of the essay discusses the ownership of productive and 'symbolic' property in this light, while in the second half the ways in which income and consumption property serve to structure inter-generational and marital relationships are examined.

Anthropology's characteristic concern is with non-industrial, 'primitive' societies where in many cases kinship organisation appears to be synonymous with social and economic organisation. While like Finnegan[3] we may marvel at people's ingenuity in creating kin links where once none existed, it is clear that kinship provides the basic model for such societies in the eyes of their members. This is nowhere more so than in the case of property where the right through kinship to specifiable areas of land or political and economic activity is jealously guarded because for the younger generation it promises access to a style of life they consider desirable but cannot otherwise obtain.[4] Provided in practice if not in theory the older generation have some discretion over this inheritance, as is normally the case, they thereby ensure the subservience of the younger generation. Peasant kinship behaviour has been analysed in this way both by anthropologists[5] and increasingly by social historians.[6] Ways of selecting an appropriate wife for the eldest son, of providing dowries for daughters and of ensuring monetary compensation for younger sons so that the patrimony is protected are issues of particular interest. What these sources demonstrate is the kinship obligation that is part and parcel of inheritance in areas where small-holding is the dominant form of production.[7] Equally American historians of the family are discovering that similar processes operated amongst families in New England in the eighteenth and early nineteenth centuries.[8]

If in the main sociologists have not been so concerned with the relationship between kin behaviour and property, they have consistently emphasised the link between family membership and social class formation. While not all would agree with Daniel Bell that the 'story of the rise and fall of social classes in Western society . . . is that of the rise and fall of families'[9] every major theorist of social stratification recognises that class is a familial rather than an individual matter. That inequalities exist within families as well as between them does not alter this. In analysing the relationship between family and property though, most sociologists have, not surprisingly, concentrated specifically on those families with a great deal of wealth. They have not really examined the role that property plays in what is traditionally called the 'normal' family – that is, families without excessive amounts of property, those not included in the top 5 or 10 per cent of wealth holders. My aim is to examine the passage of different types of property within such families and explore how this passage affects other aspects of the relationships between family members.

Despite changes in the form and extent of taxation, and despite the introduction of a range of measures at least nominally designed to increase the economic well-being of the poorer sections of the population, wealth remains unequally distributed in British society. The available evidence inevitably indicates that the majority of privately owned wealth is in the hands of a small minority of the population. Thus Atkinson and Harrison estimate that 5 per cent of the population owned (approximately) 55 per cent of the wealth in the early 1970s.[10] Statistics for wealth held by families rather than individuals are difficult to estimate with any confidence, but it seems reasonable to assume that members of wealthy individuals' families are themselves more likely to be rich than poor.

Since wealth is unevenly distributed with the majority owning comparatively little private property it might be thought that property considerations do not constrain the familial and kinship behaviour of this majority to any great extent. Such an argument would of course be far too simple in that it both fails to distinguish between different types of property and ignores the relationship between a family's property and that family's position within the wider social structure. A key distinction to make here is between productive property on the one hand and what can be termed 'consumption' property on the other. By productive property I mean property that provides one or more individuals with the means of obtaining an income. Conversely consumption property is property that is owned for its own sake, for use rather than for income. Productive property can itself be divided into primary and secondary productive property, primary being property that provides an individual's chief source of income and secondary that which merely augments his or her main source.

Family Enterprises

A good deal of previous research has demonstrated how the control of primary productive property often results in an element of control over those family members who are in a position to inherit that property. In particular, where sons expect to succeed their fathers in the family business, the cost is usually that they do their fathers' will rather more than they would if no productive inheritance were involved. The classic example of this comes from Arensberg and Kimball's 1930s study of peasant farming in County Clare, where the succeeding son's dependence on his father was almost total.[11] Only when the son took over the land on his father's death or retirement did he acquire the rights of a full adult. Even though this might not happen until he was in his thirties, he had until then virtually no control over the family economy, typically receiving 'pocket money' from his father rather than a living wage and not being able to marry. Similar though less extreme forms of parental control have been found operating in other peasant economies.[12] Analagously Leyton has shown how in the Canadian firm he studied the younger generation's dependence on their elders over financial matters extends to domestic spheres as well, with control over their marriage choice being an important element.[13]

The general picture that emerges from these studies then is that productive property can lead to the older generation's control of their descendants, particularly as it relates to their kinship behaviour and their marriage strategies. However for this to happen the income from the family property needs to be sufficiently large for the younger generation to find it worthwhile to submit to the authority of the older. That is, the rewards obtainable from the parents' property have to be significant in comparison to those obtainable from other work. The greater alternative sources of income, and status, are compared to that expected from the family property, the less the younger generation will submit to parental authority and the more likely it is they will avail themselves of these alternatives.

Now prosperous businesses and peasant farming such as the cases mentioned are hardly typical of the British economy. Leaving aside the most wealthy sections of the population, where to judge by the implications of Lupton and Wilson's study similar considerations to the above apply,[14] the most common group of the population with productive property to pass on are the *petite bourgeoisie*, the proprietors of small businesses, the self-employed, the owners of small shops, etc. But precisely because most of this property is indeed '*petite*', we would not necessarily expect children to follow their parents' footsteps nor consequently to submit to their authority. This depends on the profitability of the business and the amount of work that is involved in it. The little research that has been done on the *petite bourgeoisie* supports these contentions.[15]

So with the exception of a few occupations akin to those discussed, productive property held by the family is of relatively little significance for the great majority of the British population in the second half of the twentieth century, an era dominated by large bureaucratic institutions – possibly less so than it has been at any other time in our history. Yet somewhat paradoxically this occurs at the same time as our society becomes increasingly wealthy. Even if differences between rich and poor remain large, in absolute terms we are collectively more prosperous than in any previous era. The continual raising of poverty yardsticks indicates this, even allowing for inflation. The point of relevance here is that this increase in collective wealth has occurred with, if anything, a reduction of filial obligation. It seems clear that ultimately both these phenomena are a consequence of industrialism for not only is this form of production vastly superior to previous forms but it also entails the unit of employment being the individual rather than any larger group such as the family.[16] Thus no matter how unsatisfactory Goode's data and his specific theories are, his general thrust that industrialisation results in individuals having greater freedom by making them less dependent on their kin is evidently correct.[17]

To put this argument another way round, the increased wealth that most members of our society possess is in the form of goods for consumption rather than of goods for production. Income is earned through labour partly in order to buy these goods. The goods themselves are rarely bought to supplement this income and hardly ever in order to replace the need to labour; that is, the great majority of the objects bought are bought for use rather than for any income they may generate. Indeed rather than creating value, consumption property almost inevitably loses value from the moment it is purchased. Nonetheless because they give us pleasure or make our lives easier, most of the population prefer to hold their property in the form of items such as cars, washing machines, colour televisions, etc., rather than in share capital or other forms of investment property.[18] These objects of consumption which income is generally spent on, then, are in no manner an alternative to labour for the next generation. They cannot replace the need for an income when and if they are inherited. Consequently under industrialism the great majority in each generation is dependent on its labour power for its style of life and well-being and not on property passed on by other family members. This is not to argue that the property passed on before or after death by members has no value or consequence. It is merely to point out that for the very large majority of the population family property itself does not determine the life chances of the younger generation as it is rarely held in a form or amount that makes it a feasible alternative to wage labour.

Occupational Placement and Symbolic Property

But if family property *per se* has little bearing directly on the younger generation's life chances, what does determine them? And what if any role does the family play in it? The usual answer to the former question is 'education'. A variety of disparate theorists[19] have quite correctly pointed to the importance of formal education for structuring occupational placement, which in turn is the single most significant element governing a person's material well-being. In other words, people are located in the class structure through education, and thus to some degree this takes the place that property held in earlier theories of stratification. While not appropriate in all respects, Bernstein's analogy of education being 'symbolic property' makes this point clearly enough.[20] To argue in this fashion is certainly not to claim that our stratification system is an 'open' one, for not everyone has an equal likelihood of obtaining a successful education. Nor is it to suggest that education is the only route to social mobility. The recent research reported by Goldthorpe and his colleagues demonstrates both these points.[21] Nonetheless, the available evidence does very definitely suggest that education and occupational placement are closely linked with successful education being the chief means of ensuring an advantageous position in the class structure, especially for males though increasingly for females as well.[22]

Given this, the answer to the second question posed above – what part does the family play in determining life chances? – is clear enough. Numerous research studies throughout the 1960s demonstrated how parental social class structured children's educational success. Thus different researchers have pointed to the part played here by such variables as family size, household facilities, the normative standards of peer groups and neighbourhoods, parental knowledge and encouragement, teacher orientation, the middle class bias of schools, the language code implicit in formal education, etc.[23] The full range of such factors is seen as tending to favour middle class children over working class ones, though collectively they explain less well the greater likelihood of male than female educational achievement. If the emphasis in more recent writing has been on the school being organised along ideological and cultural premises consonant with those occurring in middle class home life, it is all the while recognised that this consonance is sustained by economic advantage. It is the middle class parents' ability to provide educationally relevant experience (as well as their knowledge of what is such relevant experience) that ensures their children's continued superiority.

It can be argued then that the most important property that families pass on to their younger generation is not material property but symbolic property,[24] though this is no more available to all than material property was 150 years ago. Generally it is through the transmission of educational and cultural advantage that middle class families ensure their children continue to enjoy superior life chances and class positions. Education is a competitive exercise in which the middle class not only have far more than a head start but will continue to take all necessary steps to ensure that they do not matter what changes occur in the internal structuring of educational institutions. Their success in doing this is nowhere better demonstrated than in Goldthorpe's recent research which shows how the sons of service sector workers (professionals, higher managers and administrators) suffer virtually no lifetime downward mobility, while, allowing for structural change in the occupational market, the sons of manual workers are no more likely to achieve positions at the top of the class structure than they were a generation ago.[25] Because educational advantage is (i) transmitted through the family from one generation to the next, and (ii) closely related to ultimate class position, this symbolic property is partly analagous to productive property. There is an important difference though. As discussed earlier, the inheritance of productive property tends to ensure the continuing dependence of the younger generation on the older. This does not happen to anything like the same degree with symbolic property, notwithstanding parental contributions to higher education grants. In this sense education can be seen as an eventual liberator, not through the generation of novel ideas or new experiences, but because it ultimately provides access to employment that allows independence from family authority. Conversely where fathers wish their sons to follow them in some family enterprise, one of the most successful tactics they can adopt is to deny their sons the opportunity to achieve educational success by, say, requiring their services for work at educationally inappropriate times.[26]

Family Solidarity and Material Property

But if symbolic property is generally far more relevant than productive property in perpetuating inherited class advantage, what influence, if any, does real or material property now have on family solidarity for the majority of people? To assess this I shall first consider inter-generational kin relationships and then examine the economic basis of marital relationships. In discussing inter-generational relationships it is useful to separate *post-mortem* from *inter-vivos* inheritance as they affect family solidarity somewhat differently.

(a) Inter-generational relationships: post-mortem *inheritance*

A basic point to make about *post-mortem* inheritance is that the amount of wealth left by the majority of the population at their death is relatively small. Reliable estimates of the distribution of the value of individual estates at death are notoriously difficult to obtain.[27] Those most frequently used are the figures the Inland Revenue derives from estate returns. However, as is well known, generalising from these estimates is hazardous as numerous more or less questionable assumptions have to be made at every level. So not only do the wealthy manage their wealth so as to minimise any estate duty due, but in addition a large portion of the less wealthy never appear at all in the Inland Revenue's official statistics. An additional problem is the remarkably small amount of research available concerning inheritance *per se,* especially for the less affluent. Concern has been focused on obtaining estimates of the distribution of wealth amongst the living, and where the emphasis is on inheritance it is on the inheritance of fortunes.[28]

Given these difficulties Atkinson and Harrison have estimated that around 10 per cent of Great Britain's population had wealth amounting to £5000 or more in 1968.[29] Thus 90 per cent of the population had less than £5000 and of course the distribution of property within this 90 per cent is biased towards those with little. If using these figures to overcome the absence of published information on the less wealthy's *post-mortem* estates is somewhat dubious because of the problems of re-extrapolating data on the wealth held by the living at a given point of time to the amount left by individuals at the time of their death, they nonetheless suggest quite clearly that the majority of the population have relatively few resources to leave to others at their deaths. Given that this property is frequently divided among various inheritors, most people can only expect to inherit rather small 'fortunes'. Moreover these 'fortunes' in most cases will not be in the form of capital assets but rather in goods of consumption for, as discussed earlier, this is how the majority of the population dispose of their income. The obvious exception here is houses wholly owned by the deceased. With the proportion of owner-occupied dwellings doubling from 25 to over 50 per cent in the thirty years since 1947 this will become an increasingly important exception as the present generation of owner-occupiers dies.[30] Apart from this, though, the property transmitted on death by the majority of people has limited value, being largely the value of second-hand consumption property.

The argument here then is that while kin generally inherit property the value of any potential *post-mortem* inheritance is, for most people, not sufficiently large to affect the character of the relationships between the testator and the beneficiary. The latter are not dependent on it in that their position in the social structure is not likely to be altered radically by receiving it. Such inheritance may well make life more pleasant in the sense it will allow various consumer goods to be purchased somewhat before they would have been otherwise, but it is not going to alter people's life chances in any fundamental way. The amounts involved are too small for this.

Certain demographic and social factors reinforce this contention assuming as seems reasonable, that the bulk of the inheritance goes to immediate descendants.[31] First, life expectancy has risen at the same time as the age of parents at the time of their last child's birth has fallen. Consequently when parents die and pass on their wealth to their children, these children are likely to be well established in their own social position. Add to this the fact that middle class parents rarely produce working class offspring, then it is evident that those leaving the most are likely to leave it to those already possessing a lot comparatively, the more so given the middle class career cycle. Equally those parents leaving little will not be altering anyone's life dramatically, though again what they do leave may prove useful as those receiving it are more likely to have relatively little.

Although *post-mortem* inheritance is unlikely to alter most people's life-style, its distribution is an expression of existing kinship solidarities. Knowledge of this distribution could therefore provide most useful data on kinship relationships, especially in cases where no will exists and the division of the inheritance is the result of a process of negotiation undertaken by the deceased's kin group.[32] Unfortunately virtually no information exists on this topic, particularly for those who leave relatively little. Occasionally *post-mortem* inheritance can itself alter the nature of surviving kin relationships as a consequence of resentment about the distribution of the property left. Indeed such resentment is the more likely where the inheritance is in the form of consumption goods as it is often harder to agree on their true value. If the property is to be shared by a number of beneficiaries, conflict is the more likely as the goods cannot be divided in an obviously proportional manner as can capital or even land. However, the extent to which ill-feeling occurs should not be over-emphasised. Firth, Hubert and Forge, who in their study of middle class kinship provide the most thorough data on this,[33] only uncovered twenty examples of such conflict amongst the kin of the sixty-six couples they interviewed about this topic. This accounts for somewhat less than one-fifth of the total number of kinship conflicts reported to them. The extent to which such conflict was manifested also varied with the majority involving private resentment rather than open quarrelling. A complete breakdown of kin relationships only occurred in some six of their cases, mainly as a result either of one sibling receiving a disproportionate share of a parent's property or of a second marriage complicating the inheritance. Even in those more common instances where conflicts over inheritance are not manifested overtly, the resentment generated can still colour the ensuing relationships and discourage social contact both between those directly involved and between their families. It may indeed be that such ill-feeling shapes kin relationships more frequently than Firth and his colleagues were able to demonstrate as their respondents would not always have known of unexpressed resentment between their kin.

(b) Inter-generational relationships: inter-vivos *inheritance*

Overall it seems unlikely that for the majority of the population inter-generational kinship control and solidarity is influenced to any great extent by *post-mortem* inheritance, apart from occasional instances of inherited productive property. However, there is evidence to suggest that this is less the case with *inter-vivos* inheritance, that is gifts between still living relatives. Admittedly evaluating the value of such gifts suffers from a similar problem to that found with *post-mortem* inheritance in that there is little reliable information available about these gifts. Official statistics derived from the capital transfer tax will provide an indication of major *inter-vivos* inheritance, but as donors making gifts of less than £2000 are not required to declare them these returns will not be useful for calculating the value of the less grand material aid that appears typically to flow from one generation to the next during the elder's lifetime. Instead we have to rely on somewhat indirect evidence from small scale surveys such as those by Colin Bell and Diana Barker.[34] The prime value of these studies is that they illustrate the underlying sociological significance of the transfers of even relatively small amounts of property for kinship solidarity.

Colin Bell sought to complement previous British kinship studies by examining the kin relationships of inhabitants of a middle class housing estate. His most interesting conclusions concerned the passage of material gifts from one generation to the next amongst occupationally stable middle class families. While these respondents were somewhat reticent in acknowledging the help they themselves had received, their accounts made it evident that middle class parents routinely give their adult children significant amounts of aid in kind or cash throughout the latter's early married life.[35] As Bell notes, a lot of this aid is dressed up as gifts for grandchildren, but however it is presented it functions to increase the standard of living of the younger generation by releasing funds for consumer goods they could not otherwise afford. The younger generation's life-style is of course not completely dependent on such aid, but as with *post-mortem* inheritance their life is made the more pleasant through receiving it. A structural feature of this type of transfer is that it benefits the receiver relatively more than it costs the donor. Because of the standard middle class family and career pattern, the parents' income is likely to be at its highest and their family and housing commitments at their lowest at exactly that period in which their adult children are most in need of assistance.[36]

Bell emphasises the way that such gifts function to ensure the maintenance of class advantage for the socially immobile middle class. For our purposes though they can be seen to have a further significance, one suggested most clearly in Barker's essay.[37] Barker was interested in the reason why comparatively few young people in a provincial town left the settled domestic world of their parental home before they married. Part of the reason was that the economic bargain to be had at home was far better than that obtainable on the open market. The 'rent' demanded by parents was far less than the real costs of housing and the varied domestic services they provided. The young people themselves clearly recognised this and uniformly spoke of their parents' generosity over and above that which they could rightfully expect. The question this raises though is why the parents are prepared to 'spoil' their children in this way. Why are they more generous than normative standards, if not common practice, require? Barker suggests that the answer lies in the parents', and particularly the mother's, desire to remain involved in their children's lives after they marry and have children of their own. By generously providing their children with a place to live and with a full range of domestic services for a rent which is recognised to be nominal rather than economic, the parents attempt to prolong their children's dependence and thereby maintain their own position of authority. Most pertinently, in the process 'material goods and physical services are translated into lasting relationships', at that very time when the elementary family is most prone to disruption.[38]

Returning now to the general theme of the transfer of material property by the older generation to the younger, it can be recognised that whenever these go beyond the prescribed boundaries a similar process occurs. Generosity results in obligation. Thus given the normative emphasis on independence the regular material support which Bell found middle class parents provided for their children's family, either directly or indirectly through gifts to grandchildren, serves not only to enhance the latter's purchasing power but also helps ensure that these kin relationships are maintained. All such *inter-vivos* gifts, no matter what their actual value, function in the same way, playing their part in structuring kinship solidarity.[39] They help stretch the younger generation's scarce resources, thereby creating obligations which help sustain the relationships.

In later stages of the life cycle the position tends to be reversed with adult children providing services to elderly parents. These services differ in important respects though from the aid discussed above. Firstly the services tend to entail contact and domestic assistance rather more than financial aid, and are consequently seen as social in nature rather than economic even though they may contain an economic element.[40] The elderly in particular have an interest in ensuring that this image of the relationship pertains, and that they remain financially independent as far as possible, as dependence for them would represent an unwelcome role reversal rather than the limited continuation of an existing pattern as is the case when at an earlier stage in the life cycle their children received aid from them. In addition of course parents whose adult children are able to give them a significant amount of financial aid are themselves more likely to be the beneficiaries of inflation-proofed private pensions and thus have little need for such aid. Secondly, the normative pressures surrounding the giving of aid at the two stages of the life cycle are rather different. Whereas parents are thought to be generous in assisting their supposedly independent children, it is taken to be more the responsibility and obligation of children to care for their elderly parents. The former is over and above normal requirements, the latter is only right and proper. Indeed it is the failure of children to look after their parents that is seen to warrant public attention and not their regular and routine provision of services, no matter how extensive these are. Consequently while parents will certainly feel obligated to their children for any help they receive and seek to repay it by whatever means they can, the giving of this aid is sociologically speaking better viewed as a consequence of filial responsibility generated at earlier stages in the life cycle than as an attempt to create or maintain fresh obligation.

(c) Marital relationships

Some have argued that the giving of gifts within marriage helps to maintain cohesion and solidarity in what is essentially an unequal relationship. For example, Bell and Newby suggest the giving of gifts by husbands in family rituals helps manage the tensions existing between 'identification' and 'differentiation', the constituent elements of the 'deferential dialectic' they identify in marriage.[41] For Bell and Newby, the asymetrical exchange of gifts within marriage 'celebrate(s), symbolise(s) and reaffirm(s) the deferential dialectic. Gifts are therefore in effect a means of social control, analogous to charity or patronage.'[42] While these authors can be criticised for placing too much weight on mere tokens or symbols, especially as one suspects relatively few husbands actually bring home the flowers – they are quite clearly correct in emphasising a point Engels made some hundred years ago,[43] and which the women's movement has brought to the fore again. This is that any understanding of the marriage bond must incorporate an analysis of its material basis, for marriage, be it termed bourgeois or otherwise, inevitably reflects the economic and occupational 'realities' of the wider society. It is the male's control of property in the form of income through his privileged position within the occupational structure, together with the conventional assumption this fosters about the proclivity of females for care of home and children, that results in the inferiority of wives within marriage. As Lee aptly notes: 'the analysis of woman's work is . . . the clue to the mysteries of family life and not *vice-versa*'.[44]

Within the home women's work is that of housewife and mother; this as far as most people are concerned is her prime responsibility. Earning the resources to enable her to do this is men's responsibility. The evident functional coherence of these stereotypes mystifies the process of subordination inherent in them. While the various consumption goods within the home are taken to be common property, income through 'productive' work is not to the same degree. Rather it is seen as being more the property of the individual worker who earns it. The use this income earner makes of unpaid labour for the provision of domestic services tends to be quietly neglected. Under capitalism, if not industrialism generally, the housewife's part of the wage is invisible: her work is not directly paid for and thus appears to play no part in the generation of the family's income.

This image of the value of different types of labour pervades family life and, as various writers have suggested, helps ensure the dominant position of the husband, the main breadwinner.[45] His work is real work, he is the one earning the money through his efforts, so he is the one who has the right to control it, to make the larger decisions and to keep the major part of any excess after necessities are paid for. Because the wage is seen as the property of the wage earner, the unpaid domestic worker also comes to be seen as dependent on the property owner rather than entitled to an income in her own right. Interestingly Hunt's research suggests that the breadwinner's control of finances does not appear to be greatly affected by the specific manner in which the income is divided.[46]

If housewives' subordinate position within marriage is partly a consequence of income being seen as the property of the individual worker who shares it as necessary with his family, how is this altered when the wife is also 'productively' employed? Surely those seven million married women who work for an income[47] are in a position to ensure a better bargain. Undoubtedly this is so in that wives equally regard the money they earn as their own to control. However it is well recognised that collectively women are in an inferior market position with few being able to match their husband's earnings. The assumptions made by employers, husbands and the wives themselves about female domestic responsibilities are ultimately self-fulfilling. Low pay and poor opportunities are justified by the fact that married women workers are not normally the main breadwinners. Because their primary responsibility is that of homemaker, the income they obtain is seen as supplementary rather than alternative to that earned by their husbands, a point underlined by the frequent claim that married women work as much for companionship as material gain.[48] In the face of these unequal employment opportunities, it is difficult to challenge the apparently natural organisation of domestic responsibilities. The Catch 22 is thus complete for without such a challenge women will retain the main responsibility for homemaking and men that for earning an income, even though both might be employed for equal hours outside the home. As the main income earner's income is generally thought of by both as more his than hers, he will be the one with the greater control of expenditure planning and the greater freedom to use his 'free time' as he wishes. If his wife works outside the home, he may well assist her more frequently than otherwise in domestic and family labour, if only by undertaking the more creative and enjoyable tasks,[49] but ultimate responsibility in these spheres is hers. This is nowhere more evident than in leisure activities. Far more than for their spouses, weekends are times for husbands to relax and recuperate from the demands of the working 'week'. Similarly should he want to go out he can normally assume his wife will care for their dependent children; she can less frequently make the same assumption, instead having to seek his co-operation.[50] In such mundane ways the male's greater control of income as property fosters his wife's position of dependence.

Given this, it seems likely that where the husband does not provide more for the wife than she can obtain without him, she will be less willing to accept this dependence. If other factors were equal we would consequently expect a greater likelihood of marital disruption the more limited the husband's financial opportunities and resources are.

This assumes however that the exchange content identified above is both the only one operating within marriage and that wives are fully aware of its basis, and clearly neither of these assumptions is entirely tenable. On the other hand, studies of 'cultures of poverty' do suggest that matri-focal family organisation is more prevalent when males are chronically unable to provide regular financial support.[51] Such a form of familial organisation can paradoxically be encouraged by the state when, as in the cohabitation rule, it provides social security to females on condition they lead celibate or promiscuous lives. To take this argument any further though and, say, to try to link male property with statistics for divorce would be foolhardy. The determinants of divorce rates are far more complex than this, with the amount of divorce and the groups having access to it depending on legal provision more than anything else. In this country legal changes have formally improved the prospects of females acquiring property from the marriage, especially with respect to household tenure, but in practice the fundamental constraint is that a single male wage is not normally able to support two families. So while in some ways divorce may result in greater female independence, it is not achieved through any reduction in the male's control of income as property. Rather as very few women benefit financially from divorce, it is the independence of a relative poverty.

Conclusion

To conclude, the aim of this paper was to examine the extent to which different types of property influenced the solidarity evidenced and the control exerted in what can be rather imprecisely termed ordinary family life in this country. It is commonly accepted that considerations of property are not as central to these relationships as they are to kin relationships in non-industrial societies, but this does not mean that property plays no part at all in structuring familial and kin bonds, even granted the claim that the family is no longer a major institution of economic production. Indeed this was my starting point. If it was in fact the case in previous times that the ownership and non-ownership of inherited productive property was the key to the individual's location within the class structure, this is no longer so in any direct sense. Instead material advantage works its effect through symbolic property, that is the ownership of educational and cultural 'capital'. It is through this more than anything else that class position is determined, and it is consequently this type of property which is the most valuable inheritance most families can pass on to their younger generation. Sociologically the most interesting feature of such inheritance is that it grants the latter rather more freedom from their elders than does inheritance of productive property. It does not constrain them nor place them in obligation in the way that receiving material property potentially can.

This pertains to the second major theme of this paper which is that while *inter-vivos* and *post-mortem* gifts are unlikely to alter people's style of life fundamentally, *inter-vivos* transfers especially function to ensure solidarity amongst some categories of kin. Certainly this seems to be the case between parents and their adult children where the giving of gifts helps ensure the continuation of a relationship undergoing gradual metamorphosis from dependence to autonomy. Far more importantly, male domination within marriage is directly related to the male's greater control of income. As his work normally results in by far the larger portion of the household's economic resources, his wage is seen as his property to a degree that ensures his wife's dependence. The role of domestic labour in producing this wage is unrecognised, so that it appears that the worker alone earns it. This ensures he receives continuing deference from his dependants and in particular provides the grounds by which an unequal division of labour within the home is conventionally justified.[52] Nowhere is the potential for property considerations influencing normal family life more evident than in this sphere.

Notes

1. I read a version of this paper in a seminar at the Department of Sociology and Anthropology, University College, Swansea. I would like to thank the participants there as well as John Hall and Peter Hollowell for their many helpful comments.
2. A good deal of data on these topics have been published by the Child Poverty Action Group and by Shelter. See also K. Coates and R. Silburn, *Poverty: The Forgotten Englishman,* Harmondsworth, Penguin, 1970 and A. L. Schorr, *Slums and Social Insecurity,* London, Nelson, 1964.
3. R. Finnegan, 'The Kinship Ascription of Primitive Societies: Actuality or Myth?', *International Journal of Comparative Sociology* **11**, 1970, pp.171–94.
4. As Goody notes, those outside such societies often fail to realise the extent to which possession of land provides forms of security in non-industrial cultures. He writes: 'It is not easy for individuals in advanced industrial economies to understand the importance of such security in other societies and other sectors when only 10 per cent of the population are engaged in primary production . . . when they are cushioned against the uncertainty of food quest by national institutions, and when the ownership of the means of primary production does not have the same significance as in pre-industrial societies.' J. Goody, 'Strategies of Heirship', *Comparative Studies in Society and History,* **15**, 1973, pp.3–20.
5. J. K. Campbell, *Honour, Family and Patronage,* Oxford, Clarendon Press, 1964; M. E. Kenna, 'Houses, Fields and Graves: Property and Ritual Obligation on a Greek Island', *Ethnology,* **XV**, 1976, pp.21–34; and J. G. Peristiany (ed.), *Mediterranean Family Structures,* Cambridge,

Cambridge University Press, 1976.
6. J. Goody, J. Thirsk and E. P. Thompson (eds.), *Family and Inheritance,* Cambridge, Cambridge University Press, 1976.
7. A story Bourdieu relates illustrates in an amusing fashion the harsh realities operating here. When an inheriting son told his father of his love for a penniless girl, his father replied: 'So you want to get married? I have paid for (three of your sisters), now you must bring in the money for the other two. A wife isn't made for being put in the china cupboard. . . . This one has nothing: what is she going to bring? What she has between her legs?' Needless to say the heir married, unhappily as it turned out, another girl, one with a dowry of 5000 francs. P. Bourdieu, 'Marriage Strategies as Strategies of Social Reproduction', in R. Forster and P. Ranum, *Family and Society,* Baltimore, Johns Hopkins University Press, 1976.
8. T. K. Hareven (ed.), *Family and Kin in Urban Communities 1700–1930,* New York, New Viewpoints, 1977.
9. D. Bell, *The End of Ideology,* New York, Collier, 1962, p.39.
10. A. B. Atkinson and A. J. Harrison, *Distribution of Personal Wealth in Britain,* Cambridge, Cambridge University Press, 1978.
11. C. Arensberg and S. T. Kimball, *Family and Community in Ireland,* London, Peter Smith, 1940.
12. Cambell, op.cit., J. W. Cole, 'Inheritance Processes and their Social Consequences', *Sociologia* (Roma), **4**, 1970, pp.133–46; and Peristiany, op.cit.
13. E. Leyton, 'Composite Descent Groups in Canada', in C. C. Harris, *Readings in Kinship in Urban Society*, Oxford, Pergamon, 1970, pp.179–86.
14. T. Lupton and C. S. Wilson, 'The Social Background and Connections of "Top Decision Makers"', in J. Urry and J. Wakeford, (eds.), *Power in Britain,* London, Heinemann, 1973, pp.185–204.
15. See, for example, F. Bechhofer, B. Elliott and M. Rushforth, 'The Market Situation of Small Shopkeepers', *Scottish Journal of Political Economy,* **18**, (1971), pp.161–80; F. Bechhofer, B. Elliott, M. Rushforth and R. Bland, 'Small Shopkeepers: Matters of Money and Meaning', *Sociological Review,* **22**, 1974, pp. 465–82.
16. As Kelly notes: 'Occupations can only rarely be purchased and sons cannot inherit their fathers' jobs in government and the large, bureaucratic organisations that dominate the economy,' J. Kelley, 'Wealth and Family Background in the Occupational Career', *British Journal of Sociology,* **29**, 1978, pp.94–109. Quote from p.97.
17. W. J. Goode, *World Revolution and Family Patterns,* New York, Free Press, 1963.
18. For an indication of this see *Social Trends,* **1**, 1970, Tables 39, 42 and 43; **9**, 1979, Table 7.6.
19. For example, R. Dahrendorf, *Class and Class Conflict in Industrial Society,* Stanford, University Press, 1959; F. Parkin, *Class Inequality and Political Order,* London, Paladin, 1972; and J. Westergaard and H. Resler, *Class in a Capitalist Society,* Harmandsworth, Penguin, 1976.
20. B. Bernstein, *Class, Codes and Control,* vol. 3, London, Routledge and Kegan Paul, 1975, Chapter 6.

21. J. Goldthorpe and C. Llewellyn, 'Class Mobility in Modern Britain: Three Theses Examined', *Sociology,* **11**, 1977, pp.257–87; and J. Goldthorpe, C. Payne and C. Llewellyn, 'Trends in Class Mobility', *Sociology,* **12**, 1978, pp.441–68.
22. While the overall connection between education and occupational placement is clear, a good deal of research remains to be done on the specific mechanisms of the occupational market, including the process of transition from school to work. As Sofer points out, there are relatively few studies of these issues which are genuinely sociological in orientation. The majority concern themselves primarily with individual choice and preference paying little heed to structural constraints on occupational opportunities. C. Sofer, 'Introduction', in W. M. Williams, *Occupational Choice*, London, Allen and Unwin, 1974, pp.13–57. An exception is K. Roberts, 'The Entry into Employment', *Sociological Review,* **16**, 1968, pp.165–84. A rather different book is P. Willis, *Learning to Labour*, London, Saxon House, 1977.
23. For a summary of the evidence see A. Little and J. Westergaard, 'The Trend of Class Differentials in Educational Opportunity in England and Wales', *British Journal of Sociology,* **15**, 1964, pp.301–16 and W. Tyler, *The Sociology of Educational Inequality*, London, Methuen, 1977.
24. The distinction between symbolic and material property has similarities with that made by Bernard and Renaud between inclusive and exclusive goods. See Kelley, op.cit.
25. The emphasis on lifetime mobility here is important as the advantages of symbolic property appear to operate throughout the individual's career and not just at first occupational placement. See Goldthorpe and Llewellyn, op.cit.; D. J. Treiman and K. Terrell, 'The Process of Status Attainment in the United States and Great Britain', *American Journal of Sociology,* **81**, 1975, pp.563–83; Kelley, op.cit.
26. On the other hand in some cases younger sons' inheritance is provided in the form of resources spent on education and occupational training. In such cases education is valued as a means of maintaining the integrity and viability of the family's agricultural holding. See, for example, E. Friedl, *Vasilika: A Village in Modern Greece,* New York, Holt, Rinehart and Winston, 1962.
27. See A. B. Atkinson, *The Economics of Inequality,* Cambridge, Cambridge University Press, 1975, for a discussion of the problems.
28. See, for example, C. D. Harbury, 'Inheritance and the Distribution of Personal Wealth in Britain', *Economic Journal,* **72**, 1962, pp.845–68; C. D. Harbury and P. C. McMahon, 'Inheritance and the Characteristics of Top Wealth Leavers in Britain', *Economic Journal,* **83**, 1973, pp.810–33; E. G. Horsman, 'Inheritance in England and Wales: The Evidence Provided by Wills', *Oxford Economic Papers,* **30**, 1978, pp.409–22.
29. Atkinson and Harrison, op.cit., p.108.
30. See A. Murie, P. Niner and C. Watson, *Housing Policy and the Housing System,* London, Allen and Unwin, 1976 and A. Murie and R. Forrest, 'Wealth, Inheritance and Housing Policy', *Policy and Politics,* **8,** 1980.
31. Horsman's evidence certainly suggests this in the case with the rich.
32. This point was suggested to me by Professor W. M. Williams who used wills as data in his study of farming in Devon. See W. M. Williams, *A West Country Village: Ashworthy*, London, Routledge and Kegan Paul, 1963.

33. R. Firth, J. Hubert and A. Forge, *Families and their Relatives,* London, Routledge and Kegan Paul, 1970.
34. C. Bell, *Middle Class Families,* London, Routledge and Kegan Paul, 1968; D. Barker, 'Young People and Their Homes: Spoiling and "Keeping Close" in a South Wales Town', *Sociological Review,* **20**, 1972, pp.569–90.
35. Research in the United States has produced similar findings. For a summary of this material, see M. B. Sussman, 'Relationships of Adult Children with their Parents in the United States', in E. Shanas and G. F. Streib, *Social Structure and the Family,* Englewood Cliffs, NJ, Prentice-Hall, 1965.
36. See Brian Easton, 'The Economic Life Cycle of the Modern New Zealand Family', *Australian and New Zealand Journal of Sociology,* **13**, 1977, pp.85–9.
37. Barker, op.cit.
38. Ibid., p.585.
39. This of course is not the only factor to structure kinship solidarity. See G. Allan, 'Sibling Solidarity', *Journal of Marriage and the Family,* **39**, 1977, pp.177–84; G. Allan, *A Sociology of Friendship and Kinship,* London, Allen and Unwin, 1979.
40. See Shanas and Streib, op.cit.; H. Z. Lopata, 'Contributions of Extended Families to the Support Systems of Metropolitan Area Widows', *Journal of Marriage and the Family,* **40,** 1978, pp.355–64.
41. C. Bell and H. Newby, 'Husbands and Wives: the Dynamics of the Deferential Dialectics', in D. L. Barker and S. Allen, *Dependence and Exploitation in Work and Marriage,* London, Longman, 1976.
42. Ibid., p.162.
43. F. Engels, *The Origin of the Family, Private Property and the State,* New York, Pathfinder Press, 1972.
44. D. Lee, review of A. Oakley's *The Sociology of Housework, Sociology* **9**, 1975, pp.518–22.
45. A. Oakley, *The Sociology of Housework,* London, Martin Robertson, 1974; W. Seccombe, 'The Housewife and her Labour under Capitalism', *New Left Review,* **83,** 1974, pp.3–24; and P. Hunt, 'Cash Transactions and Household Tasks', *Sociological Review,* **26**, 1978, pp.555–71.
46. Hunt, op.cit., p.558.
47. *Social Trends,* HMSO, 1979, p.84.
48. H. Land, 'The Myth of the Male Bread Winner', *New Society,* **29**, no. 2, 1975, pp.71–3; H. Land, 'Who Cares for the Family?', *Journal of Social Policy,* **7**, 1978, pp.257–84.
49. C. C. Harris, 'Changing Conceptions of the Relation between Family and Societal Form in Western Society', in R. Scase (ed.), *Industrial Society: Class, Cleavage and Control,* London, Allen and Unwin, 1977.
50. Hunt, op.cit.
51. E.g. R. T. Smith, *The Negro Family in British Guiana,* London, Routledge and Kegan Paul, 1956; O. Lewis, *The Children of Sanchez,* Harmondsworth, Penguin, 1964; and E. Liebow, *Tally's Corner*, Boston, Little Brown, 1967.
52. A. Kuhn and A. Wolpe, *Feminism and Materialism,* London, Routledge and Kegan Paul, 1978.

10 Career: The Claim to Job Property

Peter G. Hollowell

Work as Property – Theory and Evidence

Labour and property have long been associated in political and social theory. For John Locke, people have property in their own person and create property by mixing their labour with the things nature provides. The Marxist tradition certainly implies a strong similarity between the two institutional spheres of work and property, in its basic proposition that industrial capital is expropriated surplus value, that is encapsulated labour.[1] Work and property are thus fundamentally similar in that they are transformations of each other. Property is objectified work activity and work is potential or future property.

In more practical spheres, the idea that work is in itself a property is identifiable empirically. Various practices indicating the ownership of work could be identified in medieval industry and agriculture.[2] In the nineteenth century it was also possible to locate sentiments of jobs as property. Asa Briggs cites an 1832 publication advocating legal protection for labour since as it cannot be long withheld from the market it is 'the most defenceless of every kind of property and that which needs protection'. An instructive passage, also cited by Briggs, from a union rule book of 1869 states that

> The trade by which we live is our property, bought by certain years of servitude, which gives us a vested right, and we have an exlusive claim on it, as all will have hereafter who purchase it by the same means.[3]

Closer to our own time the significance of job property has been recognised by students of industrial relations. It is said to be important not only for issues of redundancy, but also for job evaluation, labour flexibility, effort bargaining, and the institutions of workplace bargaining. The idea of job property is put forward as a crucial one for the understanding of much of contemporary collective bargaining in the motor industry, and in other industries with similar conditions.[4] Generally many public employments, particularly the civil service and professional occupations, have the practice of 'establishing' positions, giving tenure for life. Enacted laws in Britain, such as the Contracts of Employment Act 1963, the Redundancy Payments Act 1965, and the

Employment Protection Act 1975, provide a legal basis for compensation for the loss of a job.

There is a good deal of theoretical argument, as well as empirical evidence both historical and contemporary,[5] on the view of work as property. Here the purpose is to examine a particular work situation to test the idea in some detail. In fact the occupation of printer has been assessed from the perspective of job property theory.[6] Porter's detailed case study of the International Typographical Union, based on official records, deals with two aspects of the retention of valuable work activity, namely union 'priority' rules, and union controls, giving job security. The printers' 'priority' norm had control in the three areas of hiring, promotion, and discharge of labour. Numerous agencies and institutional instruments were used by the printers to reinforce the principle of priority and to transform it into practical effort.[7]

Retention, confirmed in the case of printers, is only one aspect of job property, indeed only one aspect of appropriation. A system of appropriation will minimally feature the characteristics of acquisition, retention, and appurtenances. Railway locomotivemen are convenient empirical material to assess a second element in appropriation, namely acquisition. They are in a highly structured work situation over a long period. In particular, it is the career of the locomotiveman, a readily discernable and deeply institutionalised feature of railway life, which is most useful here.

Career: Railway Reality and Analytic Tool

Career is the major 'taken for granted' structure in the steam locomotiveman's occupational existence, and perhaps even in his total life orientation and behaviour in his work environment, a boundary for his social action constantly reinforcing his image of his identity. Considered as an abstract entity, career is not something frequently spoken of by locomotivemen. It is generally mentioned in overt terms only in respect of particular aspects, such as turning points or other critical phases. In spite of this, career is always pre-eminent in the locomotiveman's mental life. Not only does the motion of career exist in the consciousness of every individual locomotiveman, it is also clearly demonstrable in the ethos and culture of the railway industry.

Visible material artifacts relating to career, for example seniority records and proceedures, were to be found easily at the locomotive depot. As an institutional structure, career, represented by the seniority principle, was contained in a web of sub-institutional structures – job allocation between links, rules and customs about locomotivemen's 'booked work', and proceedures for relocating 'foreign' locomotivemen from other depots, which have either closed down or lost a significant amount of work. Additionally, though career is a recognisable entity in itself in the culture of locomotivemen, its existence is surrounded by highly crystallised ideational and belief systems. A notable example of this appendage to career are the patterns of belief concerning the correct privileges for a man in a particular career position.

Career has received enough attention from sociologists for it to be available as a useful analytic tool to test this aspect of the work as property hypothesis. There is enough consensus on concept components to assess the locomotiveman's career as a system of appropriation of valuable work activity. As a concept, career focuses on the dynamic. A major issue is whether the movement involved is change in a definite direction, or just simply movement. What is generally thought of as career is a discernible progression toward some more highly valuable goal. The idea has considerable status and prestige implications which reduces its applicability to a minority of life-work-spans. For the majority there is either little mobility[8] or simply movement between jobs of the same standing. The element of progress is necessary in the case of railway locomotivemen since the interest is in movement to the attainment of more and more valuable job activity.

A distinction between subjective and objective elements is basic to the career concept. Objective features of the life-work-span are generally those institutionalised elements of social structure external to the individual. These predominantly refer to the career pattern or structure, the regular stages or sequence of movement through both formally established and informal positions involving different job activities. The subjective aspect is the individual's view of himself relative to the objective elements. It is his conception of where he is now, where he ought to be, and where he is going in his work-life. Perception, of the promotion system, the value and social standing of various types of work activity, of time-scales, and of derived benefits, would all be important aspects of the subjective scale.

Property Elements in the Steam Locomotiveman's Career

The analysis makes the distinction between objective and subjective property features in the railway locomotiveman's career. Major objective features of interest are job activities, career structure, and time durations. The main subjective aspect of concern is the perception of the sequence of movement in the career structure.

Objective property elements

(i) Job activity and work organisation The job property argument requires a demonstration of differentiated activities representing the things in which the rights of property obtain. Throughout their

career, footplatemen engage in jobs with sufficiently distinctive activities to produce a well-defined status structure. These activities are thoroughly visible both before and during the actual driving part of the career.

The most humble job in the footplate grade was that of cleaner. Although frequently dirty and unpleasant, cleaning locomotives was a recognised task using specific, if elementary, implements. The swabs, cotton waste, and oil indicate a definite, albeit lowly, task, whereas the general labourer's work is much less well-defined. The fact that cleaning is organised in such a way as to give the individual an area of responsible duty means he also has a certain autonomy. Furthermore there is a correct method of cleaning locomotives, involving simple but clearly facilitating rules. Even by themselves, these aspects produce a definable specialism capable of being assessed in constellation as a property object.

The fireman's activities were a more complex job property than those of the cleaner. Unlike cleaners, who operated in squads, the fireman was alone with the driver to whom he was directly responsible for numerous operations. Putting coal into the firebox evenly and at the required intervals; monitoring the water levels in the central task of maintaining the correct steam pressure; manipulating or inspecting one or other of some fourteen levers, gauges, and valves, which were his direct responsibility; watching for signals on route, and keeping the footplate tidy were all constant activities.

Although he used only basic tools, a shovel and a hammer, the fireman was in a real sense, the essential second operator of a complex machine. His individual knowledge of job activities was more vital than in the case of the cleaner, while his discretion and responsibility were more individual. The fireman had to demonstrate a day-to-day proficiency in his tasks if he were to obtain experience in driving, the most sought after job activity for locomotivemen.

Three basic characteristics of the steam locomotive driver's activity lend support to the job property idea. The job activity itself was distinctive and had highly visible consequences. Drivers could constantly demand the services of another person, the fireman, in a very direct way. Lastly, the differences between jobs created objective categories for the demonstration of the values of different job activities.

Locomotive drivers had a considerable number of tasks to perform by themselves. Driving involved the continuous regulation of the speed of the locomotive with all the technical procedures this necessitated. As well as mechanical and other technical aspects of the locomotive itself, the driver had to meet organisational rules for running the train. The particular areas of knowledge and responsibility were explicit in a formal examination system. In general the driver's job situation was one requiring manipulative skill with the machine he controlled in order to effect an efficient working of the train.

Being in a dominant position over another worker may be a reward in itself to many drivers. It gives prestige in the eyes of others and also reminds the driver himself of his achievement. Additionally a sound fireman may bring relief from the pressure of some job activities if reliable delegation could be developed. This is an important factor as, although the driver had a clean job relative to the fireman, he had the burden and strain of having to pay constant attention to the route.

The numerous types of driving activity are sufficiently distinctive to give possibility of a generally recognised set of preferences in driving jobs. The readily identifiable varieties of driving job which can be discussed for this purpose are 'preparation', 'disposing', 'pilot', short and long distance freight, local passenger, and two types of long distance passenger job, express steam with some stops and express electric with no stops.

Preparation involves both driver and fireman going through a systematic programme, lasting about three-quarters of an hour to ensure that the locomotive is fit for its next job. Sometimes a turn of duty consisted only of preparation work but many turns involved the driver and fireman preparing the locomotive they themselves were to drive. Disposing is the most dirty and physically arduous of all 'driving' activities involving refilling the coal tender, cleaning the fire and the ashpan, and emptying the smokebox. Checks are made for defects which are noted on a 'repair' card and the locomotive is then driven away and 'stabled'. The pilot's job is mainly to assemble and break up groups of wagons by shunting in order to create trains. This job can be arduous and dangerous for both fireman and driver as there is continual change of situation and personnel.

Short distance freight work ('trips') usually involved the driver and fireman assembling the train in a siding before going with it over the running lines to a siding on the other side of the city. It thus often involved a good deal of pilot and shunting work but always a certain minimum of movement on the main running line. By contrast long distance freight working was carried out predominantly, if not completely over the main line.

Passenger jobs may involve either local or long distance working. Local passenger work often had substantial mileage values but a considerable proportion of the shift was spent at station stops awaiting times of departure. Using steam traction, long distance passenger work could be very arduous for the driver, and even more so for the fireman, as steam pressures had to be maintained to give high speeds over appreciable distances. Given the timing requirements in passenger work, manupulation of the technical elements in the situation could be very exacting indeed. With electric traction the technology is more convenient considered at the level of the individual turn of duty. In many instances the job is simply a matter of driving over long distances without stopping, although here there could be lengthy waits at the end of these continuous runs.

Turns of duty involving these clearly identifiable types of driving work are arranged into groups called links. Links are displayed on the roster boards with the appropriate names of the attached personnel by each one. By itself such publicity further enhances the discernibility of different categories of locomotivemen's jobs. The visible display of distinctive jobs is both a reflection and a reinforcement of an existing norm.

(ii) Career structure Career structure is conceived in terms of regular and prescribed movements within and between job positions. Continuity of career, or 'status passage'[9] for the individual locomotiveman is, in itself, an element of the job property system. Taking the major statuses, the analytic task is to note the progressive characteristics of each in turn.

Cleaner The initial status for the locomotiveman, the cleaner, may be an improvement for the individual relative to his position prior to joining the 'line of promotion to the footplate'. There was generally more money than in jobs outside the railway, and more dignity than in other railway jobs, such as messenger, bar boy, or 'knocker up'. Continuity or progress to different job activity is also reflected by the appropriation of increasingly 'valuable' job activities within the cleaner status. The type of work done by the cleaner, whether he cleaned wheels, boilers, or footplates, was also allocated according to the seniority of the individual, though the ranking of activities might vary from shed to shed.[10]

Of the cleaning job activities themselves, while basic and often unpleasant, it must be said that they are important for the total system. The meaning and significance of these tasks is made apparent to the individual in a number of ways, by possession of simple instruments symbolising his attachment to a defined set of activities,[11] through his membership of a squad of cleaners, his participation in the Mutual Improvement Class at the depot, and through formal instruction.[12] Once the cleaner has received formal preliminary tuition by an appointed firing instructor then he would be given firing jobs with increasing frequency.

Fireman Only after formal certification in the appropriate job requirements can the cleaner be allowed to act as fireman. Once the cleaner is on the footplate as fireman ('passed cleaner') he is socialised by the driver.[13] After becoming a regular fireman the individual can begin to aggregate significantly the number of turns of firing duty required to qualify him to act as driver. Experience over the running lines during this time enables him to acquire the essential route knowledge for driving jobs throughout the links. There was also a mileage bonus for a fireman which is a further progressive aspect for him.

Eventually when seniority and experience permit the fireman takes the most complex examination of his whole railway career in order to be allowed to act as a driver.[14] On his achievement of the status of passed fireman, the individual receives the organisational instruments – working timetables, operating notices, and wrong line orders – to enable him to carry out the job of a driver, with responsibility for the working of trains. These instruments are a significant symbolic reflection of the individual's real permission to claim a whole new range of job activities previously outside his reach.

Driver The locomotive driver's position represents at once an arrival – the achievement of stable rights in a broad range of the most valued job activities, and also an acquisitive progression – in that there is a continued movement within this category toward more complex and financially rewarding job activities. As a passed fireman the individual would still be involved in firing, as he only had a right to driving activity when there was specifically a need for this.

On becoming a registered driver his activities were limited to driving. There would be a continuous movement towards the links where the turns of duty contained more and more driving. The individual would begin with disposal, preparation, shunting and pilot jobs, gradually moving through the freight links to the long distance passenger links during his long career. Figure 10.1 is an ideal type in several ways[15] but nevertheless the time spans between various job activities are averages which are related to empirical observations.

The diagram shows that the locomotiveman's railway career could in theory span a full fifty years, from 15 years of age to 65. In practice, while many drivers have begun in other occupations, they do spend almost all of their working lives on the railways, as the average top link seniority figure (589.49 months) demonstrates.

Whereas the career construction for the lorry driver showed the typical pattern[16] as an inverted U-shaped curve, the locomotiveman's career shows a continuous rise in status throughout the entire span until the incumbent reaches his late fifties. Around 60 years of age the individual does reach a plateau. Until this time he has risen in status through the appropriation of increasingly prestigious job activities. Finally, unlike the lorry driver in the last period of his career, the locomotiveman does not suffer a reversal of prestige, by being forced on a downward course through less valuable activities, or even a pre-retirement exodus from the occupation he has followed for most of his working life. The top link locomotive driver would carry out the most prestigious duty of all, long distance passenger work, for the last three to five years of his working life.

The structure of a typical locomotiveman's career does suggest in many ways the continuous realisation over time of a claim to job property. From the financial advantages at the beginning; through the gradual attainment of intrinsically and financially more worthwhile work; to the fact that his market situation is not reduced in the last period; all these suggest proprietorial characteristics. The 'going after' something worthwhile, the acquisition of more activities, and the final retention of the most valued activity of all suggest that the locomotiveman's career is a claim to job property.

(iii) Career as an investment of time Property may be viewed as an accumulation of unconsumed wealth arising in one of several ways – a major avenue being investment of capital with accompanying effort. Career may be seen as an investment in the sense of a commitment of effort over a long period. The argument here crystallises on two problems – can time be seen as an economic factor in this way, and if so, how is such a prospective to be applied to the locmotiveman's career?

Normative intrusion, even into the seemingly objective phenomenon of time, is apparent from historical and institutional comparison. Conceptions of time have changed through the ages suggesting that there is no a priori reason why time should not be viewed as an investment under certain circumstances. In pre-industrial societies time was not the important regulator of men's activities that it became in industrial society. Agricultural production, the activity of most people, was not strict and exacting in the temporal sense. Had the routine of production demanded it, no doubt techniques of time measurement would have been more readily available. In fact, even on documents, dates would often not be recorded and the ages of important persons would sometimes remain obscure. Night and day the passing of the seasons were regulators but, relative to modern times men were indifferent to time.[17] The orientations of the worker was to the task rather than the time unit.[18]

For industrial societies time is a basic element in the rationality underlying industrialism. The rationality, which permits, or even creates industrialism, is reinforced by it over a period of time. Rationality, considered as a process of optimisation, of finding the best available means of achieving a particular goal, is often assessed in terms of time, time taken, or time spent in reaching a goal. What is

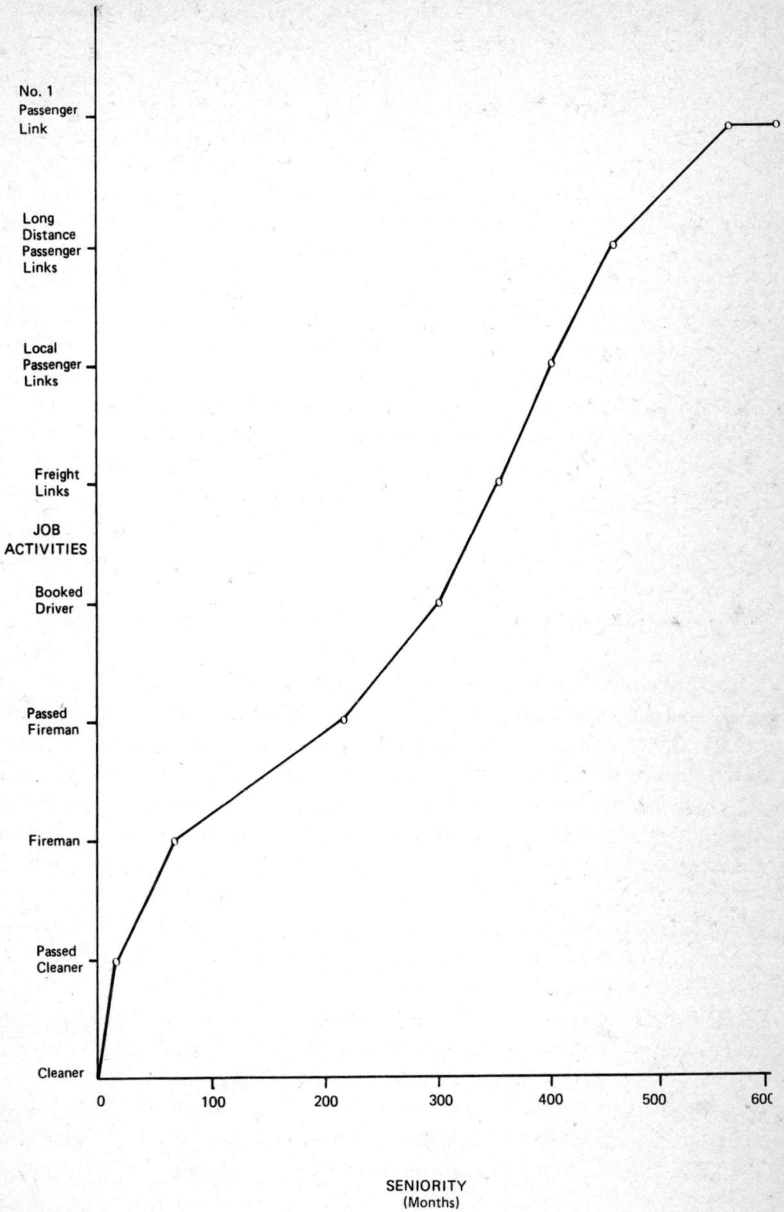

Figure 10.1 A typical locomotiveman's career pattern.

distinctive about industrial societies relative to earlier times, is that the assessment is made, and considered by those who make it to be both normal and necessary. Some analysts have made the claim that time has, as with most other things in capitalist industrial societies, become a commodity, something to be priced, obtained, and used.[19] Evidence on this point appears to be conflicting. Some studies clearly do indicate that time spent at work is something exchanged for money in itself, either with the willing, or perhaps only the grudging consent of those who offer it.[20] The full range of occupations might reduce the relevance of the commodity conception of time since many have intrinsically satisfying activities as well as extrinsic reward.[21]

The mundane nature of activity in most occupations, and even a considerable proportion in the few that are more favoured, means that some activities will be more highly valued than others.[22] Within any one occupation certain activities will be a premium of desirability with the consequence of an emergent pattern for their appropriation. Time is used in one activity with reference to the attainment of others. This is the situation for the railway locomotiveman in that there is a recognised sequence of movement from the less desirable, less responsible jobs, to the more skilled and rewarding positions. We can now deal in detail with the time durations involved in this pattern.

The overall amount of time commitment would, in itself, be sufficient to sustain the time hypothesis but a basic division in the steam locomotiveman's career doubly confirms this. The time taken to attain driver status is followed by a further substantial wait to reach the most valuable driving activity. Total time investment during the first stage of the footplateman's career is shown by considering the length of time committed between starting as an engine cleaner and being made a certified driver. On average there is a continuous decline between the 1916–20 and the 1946–50 joining periods, while there is a slight rise indicated for the 1951–55 period. Drivers who joined during and just after World War I waited on average twenty-five years to become drivers, with a minimum wait of exactly eleven years and a maximum of almost thirty-four. One driver in every two took more than twenty-four years to be certificated from the time he began as a cleaner.

Those drivers who joined in the late 1930s were luckier than their older colleagues due to the demands created by World War II, and the fact that, at this particular shed, there was almost a complete dearth of recruitment between 1921 and 1936. For those footplatemen joining between 1936 and 1940, the movement from cleaner to driver took over eighteen years, compared with seventeen years for the 1941–45 joiners, and less than sixteen for those starting in the period 1946–50. Footplatemen beginning their careers in the following five-year period took a slightly longer time, more than sixteen and a half years on average, to become registered drivers. This rise reflects a fall in the demand for railway services generally, while a sharp reduction in the range of variation suggests a more standardised market demand over the country as a whole.

The hypothesis of time investment seems well justified in real terms for the first section of the locomotiveman's career. Both the earlier average of twenty-five, and the later one of sixteen years served, before achieving the status of driver indicate considerable time commitment. In the second stage of the career there is a further lengthy period of time to be served in lesser driving activities before reaching the most favoured driving activity, express passenger work, in the top link. By taking three drivers from the top link, with seniority dates of 1916, 1918, and 1921 respectively, it should be possible to get an estimate for time investment in the second half of the career.

The 1916 man spent six years doing disposing, pilot, and shunting work. It was eight years before he drove long distance goods trains, ten before he regularly drove local passenger trains, and only after thirty-nine years did he reach the top link. There are however some special circumstances for this long haul to the No. 1 Passenger Link. By 1947, some twenty years after being certified as a driver, he had reached the No. 3 Passenger Link before taking up work on a special electric traction stopping service catering for commuters. This would give a new time of not less than twenty years to reach the No. 1 Passenger Link if it is assumed that he would have been transferred into it in the same year. In fact, given the normal rate of retirement it would have taken at least three more years to reach it. Twenty-three years would seem a reasonable estimate, though one which was perhaps on the low side. The man of 1918 seniority did five years on shunting, pilots, and shedding, and took some thirteen years to reach local passenger work. It was twenty-three years before he reached the top link. For the driver with the 1921 seniority, things were easier during the early stages of his career, with only one year spent in elementary driving activities, such as tripping and pilot work. After only two years as a booked driver he was carrying out long distance freight work. However he then took ten years to get regular local passenger work and finally reached the top link some twenty-one years after being certified as a regular driver.

Thus the time commitment in the second half of the footplateman's career reaffirms the time investment hypothesis. The typical driver can take as much time reaching the best driving activity as he spends in attaining the status of driver itself.

Subjective property elements

The idea of an essential mental side to the property institution generally is basic to the following assessment of the subjective aspect of career as a claim to property. Two subjective areas of the locomotiveman's working life are relevant – evaluation of job activities and expectations on the allocation of work.

(i) Locomotivemens' evaluation of job activity Evaluation of footplate work exhibits a definite form in terms of level and pattern. It is positive and at a high level. Of the sixty-three drivers in the sample, not one regarded his job as in any way casual. All expected to remain in driving for the remainder of their working life. Seventy per cent would not change their occupation, even if the opportunity arose. Nearly four-fifths of the sample (78 per cent) would not accept a job in a factory even for more pay. Far fewer (40 per cent) said that they would be drivers if they could start life again, and fewer still (19 per cent) felt able to recommend their occupation to others. These four subjective indicators of commitment, even the most negative, are substantial evidence for stating that the railway locomotiveman places an extremely high value on his occupation.

The job satisfaction indicator also suggests that locomotivemen value their work highly in both absolute and comparative terms. Their 85 per cent positive response over jobs is not unusual. What raises the locomotivemen's index (1.349) is the very high percentage (55 per cent) who like their jobs a great deal. The locomotivemen do not differ greatly from lorry drivers in finding autonomy, variety, and the job itself, major reasons for positive satisfaction. On this, as well as the previous subjective indicators, the locomotivemen show themselves to feel more positive about their actual jobs than other transport workers (lorry drivers), some white collar groups, (technicians, and clerical workers) and factory workers.[23]

Locomotivemen's expressed preferences for different types of jobs are another way of assessing the subjective aspect. It is clear that the most favoured jobs are those which come with seniority. It is line work, especially main line passenger work which is predominantly preferred. Sixty per cent liked passenger work most, while there was an 88 per cent preference for 'passenger work', 'main line work', and 'main line freight work'. These types of work were said to give more satisfaction, have more interest, to be more absorbing, better organised, and to be at better times of the day.

The worst job of all was that of 'pilot' (30 per cent disliked this) closely followed by 'disposing' (25 per cent). 'Freight' and 'shunting' were disliked equally (17 per cent each) while 'preparation' was negatively viewed by 11 per cent. Only a few drivers disliked passenger work (8 per cent) while a significant proportion of the reasons for disliking freight were to do with its irregularity.

(ii) Allocation expectations: the seniority system The subjective side of career structure and time investment is primarily represented by the seniority norm. Seniority is frequently defined in terms of the length of service in a particular job or firm.[24] For railway locomotivemen the seniority system is based on the date of entry to positions in the line of promotion to the footplate. A footplateman's seniority date, usually his first day of becoming an engine cleaner, would stand for the duration of his career. It affected his promotion prospects, the circumstances of his transfer to another depot, or even his leaving the occupation entirely due to redundancy.

Locomotivemen see the seniority date, and the principle of seniority as a whole, as a central condition of their working life. Furthermore it is viewed as being highly legitimate. Only four drivers of a sample of sixty-three said that they did not agree with the seniority norm. Support for the seniority system was indicated by many varieties of a common concern for the standards used in the allocation of job properties. Two replies to the question: 'Do you think the system of promotion by seniority is the right one?' illustrate this value convergence.

> Yes, you'd get the arseholes picked if it wasn't there and its like that on [a named railway]. It's the only fair way on our job – also promotion by knowledge can be misused. I had a job once which was second to none because I was being pushed. Also the firemen can learn more through the period of time spent. It [unfair allocation] can happen now with spare men – one spare man might get more work – not by knowledge but by favouritism.

> [There] couldn't be any better [way] – every man's got his proper share – its not 'blue eyes' jumping in front of the queue then.

Overwhelming support for this method of occupational advancement in terms of expressed attitude does coincide with the objective situation to a considerable extent. Seniority had the most fundamental influence in allocating work at the shed without being the *sole* principle.[25] Assessing the line of promotion links only, and these only in terms of their average running mileage, the connection between length of service and job values is apparent. In two sequential years surveyed, mileage values, and seniority show high positive correlation, 0.74 and 0.81 respectively for 1966 and 1967.

These values do show two things clearly. Firstly that the progressive character of the steam locomotiveman's career structure is just as marked after he formally reaches the status of driver as before. Second, the differentially allocated mileage with their associated bonuses do confirm the differential reward for time invested.

Line of promotion jobs: seniority and mileage

1966			*1967*		
Link	*Seniority*	*Mileage*	*Link*	*Seniority*	*Mileage*
No. 1 Passenger	589.49	82.89	No. 1 Passenger	492.30	88.89
No. 2 Passenger	377.70	74.40	No. 2 Passenger	369.52	88.10
No. 3 Passenger	349.19	72.08	No. 3 Passenger	340.94	83.80
No. 4 Passenger	329.05	71.86	No. 4 Passenger	329.46	63.64
No. 5 Passenger	318.54	62.35			
No. 6 Passenger	313.54	64.65			
No. 1 Freight	301.59	50.14	No. 1 Freight	318.54	53.55
No. 2 Freight	299.21	40.39	No. 2 Freight	299.80	37.15
No. 3 Freight	286.52	34.32	No. 3 Freight	279.30	34.82
No. 4 Freight	270.43	16.05	No. 4 Freight	266.84	24.31
No. 5 Freight	265.67	16.05			
No. 6 Freight	217.07	15.93			

Conclusion

The job property theory has considerable explanatory power for the career situation of steam railway locomotivemen. Objective and subjective property characteristics permeate the entire career structure making it a process of acquisition over time. Both intrinsic and extrinsic job values rise for the individual as he invests more time. In this sense, the steam locomotiveman's career process is a claim to property.

Nevertheless there are significant ways in which the property analogy has difficulties as an explanation of the locomotiveman's career. Some drivers in the population had career structures more attributable to welfare than property criteria. Men were able to come out of the line of promotion on either a temporary or a permanent basis. There were links containing only work considered more suitable for men with disabilities.

Perhaps more important is an inconsistency in the 'property' system itself. Systematic integration would lead to the requirement of a high positive correlation between the major elements of the system – legitimating attributes (health, merit, seniority), job properties (differentiated activity in the link structure), and appurtenances (wage rates, earnings, intrinsic job satisfaction). In fact the signs of horizontal integration are there to a high degree except when earnings are considered. Here the correlations with legitimating attributes indicate the predominance of a merit/effort system rather than a seniority/property system.

The job property theory may still be the most pertinent in explaining the career of the steam locomotiveman in a priori terms.

Where basic wage rates apply, and the formal location of mileage bonuses, then there is a high degree of integration between system elements. In real life it is earnings which are crucial.[26] The inverse relationship between seniority and earnings does suggest an informal system of effort departing from the property system.

Contrasting social patterns within or around the broad structure is a feature well known to sociologists, criminologists, and students of industrial relations. In the economy there is 'hidden' or 'black' activity as well as the official kind.[27] Three contrasting systems in the locomotiveman's career are thus not extraordinary. The interest will rather be centred on which is pre-eminent normatively and the factors influencing such superiority. Clearly the job property system of locomotivemen is technologically based and will be affected greatly by traction changes. Against the survival of a job property system is the rigidity it induces into an occupation and even the economy at large. More in its favour (or perhaps a surrogate), is the contribution to the meaning of occupational activity in a situation of ever increasing mundanity (if not alienation) at work.

Notes

1. '. . . though private property appears to be the source, the cause of alienated labour, it is rather its consequence . . .'. Marx's essay on 'Estranged Labour' in *The Economic and Philosophic Manuscripts of 1844*, edited by D. J. Struik, New York, International Publishers Edition, 1964, p.117. See also David McLellan's summary in *Marx's Grundrisse*, UK, Paladin, 1973, p.122 in that the capitalist does not acquire man's products even by exchange 'Since what he exchanges for them is previously appropriated surplus labour'.
2. See Max Weber, *The Theory of Social and Economic Organisation*, New York, Free Press, 1964, p.236. Weber wrote these essays the early years of World War I. For a summary of the effects of workers appropriation of rights in their jobs see T. Parsons, 'Max Weber's Sociological Analysis of Capitalism and Modern Institutions', p.304 in H. E. Barnes (ed.), *An Introduction to the History of Sociology*, Chicago, University of Chicago Press, 1961, who suggests that the general consequences of the increase in such rights means a restriction on the formal rationality of the economy.
3. 'Rules and Regulations of the Birmingham Society of Wire Workers', in A. Briggs, 'Social Background', Chapter 1 of A. Flanders and H. A. Clegg (eds.), *The System of Industrial Relations in Great Britain*, Oxford, Blackwell, 1967, p.13. The 1832 publication is J. Wood, 'The Right of Labour to Legislative Protection'. Other examples include watchmakers, (Report from the Committee on Petitions from the Watchmakers of Coventry, Parliamentary Papers 1817 IV, Minutes of Evidence, p.47), and cotton weavers (Cotton Weavers Manifesto 1823 quoted in J. L. and B. Hammond, *The Town Labourer*, (1978 edition), p.205).
4. See H. A. Turner, *Trade Union Growth, Structure and Policy*, Allen and Unwin, 1962, pp.110, 111, 254 and 262. H. A. Turner, G. Clack and G. Roberts, *Labour Relations in the Motor Industry*, Allen and Unwin,

London, 1967, pp.337–8. The question of job property rights and the 'effort bargain' in workplace negotiations have a place in an earlier piece on strikes by Turner. H. A. Turner, 'The Trend of Strikes', Inaugural Lecture, Leeds University, 1963, especially p.18.

5. A study of a pre-outmoded tinplate works suggested that 'the production jobs (were) tending to become a pseudo-property right inherited through relatives. Entry to the steel plant was by father – son succession in the case of more than half the interviewees of both samples.' J. Chadwick-Jones, *Automation and Behaviour*, London, Wiley, 1969, pp.41 and 44.
6. A. R. Porter, *Job Property Rights*, Columbia University, New York, Kings Crown Press, 1954, says, 'A man's job is admittedly intangible but nor more so than good will, a copyright, or a patent.' p.7.
7. Porter, op. cit., p.83. See also material on hiring and priority in R. Blauner, *Alienation and Freedom*, Chicago, University of Chicago Press, 1964, p.39, and S. M. Lipset, M. A. Trow and J. S. Coleman, *Union Democracy*, Glencoe, Ill., Free Press, 1956, pp.284–6.
8. See the discussion by R. Mansfield, 'Career and Individual Strategies', pp.107–32, in J. Child (ed.), *Man and Organisation*, London, Allen and Unwin, 1973.
9. An extremely useful framework for the consideration of career is that offered by the concept of 'status passage' defined in terms of properties which can be specified as operational variables, i.e. elements existing empirically in varying degrees in a particular situation, for example regularity and prescription.
10. N. McKillop, *How I Became an Engine Driver*, London, Nelson, 1960, p.6. Also T. A. McCulloch, *Working on the Railway*, in Jack Common (ed.), *Seven Shifts*, London, Secker and Warburg, 1938, p.250.
11. The 'cleaner's box, swabs, tallow and oil', may be of minimal status as tools, but they serve to mark off an entitlement to a distinct set of activities. As such the cleaner is immediately different from the unskilled labourer who in many cases may be ordered around at will to perform a wide range of different tasks. See McCulloch, op. cit., p.250.
12. McKillop, op. cit., p.10–11 describes the classes run by the enginemen themselves so that newcomers and others could learn the requirements of their occupation. Cleaners and firemen were helped to pass their examinations through such classes. When the time comes near for his turn to act as fireman the cleaner is given two weeks of formal tuition by an appointed firing instructor.
13. The 'booked' driver's role in teaching the fireman is a clear policy of the formal organisation:

    > A Fireman or Passed Cleaner acting as a fireman is under the control and supervision of the Driver upon whom falls the responsibility of assisting in training him in the early stages of his career. By tactful and careful instruction the driver, by recalling the time when he himself was in a similar position and acting on his own experiences, will have considerable influence which will reflect credit upon him, in addition to making each working day satisfying to both, in the knowledge of a job well done.

    British Transport Commission, *Handbook for Railway Steam Locomotive Enginemen*, London, 1957, p.22. See also M. Reynolds, *Engine Driving*

Life, London, Crosby Lockwood and Son, 1894, on the teaching functions of the driver, p.17.

14. Associated Society of Locomotive Engineers and Firemen, *Rates of Pay and Conditions of Service of Men in the Line of Promotion for Footplate Staff*, 1964, pp.28–32.
15. It brings many of the hypothetical elements into equal emphasis. The relationship of these elements is deliberately constructed for analytic purposes. Lastly it comprises variables relevant for both causal and meaning analysis of social action.
16. P. G. Hollowell, *The Lorry Driver*, London, Routledge and Kegan Paul, 1968, p.67.
17. Between the tenth and twelfth centuries in Europe it would appear that 'it was not the notion of time only, it was the domain of number as a whole which suffered from this haziness'. See M. Bloch, *Feudal Society*, Vol. 1, Chapter 5, 'Modes of Feeling and Thought', p.74, London, Routledge and Kegan Paul, 1965.
    The limited view of time in the middle ages has to be seen in the context of the absolute subordination of society and the individual to the will of God. Need for conformity could only be satisfied by making man's use of time subordinate and passive and therefore separating it from God as an immutable eternity. R. Glasser, *Time in French Life and Thought*, Manchester, Manchester University Press, 1972, pp.50–53.
18. 'For the primitive food gatherer or peasant cultivator time as such is not economically valued. He pursues a particular task, or set of tasks steadily, except as he is interrupted by darkness or fatigue, until the work is completed, and then may spend a variable period "doing nothing" until the next endeavour is started.' W. E. Moore, *Man, Time and Society*, New York, Wiley, 1963, p.25. See also the summary by E. P. Thompson, 'Time, Work Discipline, and Industrial Capitalism', *Past and Present*, **38**, 1967, pp.60–1.
19. See Thompson, op. cit., pp.90–1. 'In mature capitalist society all time must be consumed, marketed, put to use; it is offensive for the labour force merely to "pass the time".' Time may be a commodity in itself or its 'use' may be the basis on which relationships are reduced (if one takes the usual moral position) to commodities. '. . . time appears as a commodity men request from one another, one which they mutually give and take, steal and grant. This conception, a commonplace with us, was unknown to the Middle Ages.' Glasser, op. cit., p.200.
20. The evidence on motor car assembly line workers is the case which is most obviously appropriate.
21. A summary of studies made between 1935 and 1957 suggests that over the whole range of occupations there is much intrinsic satisfaction to be derived from work. See R. Blanner, 'Work Satisfaction and Industrial Trends in Modern Society', in W. Galenson and S. M. Lipset (eds.), *Labour and Trade Unionism*, New York, John Wiley, 1960.
22. Studies of factory work, even the most mundane kind, suggest that operatives do differentially evaluate separate operations making up the whole task. A public service occupation provides an example in the tertiary sector. Policemen dislike routine checking of premises or attending domestic disputes relative to crime prevention and detection.

See R. Reiner, *The Blue Coated Worker*, Cambridge, Cambridge University Press, 1978, especially Chapter 10.

23. Comparative sources here either originate or are quoted in Hollowell op. cit., p.88.
24. A useful discussion of the functions of seniority is that of F. Meyers, *The Analytic Meaning of Seniority*, Institute of Industrial Relations. Reprint No. 156, University of California, 1966, since it shows the importance of the seniority concept in the action approach to career as appropriation.

    > Career progressions of some kind are the usual though not the universal concomitant of seniority rules. p.8.

    > . . . the affirmative function of seniority – to allocate claims and to establish priorities as between conflicting claims. pp.1–2.

    > [Seniority involves the notion that] people acquire propertylike rights in employment opportunities, and the prerogatives that are to be shared within given boundaries, pp.8–9.

25. Welfare criteria operated significantly in the allocation of locomotive work off the main running lines. For example the disposal of steam locomotives could be used to give employment to men whose health would be a potential safety risk on the main line.
26. The effort system worked most significantly for the men in the freight links who had considerably higher annual earnings than the passenger link men. In the freight links, the effort factor relating to the accepted opportunities for overtime, clearly outweigh the pecuniary advantages of the possession of job property in the passenger links. Average annual earnings for passenger link men was £1267.17 compared with the freight link men's £1314.97 in the period 1966/67.
27. The Hawthorne phenomenon can be extended from the world of work to the world at large. Strategic effort is shown in informal behaviour patterns at the workplace (G. Mars, 'Chance, Punters and the Fiddle: Institutionalised Pilferage in a Motel Dining Room', in M. Warner (ed.), *The Sociology of the Workplace*, London, Allen and Unwin, 1973. J. Ditton, *Part Time Crime*, London, Macmillan, 1977. In the wider social sphere 'hustling' is an alternative to 'shit-work' (K. Pryce, *Endless Pressure*, London, Penguin, 1979) in inner city deprived areas, while in the economy at large there is a considerable secondary system. S. Henry, *The Hidden Economy*, London, Martin Robertson, 1978.

Index